More
of a Certain Age

More of a Certain Age

NAIM ATTALLAH

QUARTET BOOKS

First published by Quartet Books Limited 1993
A member of the Namara Group
27/29 Goodge Street
London W1P 1FD

Copyright © by Naim Attallah 1993

All rights reserved. No part of this book may be reproduced in any form or by any means without the prior written permission of the publisher.

A catalogue record for this title is available from the British Library

ISBN 0 7043 7016 6

Typeset by Contour Typesetters, Southall, London
Printed and bound in Great Britain by
Bookcraft Ltd, Midsomer Norton, Avon

CONTENTS

Lord Amery	1
The Rt. Hon. Tony Benn	23
The Duke of Devonshire	47
Mary Ellis	63
Lord Forte	79
Lord Hartwell	93
Patricia Highsmith	117
P. D. James	131
Lady Longford	155
Sir Bernard Lovell	177
John Mortimer	195
Marjorie Proops	215
Kathleen Raine	235
Dame Cicely Saunders	261
Lady Soames	283
Sir Laurens van der Post	307
Lord Wyatt	329

LORD AMERY

LORD AMERY

Julian Amery was born in 1919 and educated at Eton and Balliol College, Oxford. He was a war correspondent in Spain during the last part of the Spanish Civil War. He joined the RAF and served as sergeant from 1940-1 after which he transferred to the army and fought in the Middle East, Malta and Yugoslavia. In 1941 he organized the first military missions to the Yugoslavian Resistance Movement and in 1944 was wounded in Albania when leading a force of escaped Russian prisoners. His brother John, who made pro-Hitler broadcasts from Berlin, was later tried for high treason and hanged in London in 1945. In 1950, Julian Amery married Catherine, daughter of Sir Harold Macmillan, and in the same year he was elected MP for Preston North. He was defeated in 1966 but was elected for Brighton at a by-election in 1969. As Minister of Aviation he was responsible for signing the agreement with the French Government on the Concorde project.

Lord Amery

You grew up in a family which was as much part of the Establishment as any could be. Has that ever worked to your disadvantage, do you think?

It worked both ways, though I don't agree that my family was so very much part of the Establishment. My father was a fellow of All Souls, but he didn't have money or any particular family connections. He got on to *The Times* and later became a leader writer and a supporter of Joseph Chamberlain in the tariff reform campaign, but that hardly puts him in the Establishment class. Perhaps at the end of it all he had graduated into it.

But you went to Eton, did you not?

Yes, of course. That was not a difficult thing to do, however, and it hardly makes me part of the Establishment.

Was your father the most influential figure in your life?

Certainly. He always treated me as an adult and would talk to me about economics when I could hardly understand it. I grew up imbibing the atmosphere of politics and I met Churchill and other leading figures when I was seventeen or eighteen. It was part of the air I breathed. And later in the early part of the war when I was catapulated into the whole morass of Balkan intrigue, we had the shared experience of political interest in that part of the world. This made a great difference and established a partnership between us which otherwise might have been difficult to achieve.

Most children seem to have a period of rebellion, quite often when they are students. They become Marxists for a while or hopelessly idealistic about the world. Did you ever waver from the Tory traditions in which you were reared?

Yes, indeed. My youthful political career was not exactly straightforward, and not all that Tory. When I was eleven years old my father took me to the House of Commons where I met Lloyd George who asked me what I wanted to do when I grew up. I told him I wanted to go into the navy. 'Why the navy?' he asked. 'There are much greater storms in politics, you

3

know. If you really want the broadsides, walking the plank and blood on the deck, this is the place.' The scales fell from my eyes, and his comparison of modern parliamentary life to *Treasure Island* made me opt for politics. My father was of course delighted, but I kept in touch with Lloyd George, and whenever we had mock elections in my school I was always a liberal candidate. Then I examined Communism and Fascism and it was only when I went to Oxford that I opted for the Conservative Party, though I also joined the Labour and the Liberal clubs so as to be able to go to their meetings.

Some people have suggested that the driving force of your ambition may have been a determination to honour a well-loved father's memory. Do you see it that way?

I certainly inherited my father's views on the Commonwealth and the importance of Britain as the centre of the Commonwealth and a leading power in Europe, and all my life I was greatly influenced by his thinking. The year after he died I fought what I thought was the last great battle of the Commonwealth, the battle over Suez. When we gave in at Suez it was really the end of the Middle Eastern and African empire which Britain had built up over many decades. I was very sad at that, and it seemed to me then that our only chance of playing an important role in history was within Europe; and so while I did my best to defend what was left of the imperial position, in Cyprus, in Aden and elsewhere, Europe has become increasingly the important area for British influence to exert itself. I see no other.

At the Oxford Union you spoke in favour of conscription which reversed the notorious 'We will fight for King and Country' motion of some years previously. Did your conviction spring from the mood of the time or was it ingrained in your background?

It had been ingrained. My colleague in the debate was Randolph Churchill, who had by that time become a friend. It was the first of several campaigns that we fought together. When I left the debate, I went at once and joined the Royal Air Force reserve.

Lord Amery

You had what people would call a good war, risking your life many times in undercover operations. How do you look back on these years . . . with pride, with nostalgia, perhaps with incredulity?

I have to confess, with enjoyment. There were of course moments of danger, moments of discomfort, but if you look at the whole spectrum of that sort of life it was pretty agreeable. Sometimes there were three or four days without anything to eat at all, then there would be a roast sheep. And then there were the times when we were sitting around in Cairo waiting for the next assignment, where all the delights of the flesh were available. Denis Healey once said I was nostalgic for the life of Richard Hannay in the Buchan novels. I don't think that's true, but I did enjoy those days.

Didn't you work for the Secret Service?

There were always two secret services, intelligence and operations. I was in operations. My role was always to do things, to blow up trains or bridges, or to shoot convoys. One of our more dramatic coups was when the Bulgarian government wanted to arrest, and perhaps to kill, the leader of the peasant party. I supervised the arrangements which brought him out of Bulgaria in a diplomatic bag. He was transported to Istanbul where we unpacked him and released him for his future activities.

Were you ever a spy?

The word is of course derogatory, and a spy is someone who learns or acquires information. If the spying side involves itself in operations it loses its security.

Apparently you made the suggestion to Churchill that he visit his weary troops in the desert, and as a result you are sometimes dubbed 'The Victor of Alamein'. Do you think that visit had a significant impact on the outcome of the war?

Who shall ever say? What happened was this: I was flown back from Cairo to London to report on our plans, and when I came to my father's house, I found him lunching with Harold Macmillan, then a junior minister. They

Lord Amery

asked me what the mood of the troops was and I told them I thought the 8th Army was rather demoralized. When they asked what could be done, I told them that it would be difficult to change the balance of forces, but the balance of morale could conceivably be altered by Churchill visiting the troops himself. I then went on to the SOE headquarters where I received a telephone call summoning me to Downing Street. When I arrived, there was the Prime Minister in a boiler suit with a rather weak whisky and soda in front of him. Alanbrooke, the Chief of the Imperial General Staff was also there, and the PM asked me to tell my story. Of course the Field Marshal didn't like the idea of a junior captain, not even in a regiment, criticizing the morale of the army and he kept trying to interrupt, but Churchill said, 'Let him talk.' I told him if he went out and talked to the troops it would have a dynamic effect on morale. When I left Churchill thanked me, but I heard nothing for a while. Later of course he did go, and it was his private secretary, John Martin, who said to me afterwards that my talk had inspired Churchill with the idea, so to that extent I could claim to have won the Battle of Alamein.

You were a war correspondent during the Spanish Civil War. Did you have any sympathy with the Republicans?

I went three times to Franco's Spain. The first time was in the spring of 1937, and I came away rather pro-Franco. I went again in the summer of the same year when I met Philby, who was then *The Times* correspondent, and very pro-Franco, rather more than I was myself. Then in a hotel bar I ran into a German colonel of my acquaintance who was fighting on Franco's side. We had a drink together and, referring to the Munich agreement, he said, 'I think we've got the better of you this time.' That was the moment I understood that the Germans and the Italians were about to fight against us, and this changed my whole attitude. The Germans and the Italians were using Spain to advance their control of Europe at our expense, and once I realized that, there followed a kind of Pauline conversion. I came back to England determined to see what I could do to oppose it.

You mentioned Philby. Did it ever occur to you that he could be a Communist spy?

Lord Amery

No, I met him once during the war and once after the war, and he appeared on both occasions to be a rather right-wing Conservative.

In 1950 you married Harold Macmillan's daughter. In political terms I imagine this was a mixed blessing in that there were the inevitable cries of nepotism and an element of resentment that you had a direct line to the Prime Minister. Was that difficult to deal with?

I would want to get the story in perspective. Macmillan was then not even in office, and when he did get into office it was as Minister of Housing, so he wasn't at all a senior figure. I'd also known him before because his son Maurice was one of my closest friends at school, and I had often been to their house. But there were many steps between him and the premiership. I liked Harold but my affection for his daughter was entirely personal.

Macmillan aroused very different opinions, both as a man and as a politician. Some people thought him devious, a charlatan and ultimately a very cold man. In so far as you could stand back from family ties, how did you view him?

Every Prime Minister has to be to some extent devious and cold; he has to sacrifice people. If you're at No. 10 Downing Street you have to keep the Party together, the Cabinet together, you have to drive through the policies to which you're committed. And Macmillan served all these well. He was enthusiastic for Europe, though it took him a long time to get the Cabinet and House of Commons to accept his proposal to join Europe, and then he was defeated by De Gaulle. He was always determined to maintain Britain as a nuclear power which now everybody accepts, even the Labour Party; but it wasn't accepted in those days, and he fought a good battle. As Chancellor of the Exchequer he gave in too soon to American pressures over Suez – I don't want to say he lost his nerve, but he became frightened by the run on sterling. He then made it his first objective to repair relations with the Americans, which he did. And we have to remember that inflation in his time never topped three per cent.

And yet people call him the father of inflation.

Lord Amery

There's a lot of nonsense talked now about the Macmillan government and its effect on the economy, but in the light of the circumstances of the time he was doing just about the right thing.

But how would you rate him as a Prime Minister?

I wouldn't put him in the Churchill or perhaps even Disraeli class, but I think he held his Party together, he held the country together and he was vindicated at successive elections. He was a very remarkable political operator.

When I interviewed Mollie Butler there was no doubt in her mind that Macmillan was determined from the first day of his leadership to the last never to be succeeded by Butler, even though Butler was the obvious candidate. Do you think that's true?

Yes. He thought of Butler as an extremely able, intelligent political leader, but he didn't regard him as a commander-in-chief. I don't think it was jealousy – in fact he had very good personal relations with Butler.

Most people believe that Macmillan rigged the results of the investigation into whom the Party wanted as his successor, and Enoch Powell even wrote an article entitled 'How Macmillan Lied to the Queen'. What view did you take at the time and what view do you take now?

I don't think he rigged the election. What happened was fairly simple: the Lord Chancellor and the Chief Whip consulted the members of the Party as to whom they would like as leader. There was a strong vote for Quintin Hailsham and a strong vote for Butler. We were all asked, myself included, whom we would choose if we couldn't get the candidate we favoured, and there was a very large vote in favour of Alec Home. The Prime Minister had no alternative but to tell the Queen that the Party was divided between Hailsham and Butler, but there would be a consensus for Sir Alec Home; and so Home got it. I don't call that rigging it.

Why do you think Enoch Powell in particular opposed Alec Home?

The official reason was that he didn't think a fourteenth earl had the right image for the modern Tory Party, but I think it was really that he wanted Butler to succeed. He thought that if the leadership of the Party refused to accept Alec Home then Butler would have it, but when the time came Butler wasn't prepared to throw his hat in the ring.

That Butler was prepared to serve under Home was commendable in itself, was it not?

It was a matter of political morals.

What did you think of Enoch Powell at the time? I believe you have described him as something of a werewolf.

He was always a friend of mine, I always liked him, but he does have some of the characteristics of a strange creature.

Butler is often referred to as the greatest Prime Minister we never had and indeed people often say you are the greatest Foreign Secretary we never had. Do you think these labels are ones which emerge only when we have events in some kind of historical perspective, or is it the case that you felt at the time you were being passed over?

Let's take Rab Butler first. I think if elected he would have been a great Prime Minister; what I'm not sure about is whether he could ever have been elected by the people. Of course he was an able man, but he lacked charisma and I don't think he was a natural leader, though he was a great chief of staff. In my own case, the only comment I would make is that there is a difference, not always appreciated, between diplomacy and foreign policy. Diplomacy is the art of negotiation; foreign policy is determining where the interests of your country lie. Looking back on the years between the wars I had a clearer view of where the interests of our country lay and would have fought for those rather than attempted negotiation. Anthony Eden, who was perhaps the greatest negotiator we ever had, fought very hard over Vietnam, where there was no great British interest, yet he surrendered in what I thought was an area of vital interest, in the Suez Canal Zone in 1954. This effectively meant the end of the

Lord Amery

Commonwealth as a world force, and a major defeat for Europe, and for British influence in Europe. Later on there was the Rhodesian crisis where again Lord Carrington achieved a great success in producing agreement between the different sides, but in my view at the expense of vital British interests in Southern Africa. So I have sometimes said that we have to be careful not to let diplomacy triumph over foreign policy; I would have put the latter ahead of the former.

Don't you think the loss of the Commonwealth, or the loss of the empire, was only a matter of time?

Not necessarily. It might well have survived. The resilience of the old Commonwealth was quite remarkable – in 1931 when we went off gold, in 1940 when we went into the war, in 1945 when we came out of the war – and with a little encouragement we could have kept the system going for quite a long time, perhaps indefinitely.

Would it be fair to say that your views are right-wing as opposed to middle-of-the-road?

I never know what people mean by right-wing. My views on domestic policy have been rather centre, some might say slightly wet. Where foreign policy is concerned I've always taken the Churchillian view that you first of all identify the enemy, and having made up your mind where lies the threat, who is the enemy, you must stand up against them and take whatever precautions are needed to counter them. I've always thought it right to defend British interests and to take a fairly long-term view of what they are.

When Alec Douglas Home became Prime Minister your position became increasingly difficult and there was a move to oust you from government. Do you look back on that period as being particularly difficult?

Unpleasant... but these things happen. I was perceived as an extravagant minister, with Concorde, TSR2 and space projects, and people were beginning to say we must cut back on public expenditure.

Lord Amery

Do you think they were justified in trying to remove you?

No, I think I was right. Concorde has been a great technological success. It may not have been a moneyspinner but it's been our little space programme and it hasn't lost any more money than space has lost to the Americans and the Russians. And the TSR2 and the P1154 would have been remarkable aircraft – they haven't found anything better twenty years later.

I suppose you came closest to becoming Foreign Secretary when Lord Carrington resigned over the Falklands. Were you disappointed not to have been chosen?

I don't think politicians should be disappointed. But it was perfectly true, there was a strong movement from the Tory backbenches to make me Foreign Secretary at the time, and I would have enjoyed the opportunity.

Your career was badly damaged during your time at the Ministry of Aviation in the last days of the Tory government – I'm thinking of the Ferranti business. How serious was the damage in your view?

Not very serious. I think I overcame that. The Ferranti family were prepared to cough up the money which we thought they had unduly gained. They repaid the debt, perhaps even more than they should have done.

Before 1962 your career was extremely promising, and you were tipped as a possible Minister of Defence. Are you philosophical about the volatility of political life?

You have to be, otherwise you couldn't go on in politics. I've never been very keen on securing a particular job; it's been much more important to achieve certain policies and objectives. There's no point in being embittered.

You were Aviation Minister when Profumo ran the War Office. What view did you take of the Profumo scandal?

Lord Amery

I supported him as far as I could. He was a friend, he's remained a friend, and I thought he was not really as important as the media made out.

The official reason why Profumo had to go was that he lied to the House of Commons, but of course the real reason was his involvement with a prostitute. Isn't that the ultimate in British hypocrisy?

I think they could have tolerated the involvement with the prostitute; the real reason was that he was led into a situation where he told a lie to the House, and this was an indefensible position to be in. Had he not lied to the House, and had simply admitted to the affair, he might still have had to resign but would have remained in the House of Commons, and continued to claim the viscountcy which was the right of any Secretary of State in those days.

The number of scandals involving MPs has increased over the years, or at least the diligence with which the media expose the scandals has increased. Do you think the private lives of MPs are a legitimate area of public interest?

In principle no, but of course if an MP or a minister gets himself into a flagrant position it's bound to be discussed.

Discussed is one thing, but hounded out of office is another.

Where do you draw the line between the two? None of this is new . . . it went on in the last century, and it goes on today. I think the public will accept a good deal, and any incidental action on the part of a politician does not necessarily render him incompetent; on the other hand, a man who gives a lead in not only political but moral affairs, obviously can become a little ridiculous if he's caught in the wrong situation. Before the Second World War, the rule was that if the wife didn't complain the press had no right to complain, but in those days a divorce was a clear block to continuing in political life. That convention has now disappeared; indeed it's sometimes said that you can't get into the Cabinet unless you're divorced. But the balance has not changed very much; things go on very much now as they did before.

Lord Amery

Thirty years ago you signed the Concorde deal with the French. Was that your proudest moment?

No. I suppose my proudest moment was when Nasser proved me right about the Suez Canal, and I was able to say in the House of Commons, much more politely than I'm saying it now, 'I told you so.'

You seem always to have had a thinly disguised suspicion of America and the Americans. Even in the 1960s when the cold war with Russia was at its height, you said you were more alarmed by the Americans than the Russians . . . what was the origin of this alarm and suspicion?

Objective historians recognize that it was the aim of American foreign policy to destroy the British, French and Dutch empires. I myself became aware of this during the Second World War when I was attached to Chiang Kai Shek's headquarters in China. It became quite clear that although American policy was well aligned with our own in Europe and the Middle East, it was quite plainly anti-British, anti-French and anti-Dutch in the Far East. And Suez was the touchstone, Suez was the *coup de grâce*.

So you don't believe in the so-called 'special relationship' between Britain and America?

On the contrary, but it doesn't alter the fact that there was an American policy to destroy the British Empire; and it succeeded.

Do you have difficulty in accepting the view that without the Americans we would not have won the Second World War?

I don't see how we could have won without the Americans. I remember a curious occasion – January '41 I think it was – when I was invited to a little dinner party where Churchill and Harriman were the principal guests and the talk came round to how the British were going to win the war. There were still oranges on the table, though they became rarer as the war went on, and Churchill picked one up and said, 'If I were a worm wanting to get into this orange I would crawl round it until I found a rotten spot.' He then turned to Harriman and said, 'But you've got to keep the worm alive

13

until it finds the rotten spot.' Without the Americans I don't think we could have won the war, but we'd already got to the point where we weren't going to lose the war.

Did you yourself ever have any doubts about that?

At the time when Rommel came to Alamein, I think my heart never doubted, but my head may have wondered a bit.

Your own patriotism during the war must have made your brother's behaviour all the harder to bear. I wonder how you think it was possible for two brothers born of the same parents and brought up in the same environment to have turned out so differently. You must have asked yourself this a million times – what is the answer?

Although you talk about the same environment, he had in fact lived on the Continent for several years, and that made all the difference. He'd been involved in the Spanish War, and then came very much under the influence of Doriot in France. He was convinced the Germans were going to lose the war and that the Communists would sweep over the whole of Europe. This was a view that became increasingly prominent in the occupied countries. Of course it was not for him to intervene, and he was able to do so only because of my father's standing. He should have kept his mouth shut, but he felt he had to say something. It was regrettable but understandable.

It is difficult to imagine the depths of disappointment, the shame, the anger which must have been wrought on the family at the time, feelings which must have been made worse by the heightened tension of the war. How did you all cope? Did you talk about it, or was it suppressed?

It wasn't suppressed. My father offered his resignation and I offered mine; we were both quite clear that it was the right thing to do, but we were both refused.

Did your father ever manage to come to terms with what had happened?

Yes. He came with me to say goodbye to my brother in prison and indeed he wrote a short verse in the taxi which took us there, and I think it sums up his feelings: 'At end of wayward days / You found a cause / If not your country's./ Who shall say whether that betrayal of our ancient laws/ Was treason or foreknowledge? / He rests well.'

In the course of my research I was struck by the fact that although you said you might have killed your brother with your bare hands if you had met him during the war, after you saw him in prison your feelings changed. Compassion took the place of anger, blood was thicker than water perhaps?

I think that is about true. Also, if I had seen him during the fighting he would have been with Hitler and I would have been fighting against Hitler, but when I saw him in prison the war was over and the Russians were dominating half of Europe.

Did your brother's plea of guilty come as a shock especially after all your efforts on his behalf?

No, I think it was a logical act.

Albert Pierrepoint, the famous hangman, said that of all the people he executed your brother was by far the bravest. Did that make the pain all the harder to bear?

No, I think it was appropriate. He was an Amery.

As an MP you have consistently voted against capital punishment. Is that shaped directly from your personal experience?

It has been influenced by it. Within our legal system when someone is charged for a potentially capital offence there is a considerable delay while the lawyers prepare their case, then there's the trial, the appeal, and even when that is rejected there is the appeal for mercy. All this takes a long time

Lord Amery

and it exacts its toll on all concerned, especially the family, quite apart from the person charged.

You were a vociferous opponent of the Official Secrets Act and were against the lifelong confidentiality imposed on former members of security and intelligence services. Why was that?

There used to be a very flexible arrangement under which former secret agents could publish their memoirs if they had first of all submitted them to the proper authorities. This was a very good system and it should be allowed to continue, because it is right that people who spend their whole lives in the Secret Service should be able to explain to their family and friends what they've been doing, provided it doesn't endanger future operations. It is wrong to have a blanket veto on anybody writing anything, even about what they saw of butterflies in Anatolia. I produced what I thought was a rather good amendment which was accepted by the Home Secretary of the day. But he then went back on it – orders from No. 10.

Do you think Mrs Thatcher made herself and her government look foolish over the Peter Wright memoirs?

Yes. She was his best publicist.

In a BBC interview with Robin Day in 1979, just after the Commons debate on Anthony Blunt, you remarked that there were a dozen traitors in the House of Commons, a remark which you later – under pressure – unreservedly withdrew. Why did you make that remark in the first place, and why did you then feel bound to withdraw it?

I was not in a position to prove that the members concerned had been bought by the enemy; I could only have attempted to prove that objectively they were siding with the enemy. Mr Speaker asked me to withdraw my remark, otherwise there would have been a long and complicated debate. And so I withdrew.

Lord Amery

You had great doubts about American foreign policy, especially in South East Asia and in the Middle East. Did you therefore have doubts about the Iraqi war and the reasons, largely dominated by America, for going to war?

I had no doubt about the American decision to go into the war. I still have the greatest doubts about their decision to stop. In Churchill's famous words: 'I don't know whether I would have dared to start; I would never have dared to stop.'

You once said of Mrs Thatcher: 'Her aims have usually been defensible, but her methods deplorable.' What did you mean by that?

I don't remember ever saying that, though I remember seeing it in print. I've always had great respect and considerable admiration for her. We didn't always agree about Europe, but she made a great Prime Minister.

You have crossed swords with Ted Heath in the past over oil sanctions and he sacked you from the opposition front bench, and yet on other matters you have been closely aligned. Am I right in thinking you have a high regard for Ted Heath?

We've known each other since student days at Balliol. I've always liked him, and I am a strong supporter of European union, though I think he goes sometimes too far in that regard. I thought he was wrong about Rhodesia, and wrong about the Suez Crisis when he was Chief Whip, but we have a good relationship.

And was he wrong about Mrs Thatcher?

Well, that was his opinion.

You're very diplomatic. It has often been said that personal loyalty is one of your best attributes. Do you regard loyalty as a necessary political virtue?

Personal relations play a much greater part in politics than is generally

17

understood, and loyalty to friends at home and abroad is of great importance. Sometimes necessity makes you change friends, but if you have to change friends you should always take steps to ensure that it is done with proper decency and decorum.

The Tories at the moment seem riven with disloyalty . . . but isn't that ultimately a more honest approach than the normal closing of ranks in political parties?

I'm not a great believer in open government, and I confess I'm rather shocked by the speed with which friends of mine publish their memoirs. They bare all sorts of secrets which would have been thought very indecent until quite recently.

Politics can sometimes be a dirty business. Have you ever felt a distaste or at least an ambivalence towards the political life?

No. If you go into the business you should be prepared to get your hands dirty.

As a politician you concentrated your energies on the wider issues of national importance – some said at the expense of your own constituency and the local interests of your own people. Do you think that is a valid criticism?

Not really. I managed to retain the wholehearted support of both my constituencies, in Lancashire and in Brighton. But I've always thought that the fate of more people is determined by what goes on abroad than with what goes on at home. Whether with the old imperial connection or the modern European connection, or issues of peace and war, or issues of export and import, the British people are terribly dependent on what goes on in the world.

What would you describe as your greatest failing?

Perhaps it was to take up positions that were not popular at the time – I'm thinking of my support for Britain's imperial and Commonwealth role when it was unfashionable (though probably right), and my tendency to make realistic judgements in foreign affairs when these were thought rather reactionary. I've usually been a little out of phase with the mood of the time.

If you were to relive your political life, would you do it differently?

I don't think so, I might have made greater efforts to soften some of the things I said, and I might have tried to sell my views rather more plausibly to audiences who didn't want to hear the truth; but I would still have taken the same line.

Do you think you will be vindicated by history in all the causes you have chosen to champion?

All is saying a lot, but I've already been vindicated to a very large extent in many of them. The chaos that has overtaken Africa as a result of a premature decolonization speaks for itself; the successive Arab-Israeli wars came about directly as a result of Britain's withdrawal from the Suez Canal Zone; and the anxieties I expressed about Soviet domination of Eastern Europe, alas, were proved to be well-founded.

You were an adviser to BCCI. Wasn't that a major embarrassment to you in view of what happened?

No, because I was merely a consultant. I was only ever asked for my judgement on the political climate, the validity of investing in Africa or in Europe. I was never involved in the banking or the finance, nor would I have been capable of helping in that way; they simply wanted political advice, which I was happy to give them at the invitation of the Sheikh of Abu Dhabi, who was a good friend of this country and a friend of mine.

But didn't you suspect anything at all? Weren't you taken in?

I was never anywhere near their books. I had no idea what they were doing. I certainly don't think I was taken in.

Lord Amery

You began life with many advantages: financial independence, public schooling, intellect, powerful connections. You still live in the house in Eton Square in which you were born. Do you ever think that these factors have effectively removed you from the lives of the vast majority of people in this country?

No. Don't forget I was for eighteen years Member of Parliament for Preston in Lancashire, a very marginal constituency, and in order to keep the seat I had to see very much how everybody else lived. I never felt out of touch.

How did you cope with the death of your wife, your companion for forty years?

Of course it was a terrible blow, I can't conceal that, though up to a point I was prepared because she had been ill for a couple of years.

Do you ever think you might see her again in another life?

I don't know. These are mysteries which are not unveiled to me.

Were women very important in your life?

The whole problem is this: Which is more difficult? To have to do with women or to do without them?

And what is your answer?

It is a dilemma. Further disclosures will await my memoirs.

Though you have had a very distinguished career in politics, many have remarked that it is so much less than you should have had. You give no outward sign of being disappointed. Does that reflect your inner feelings also?

Lord Amery

What is the use of being disappointed? In life one learns that the prizes don't always go to the ablest or to the ones who were right; they go to people who are better connected, or have the ear of the powers that be. It's stupid to be disappointed.

THE RT. HON. TONY BENN

TONY BENN

Tony Benn was born in 1925, the son of Viscount Stansgate. He was educated at Westminster School and New College, Oxford, and served as an RAF pilot from 1943–5. Between 1950 and 1960 he was Labour MP for Bristol before being compelled to leave the House of Commons on inheriting his father's title. He fought successfully to renounce the peerage and in 1963 he was re-elected to Parliament. He has served on the Labour Party's National Executive since 1959 and has held a number of ministerial posts including Postmaster General (1964–6) and Minister of Technology (1966–70). His publications include *Arguments for Socialism* (1979), *Writings on the Wall* (1984) and several volumes of *Diaries*.

The Rt. Hon. Tony Benn

There are many routes into politics but yours seem almost to have been predetermined genetically. Have you ever regarded your political orientation as an accident of birth in the way people often regard religion?

Both my grandfathers were Members of Parliament; John Benn was elected a hundred years ago for East London, and my mother's father in 1911 for Govan. My own father was elected in 1906, so I was brought up in a very political household, and my political memories go back to the time when I was three or four. In 1928 I went to the house of Oswald Mosley who was then a Labour MP, and I remember the 1929 election when I was four, and visiting No. 10 Downing Street when I was five. I met Ramsay Macdonald and in 1931 I met Mr Ghandi when he came to London. I only ever wanted to be in political life, not so much from ambition, but because this was an area of great interest where you could contribute something. I wouldn't call it genetic, I would simply say this was what my life was like, and just as a doctor's son might want to be a doctor, or a miner's son might want to be a miner, I wanted to go into politics. I was very lucky, and I entered Parliament when I was twenty-five.

The twin pillars of religion and politics are a feature of your family history as far back as it can be traced. Did you ever feel a pull in the other direction, to the Church?

Not really. My brother Michael who was killed in the war wanted to be a Christian minister, but as far as I'm concerned my own interest is confined to the social ethics of religion, the teachings about humanity and community rather than the mystery of life. The work of a local Member of Parliament, however, is very like that of a conscientious minister. People come and seek my advice and tell me their problems, and I find that the most satisfying part of my job.

According to your brother, you both had a very good political upbringing but a very poor cultural upbringing. Is that something you felt to be a handicap in later life?

It's true that we never went to museums or art galleries and my father wasn't very musical. I suppose if you concentrate on one particular part of life you are deprived in other areas. You can't be competent and interested

The Rt. Hon. Tony Benn

in everything, and I sense that a bit in my life. My children are very musical, and my wife is a great opera lover, but my horizons may be a little narrower than they should be.

You were greatly influenced by your father's politics and ideas. On a personal level, were you very conscious of the age gap which could have made him a rather remote Victorian figure?

He was born in 1877, and when I was born he was forty-eight which is quite old for a father. But he had a very young mind and in terms of his behaviour and his vitality he never quite grew up. He was a mature and wise person but there was no sense of remoteness, no sense of his being a Victorian grandfather whom you had to look up to.

Your mother gave to you, in your brother's words, 'the precious gift of religion'. How important has that been in your life?

Very important. My mother's grandfather was a very strict Scottish protestant. He was a member of the Irvine Brethren, much the same as the Plymouth Brethren in England. This drove my mother's father to atheism, and the atheism drove my mother back to religion. It was like the shunting of coaches on a train. She came to religion, not because of any belief in the mystery of it, but because she believed there must be a good spirit behind the creation of the universe. It was never the idea of the sacred nature of Jesus, but she saw that his life embodied the spiritual community which she believed existed, and at the end of her life she became the head of the Congregational Federation. Independence of mind, both in religion and politics, contributed very strongly to my upbringing. Since my wife is of Huguenot stock from France via America, that same quality has been fed in through my marriage, and it gives me a rock on which to stand when things are very difficult.

You were devastated by your brother Michael's death in 1944. Was the family's grief more easily borne, do you think, because of faith in God?

As far as my mother was concerned, yes, but my father was absolutely shattered by it. My mother had a stronger personal religious faith, and she

The Rt. Hon. Tony Benn

survived it. I myself was terribly distressed. I was in Rhodesia at the time learning to fly, and I had just turned up for a lecture one morning when somebody gave me a telegram which announced he was dead. I had to sit there for an hour in the class pretending to listen, overcome by sadness. I was very fond of my brother. He and I had a lot of correspondence together during the war, and when I look back on it it's not only his strength of character that comes through but also what it was that young people were thinking about, even during the destruction of war; what the post-war world would be like. His letters were full of hope, the very opposite of the pessimism and cynicism of today. That is an important element to keep in mind; fear drives you into yourself and encourages fascism, but when you have confidence and hope you can look at the world straight in the eye and not be frightened by it.

Your mother was a lifelong campaigner within the Church and notably for the ordination of women. Do you support the idea of women priests?

Oh absolutely. I can't think of many central beliefs of my parents that I have repudiated. She was a member of an organization committed to the ordination of women called the League of the Church Militant and she was summoned to Lambeth Palace in 1925 and rebuked by the Archbishop of Canterbury, Randall Davidson. She left the Church of England in 1948 because they would not move on the question of ordination of women, and became a member of the Congregationalist Church where there have always been women ministers. I feel very sorry that she died a few months before the Synod agreed to women priests but she knew it was coming and the appointment in America of Bishop Barbara Harris, the first black woman bishop, gave her such pleasure.

Although you describe Westminister as your local school, it nevertheless had all the trappings and rituals and customs of the famous public schools. Did that make you feel at all uneasy?

I didn't like the politics of it. In 1938 there was quite a strong political strain developing and the headmaster was very right-wing. I can't say I cared for it very much and I never felt that it gave me anything of real value in my subsequent life. My children all went to the local comprehensive school and even if they had won the pools you couldn't have induced them

The Rt. Hon. Tony Benn

to go to a public school. Westminster was a part of my childhood but I can't say it really influenced my thinking, except perhaps to make me more determined to be independent. I can't say I was very happy there but in the end you make your own life wherever you are. They always say that public schoolboys can cope with prison because they are familiar with the circumstances of prison life, and I can understand that.

At a school debate you denounced the English public school system as 'the breeding ground of snobbery'. Did you experience discomfort at being part of that system?

Yes and no. There were no comprehensive schools at the time and my parents sent me there as a sort of normal thing to do if you were middle-class parents. I can't say I felt very much at home there but I've always been an easy-going person, and wherever I am I try to fit myself in.

Would you accept that but for your schooling at Westminster and your father's eminence, entry to Oxford might have been more difficult?

There was a kind of automaticity about it; I'd been to Westminster so I was admitted to New College. But you must remember that it was quite a different period of history. I was there for six months in 1943 and then I joined the Air Force. When I came back at the end of the war, university life was quite different; it was serious and informal and modest in life style, so it is misleading to think of that period of university life as having much to do with the Oxford you may visit now or the Oxford that existed in the 1930s. The luxury and splendour one associates with Oxford was not a feature of my time there; it was just like serving in an Air Force camp in Egypt, except there was enough to eat.

By the age of sixteen you had drawn up a list of things to achieve – to become an RAF pilot, to become an MP, to marry and have a family. All of these were realized within ten years. That suggests an extraordinary degree of self-knowledge and self-confidence.

I don't know whether it was self-knowledge or planning of a kind that has characterized my life from then till now, but I still look ahead. I have a

The Rt. Hon. Tony Benn

diary that goes up to my hundredth birthday. If I live to be a hundred I have another thirty-one years to fill, and I find it a very good way of focusing my mind. For example, in 2025 I've marked in my 100th birthday on 3 April; my wife will be ninety-nine that year, and my older son will be seventy-eight. It is a way of developing your capacity to use every moment of the day.

You have often achieved a goal by means of what you call the stiletto principle – i.e. putting all your weight on one point. Has the principle ever let you down?

I've certainly made lots of mistakes. The only difference between other political people and myself is that I publish my mistakes in my diaries, whereas other people in their memoirs forget theirs. But it is true that if you really do press very hard on something you can win, just as a woman with a high-heeled shoe can go through a parquet floor.

You were the first man in history who, by Act of Parliament, was allowed to forgo a hereditary peerage. Your long battle was essentially to enable you to continue to serve in the House of Commons, but there was surely an underlying ideological battle of Benn versus the Establishment.

Yes, but it wasn't, as people think, an ambition to be Prime Minister. I deeply resented being expelled, having been in Parliament for ten years and elected many times by Bristol. My father, who was a very radically minded man, took a peerage in 1942 when he was sixty-five because Attlee wanted some Labour peers. There were no life peerages at the time; all peerages were hereditary. He consulted my brother who wanted to be a Christian minister and didn't care if he became a peer, but he didn't consult me and I was very angry with him that he didn't. When my brother was killed my father was full of guilt, and he said, 'I've landed you with this – you'll have to try and change it.' It took me ten years to change the constitution, and I learned a very great deal in the process. Resentment of the idea that privilege should take precedence over democracy was the principle of it. Other people saw it as a human interest story of the 'man bites dog' variety, but it was a long and very worrying period. It worked out all right in the end and I learned the most important political lesson in my life: never rely on judges, cabinets, or parliaments to give you justice; if you've

The Rt. Hon. Tony Benn

got a case take it to the people and get public support. I've never forgotten that and I've applied it many times to other issues.

Before you achieved your victory, most people thought you could not possibly win. Did that make success especially sweet?

It had been a long battle, but it was about the winning of it, so success was sweet in that sense. After the by-election in 1963 I went to the House one day when it was empty and I just sat there and thought of what a struggle it had been. It didn't make me bitter in any way, but it made me very strong against the privileged people who thought they ran the world. They didn't, and they don't.

But would you consider that single act as your greatest achievement?

Not at all. It was a very inconsequential thing politically, and I would be very sorry if when I die that were the only thing in my obituaries. I would like to be remembered for totally different things.

It was the same Renunciation Act that allowed Alec Douglas Home to become Prime Minister. Was that a bitter irony for you?

It was a bit of a disappointment on the day, but on the other hand it was the same act that made Harold Wilson Prime Minister, because if it had been Iain MacLeod rather than Home, Harold Wilson wouldn't have won. I made it possible for the Tories to pick a leader so weak that Labour could win.

From as far back as the 1970s you argued that the principles of Socialism were being betrayed by Labour leaders. This was a view that did considerable damage to the Party you loved. Is it a view you still adhere to?

It depends on how you define Socialism. For me Socialism has a moral basis going back to the book of Genesis and to the New Testament: 'Am I my brother's keeper?' and 'Love they neighbour as thyself.' Politics are based on a moral judgement of what is right and what is wrong, and not on

The Rt. Hon. Tony Benn

what is profitable and what is loss making. No one wants to run a business that is loss-making, and everybody wants to get a return for their labour, but to run a society where the main criterion is profit and loss is criminal in my opinion. Homeless people don't get houses because it's not profitable; Canary Wharf which nobody wants was built because the government though it would be profitable. The permanent critique of any society – Capitalist, Communist, Fascist – is right and wrong in a moral sense. The second thing about Socialism is that it is about democracy. If we are brothers and sisters under God then we have equal rights to govern ourselves and to enjoy a full life. The democratic argument is also very threatening to Communism, Fascism and Capitalism, because none of those systems really believes that ordinary people have rights, save to be put down, kept down, brainwashed, manipulated, told what to do, told to bow and scrape. The third thing about Socialism is that because it analyses why things happen and tells you there is a conflict between those who create the wealth and those who own the wealth, it helps you to understand what's happening in the world. And the fourth thing is that it tells you that if you band together and you don't depend on a benevolent prime minister or leader or landlord to help you; you can do it yourselves. When you look at all that, the idea that the Labour Party could win by deliberately and explicitly repudiating its history and tradition – particularly at a time when the slump is worse, injustice is worse, the gap between rich and poor is worse, the world is in a mess – is very foolish. The only time we have ever won an election is when, as in 1945, it was fought on principle; 1964 and 1974 were also quite strong on principle; every other time we've put forward this milk-and-water liberalism, and we've lost. So I don't see any conflict between taking a strong position and winning support. After all, to look at the other side, Mrs Thatcher wasn't exactly a compromiser; people knew where they stood with her. But with the Labour Party you don't know where you stand; Dr Gallup writes our manifesto, so people don't believe us.

I'm intrigued that you mention Mrs Thatcher . . . if you could detach yourself politically, how would you assess her?

She was a strong, principled woman who defended her class with absolute commitment, and was determined to crush trade unionism, local government and democracy itself. I regard her policies as absolutely evil and destructive, but at least you knew where you were with her. By

The Rt. Hon. Tony Benn

contrast Labour Party policy is like a bit of cloud blowing up – you don't know where it is, what it's covering up, and where it's going next. I'll tell you an interesting thing. When Eric Heffer died, there was a memorial service in St Margaret's Westminster at which I gave the address. The Labour Party didn't send anybody, but Mrs Thatcher was there, standing just behind me. As I get older what matters to me is not so much whether I agree with people but whether I respect them, and I can respect people with whom I profoundly disagree if I think they mean what they say and say what they mean.

Your biographer Jad Adams acknowledged that you wanted to be leader, but not at any price. He writes: 'He would be leader if they acquiesced in his judgement, but he would not bend his principles to them.' And in that respect he suggests you are more of a Coriolanus than a Macbeth. Is that how you see it yourself?

There's not much point in leading a party that elects you without knowing what you stand for. People used to say to me regularly that if I just kept quiet about this or that I would become leader, but the idea of getting there by stealth, slithering up by concealing my real intentions is false, and it would have destroyed my self-respect. Leadership must be based on integrity and some understanding and acceptance of what you're saying, and that was the principle I worked on. I fought four elections, two for the deputy leadership and two for the leadership, and I didn't win any of them, but ideas were planted then and are beginning to grow now. As far as I'm concerned I'm a teacher, not a would-be managing director, so I judge my electoral campaigns in quite a different way from the way the political correspondents do, where everything is judged in terms of how far you have climbed up the slippery pole.

But had you been elected, do you think you would have made a good leader?

I don't know, but I would certainly have regarded the leadership as having a very different sort of function. My view, particularly as I've become older, is that the real political role is as a student and a teacher. I do hundreds and hundreds of meetings around the country, and everywhere I go I learn something, and I also try to teach something. That is very different from the modern view of political leadership which is that if you haven't got a policy you buy a new suit, you engage a new adviser, and you smile more. But you cannot build a political movement on sand. The Labour Party doesn't believe in public meetings any more; they believe in soundbites and photo opportunities. We're witnessing the destruction of democracy, not by Communists or Trotskyists, but by a conspiracy between the political leaders and the political correspondents that there will be no discussion allowed. However, you stir me too much . . .

Most politicians would prefer to be compared to Coriolanus rather than to Macbeth, but the tragedy of Coriolanus was that he believed that a statesman could act alone without bowing to others, and in the end his obstinate pride and lack of self-control got the better of his nobility and heroic virtue. Do you see anything of yourself in Coriolanus?

I'm not sure I know enough about Coriolanus to answer your question, but this theory that I'm isolated is without foundation. I've been on the National Executive longer than anyone in the history of the Labour Party, so if I'm an isolated figure, why do the constituencies still put me there? I've been elected without having to make the concessions that you're supposed to make in order to get to power. The idea that I have hovered on the margins out of obstinate pride is simply not true. The truth is I've been much influenced by what I've seen and I've had some influence in persuading other people. Where are the great figures who fitted all the patterns you describe, where are they, what footprints have they left in the sands of time?

Peter Riddell observed of you: 'For all his energy and affability, Tony Benn's inability to trust his fellow politicians means he has never really understood what politics is about.' Do you accept that this inability to trust has been a weakness?

No. Peter Riddell's idea of politics is that you say anything to get personal power. That's not the politics I'm interested in, not the politics of any durability. The trouble with political correspondents is that they are interested in politicians' careers, which have very little to do with politics. The most influential people in the history of humanity have been Galileo, Marx, Freud, Darwin, and so on, but who are the people who have held

The Rt. Hon. Tony Benn

political office? They simply disappear. My mother taught me, and I never forgot, that the Old Testament story was a conflict between the kings who had power and the prophets who preached righteousness, and if you ever think that power without righteousness is satisfying, then you disappear. Peter Riddell is a courtier of the governing class; he hovers round hoping for titbits from somebody who can tell him what happened in the Cabinet. In any court in medieval Europe there would have been a Peter Riddell. I don't mean to be personal, but the cynicism of the political correspondents, of the disillusioned liberals who hover in the lobby, of these people who were once progressive and now can't bear to think that anybody can have any legitimate reason for hope, that cynicism destroys democracy. If democracy goes it will be due to that view of politics, not the militant tendency. Peter Riddell's review of my book was the most revealing I ever read; it told me so much about Peter Riddell and very little about myself.

Political observers have often drawn a comparison between you and Enoch Powell, pointing out that you are both great debaters, both brilliant, evangelical and romantic. Does the comparison strike you as absurd, or even offensive perhaps?

I've known Enoch for years, and I respect him in the way I respect Mrs Thatcher. He made one terrible mistake in the speech about rivers of blood, but he is a thoughtful academic, and I'm not an intellectual in the way he is at all. People compare me to Enoch in order to make me seem extremist, but the difference between Enoch and myself is that he has never been elected to any position in the Conservative Party, while I have been elected for thirty-odd years to the National Executive. Enoch is worth listening to; you can disagree with him but at least he is motivated by a desire to illuminate. There are three ways in which politicians can operate: they can oversimplify like the demagogues, they can mystify like the people who say you can't discuss unemployment unless you have a PhD in economics, or they can clarify. Enoch is a clarifier. I also try to be a clarifier, and I like him very much.

Enoch Powell's 'rivers of blood' speech and your own riposte in which you evoked images of Dachau and Belsen came to be regarded as suicidal in political terms. Was it not one of the great political ironies of all times, i.e., that in attacking what you saw as the great evil of racialism, you should have done yourself untold damage?

Racial questions are so explosive that political leaders have a conspiracy of silence about them. When Enoch made that speech I did not think the issue could be allowed to rest, so I made the speech I did about the flag of Dachau. I wondered whether I was right to make it personal to Powell, but the argument itself was absolutely right. Wilson was furious with me because he and Heath had agreed that race would not be an election issue, but Enoch was right to open up such a big question. He opened it up as a white nationalist, while I opened it up as an anti-racist. On these matters you do have to take a stand, and looking back on it I'm glad I did.

You felt uneasy afterwards about having made the remark so personal, but you claimed that it was a statement which 'came out of my stomach'. Do you think the political arena would benefit from more remarks from the stomach and fewer from the collective Party brain, so to speak?

I don't know that there is a collective Party brain, more a collective Party public relations officer. If I thought a great brain was working at the top I might be more at ease with myself. You have to say what you think. I don't want a peerage, I don't want cash, I don't want office; all I can do is to use my experience to convey my convictions, and if I'm wrong I'll be criticized, if I'm right I'll persuade. When I look back I wish I'd done more of that. You compared me to Coriolanus, but I was rather slow in many respects to say what had to be said. The one principle I've always tried to work on is 'Don't make it personal', because if you do you reduce the issue to the yah-boo of politics, which is an absolute switch off; the public hate it, and it doesn't influence anybody.

Michael Foot, in one of the most remarkable denunciations of our time, argued that after 1970 you underwent a radical change and in the eyes of political associates and cabinet colleagues you became 'someone not to be trusted'. Can you see how that impression, however erroneous, might have arisen?

Michael began as a left-winger and ended up as a right-wing leader whereas I have radicalized with the years. It was actually in 1968 that I decided, having been a minister for four years, it was time to come out with a lot of serious political thought, and I made a series of speeches, long before we were defeated, about the referendum, the Party, Socialism, the media, and so on. Michael, who was not a member but a critic of that government, though it was only after we were defeated that I spoke out, which wasn't true at all. I was saying it all when I was in office, and being attacked for it too. Michael's own position, however, has changed on everything: he's no longer a unilateralist, he supported the Falklands War, and so on. That of course is his right, he can do what he likes, but I don't accept this idea that trust must require you to move to the right as you get older.

Would you say that Foot's attitude was based more on rivalry than substance?

I don't think so. He became leader of the Party by following the principles you describe. What's interesting about both Foot and Kinnock's election is that the Party picked people with left-wing credentials to destroy the left. Michael's function as leader was to secure victory over the left on behalf of the right, and Neil's function was to do the same. Clearly I had a different approach.

Your biographer's comment on Michael Foot's list of recriminations against you is: 'Indeed there are no friends at the top.' Have you felt the acute loneliness of political life?

It is a very cynical phrase, but it is true that alliances move, and only very good friendships can survive differences of opinion. Clearly my personal relations, though courteous, lack warmth if I have been engaged in a real argument with somebody; that is true, I must confess.

It has nevertheless been a common criticism of you that you have regarded your reputation and ideas as more important than the Party you have served. How would you defend yourself against that charge?

I don't honestly feel I have to defend myself against any charge; I'm not a criminal coming up for trial. All I can say is that I've tried to speak my mind and I've been elected. It's not a charge ever made against David Owen, Roy Jenkins, George Brown, Hartley Shawcross, Dick Marsh or Reg Prentice; but only against me. I've seen other people who have been carried to the top on the shoulders of the Labour movement, people who have kicked away the ladder and yet are treated as men of principle. For example, David Owen has been in six parties, yet he's now 'a man of principle'. Just exactly what is it about his political life that makes it in some way more uniquely principled and trustworthy than mine? It's a charge motivated by political disagreement, and without substance.

Perhaps another way of putting it is that you have been loyal to principles and ideals rather than to people, something which has led you to argue with all the leaders of the Labour Party in your time, Wilson, Callaghan, Foot and Kinnock... have you ever regretted that particular price of principle?

I have had good relations with them all. I was out of Parliament when Wilson was elected but I voted for Wilson when he first stood against Gaitskell in 1960, just before I was thrown out of Parliament on the grounds of my peerage. Wilson made me a minister, and I was very close to him. Though we had our arguments, I regarded him as a Prime Minister with a capacity to keep the Party on the road. I didn't vote for Callaghan, but I liked him very much, and preferred him in many ways to the latter-day Wilson because he was straightforward. After Callaghan came Foot, and I voted for him. Healey didn't vote for Foot, Silkin didn't vote for Foot, Shore didn't vote for Foot, but I voted for Foot. Kinnock I've known over a long period; he supported me when we had the so-called left-wing dominated National Executive, and then when he was elected I wasn't in Parliament, so I wasn't able to vote for anybody. I stood against Kinnock in 1988 because I thought his policies would lead to defeat, and they did. But it was a principled thing, nothing personal about it, so this idea that I've fought with everybody is just an illusion. You put me in a position where I appear to be defending myself; I'm not interested in defending myself, only in putting the record straight. The theory you suggest is put about because people disagree with me, which they are quite entitled to do; but they don't have to cook up imaginary arguments.

Harold Wilson is probably the least respected or talked about former Prime Minister. Why do you think this is?

The Rt. Hon. Tony Benn

Harold is not very well, but when his life comes to be assessed, he will be remembered for three things. First of all, for getting Labour elected four times, a formidable achievement after many years in opposition. Secondly he reminded the public that without careful planning the technological revolution could destroy communities, as it has done. The third thing he will be remembered for is the Open University, and any man who founds a university is a man whom history will honour and praise for all time. He was also very committed to third-world matters, but of course he was always hated by the right. When he resigned with Bevan in 1951, he was treated with contempt by the right wing of the Party. They loathed him and called him Nye's little dog, but he came through it all with considerable dignity, became leader, won us the election of '64 and carried through '66, '70, '74 and then retired. At the end of his political life he was a bit of a spent force and I had many arguments with him about policy because I thought he was a bit technocratic and centralized, not democratic and open enough. I'm bound to say, however, that his was a successful life, more successful than Callaghan's or Kinnock's or Foot's, more successful than that of Gaitskell who fought an election and lost it. So the man will be remembered in a rather different way from that in which the scornful Peter Riddells dismiss him.

A common complaint is that you are out of touch with the electorate and even your own party. Bill Deeds in an article in the Telegraph *a few years ago wrote: 'Tony Benn, though a highly sensitive man, is not sensitive to what's going on around him if it is not what he wishes to see. He lacks political feel because his mind is dominated by the kind of society he desires to bring about.' How do you go about countering that rather deep-rooted idea of you?*

It's very simple. I've been elected to Parliament sixteen times which is a record in the House of Commons, and every year for all those years I've been elected to the National Executive. I receive 15,000 letters a year, a thousand people a year come to my surgeries for advice – I couldn't be more in contact with the life and opinions of people except if I were a priest perhaps, but then it would be very much more personal and rather less political. The test of my credentials is straightforward: if the local party wants me I am nominated as a candidate, if the electorate wants me I am elected. These arguments you put are just a way of trying to undermine the position I hold; I don't mind at all, they don't worry me, but if I'm

The Rt. Hon. Tony Benn

asked then I'm bound to give the answer. I like Bill Deedes very much but all he is saying is, 'Mr Benn is not in touch with what is happening in the Carlton Club', and I confess that is correct; I'm not.

Bill Deedes in the same article wrote: 'There has been a marked petulance about his behaviour in recent years, when his main achievement has been to raise the standard of the wild miscellany of extremists who have done the public life of this country no good at all.' You will perhaps say that this is standard Telegraph fare, but isn't it a perception which goes beyond the columns of the Tory press?

The wildest extremist I've ever come across in my life was Mrs Thatcher. She destroyed trade unionism, she destroyed local government, democracy, she took us into the Common Market and the single European Act without a referendum . . . so it depends on how you define extremism. I've argued a case which would only succeed if I could win a majority. Bill Deedes probably represents his class very well; I try to do the same.

Your last volume of diaries 1980–1990 was called The End of an Era. *Presumably the era referred to is the Bennite era?*

No. It was the end of Thatcher, and the end of Communism. It wasn't the end of my era – in fact, there's probably more public support for my ideas now than there's been at any time in the last ten years. People have rejected Thatcherism, they've rejected selfishness; they see our industry being destroyed, they see homeless people, unemployment, and much of what I have argued for has now won support. People wrongly thought it was the last volume of the diaries, but I'm working now on 1942–1962, and the one after that will be 1990–2000, and the final one will take me up to my 100th birthday.

How would you like to celebrate your 100th birthday?

I'd like to be re-elected to Parliament on that day for the first five years of my second century.

The Rt. Hon. Tony Benn

In the volume 1980–1990 Neil Kinnock is vilified again and again as someone shallow, ambitious and a traitor to the left of the Party. Wouldn't you allow that there is a good chance that history will come to judge him as the man who reformed the Party for its own good, something which had to be done to avert disaster?

I don't know how many times you have to be defeated to prove that you're unelectable. To be candid, nobody believed a word that was said. Election policies were made on the hoof, but I've never blamed Neil for this; I've only commented on his contribution. The people who accepted Neil were the National Executive, the Shadow Cabinet, the Parliamentary Party, and what interested me about the recent conferences of the Party was that the delegates were cheering because they thought Kinnock was going to win, and the media people were cheering because they knew he was killing Socialism. What neither realized was that he would not kill Socialism because it's alive, and that he would not win.

But did you think he would win the election?

I obviously hoped that we would win, but I had grave doubts about our capacity to win because it was very difficult to know what we stood for. For the first time in my life I voted against the manifesto along with Dennis Skinner. It never came out since they didn't want it to be known that there was a disagreement within the Party on the manifesto, but I put up my own posters in Chesterfield and told the voters what I believed in, and my vote increased. I did not think it made sense in the middle of a slump and with the Cold War over to give high priority to nuclear weapons, to abandon commitment to a democratic economy and go over to Maastricht. It was a terrible manifesto which had no credibility. It was not laying the foundation for victory; it was laying the foundation for a fourth defeat. But I can't blame the leader because he was supported by everybody.

Would it be fair or accurate to say that the extremely gifted and talented tend not to enter politics nowadays, and that consequently our lives are governed by rather mediocre people on the whole?

No, I don't think so. Clever people can be very stupid and I have known

The Rt. Hon. Tony Benn

some very clever fools in politics and also some very simple people who are wise. Eric Heffer, who was entirely self-educated, was one of the most intellectual men I knew; his library and his knowledge were phenomenal. Then there are people with top degrees who haven't had a single thought since they left college. Politics has always attracted ambitious and shallow people, and also very good and gifted people. In the end the public have to choose; they get the government they want or deserve, whichever way you look at it.

I have the impression that you see yourself as being on the side of the angels. Does this stem for your radical Christian upbringing, do you think?

I don't think that's true at all. I'm an ordinary human being who has had a lot of experience, doesn't want anything and speaks his mind. I'm sure Neil Kinnock thought he was on the side of the angels, but the angels in his case were all newspaper proprietors. I think I'm a hard-nosed realist who's confronting the harsh reality that Britain is rapidly declining and becoming a third-world country, losing its democracy, its morale, its self-confidence, and its hope. The dream that somehow you can get into power by joining with the liberals, having proportional representation, keeping the bomb . . . I would call that romanticism of a foolish character. It depends entirely on how you use language.

'In the end,' as Rab Butler famously remarked, 'politics has to be the art of the possible.' Is that a maxim which you have tried to keep in mind?

Of course. I've never been able to do anything without consent. I've said things that were unpopular, I've been defeated sometimes, and other times I've won, but everything that's ever been achieved has been by consent. It's terribly interesting being interviewed by you because you produce all the language of the right, and when it's examined it's found to have no substance. I didn't become leader of the Labour Party, but the elected leader, although he had the support of the Party, failed to persuade the public. What I try to do is to get people to see a different point of view, a different perspective.

You have been described as a compulsive optimist, a natural leader always rallying the troops. Do you see despair as the worst enemy?

The Rt. Hon. Tony Benn

I see it as very dangerous because when people are despairing, they look for a Hitler or a Mussolini. You can't be foolishly optimistic, but hope is the great fuel of social change, hope keeps you going, the idea that we will reach the promised land, we will get there one day. 'I have a dream,' said Martin Luther King, and that is what makes people work. Cynical journalists try to eliminate hope and there's a great deal of anger directed against anyone who tries to spread hope. For years the *Guardian* has attacked anyone who has had anything constructive to say, and when they've cleared the board of anything hopeful, then they say there's no vision. It is *la trahison des clercs*, a defect of the chattering classes.

In 1983 you were devastated to lose your seat in the General Election. How did you come to terms with this defeat and find the strength to fight another day?

I decided to be defeated in 1983. When my constituency was abolished I had six invitations to go to safe Labour seats and I refused on the grounds that I had been a member for Bristol for thirty-three years and I owed the people of Bristol everything. I chose to stay and be defeated, and I'm pleased that I did. I couldn't have walked away from the city that had supported me through the whole peerage case and just leave them to their fate; and it was the best decision I ever made. But you mustn't misunderstand me; to be defeated in the city I'd represented longer than anyone in the whole history of Bristol was a terrible bereavement.

How much have you relied on your wife and family for support during difficult times?

Oh enormously. My wife is an intellectual of formidable proportions and her understanding and academic capacity are far greater than mine, but she and my children have been very supportive. They've all paid a price for living in a house with somebody who has been engaged in lifelong controversy, but as far as I'm concerned it would have been quite impossible without the help of my family – parents, children and grandchildren. My little grandson came to Chesterfield on May Day and said afterwards, 'You weren't half as boring as you were last year.' Now when your grandchild tells you that, you know you've got a valuable adviser, and I take more notice of him than of Peter Riddell or *Guardian* leading articles.

The Rt. Hon. Tony Benn

Divorce seems to be an occupational hazard in political life. To what do you attribute the success of your own very long and happy marriage?

It's been a very good partnership and friendship, and I'm very fortunate in it. I met Caroline in Oxford and proposed to her after nine days, and from then on it's just been a very happy life together. We are very lucky.

You once advocated that instead of making divorce easier, marriage might be made more difficult, and that there might be compulsory education for the engaged couple. Was that a serious workable proposal in your view?

You must have done a lot of research into my writings. I remember writing that somewhere, but nowadays marriage is really more optional; it's partnerships that are developing now. In the end everything hinges not upon the formalities but upon the confidence of the relationship and the safeguarding of the children. So it is not now a question of making marriage more difficult because nowadays you don't have to marry at all.

Do you approve of that?

Oh yes. Marriage in one sense has been an enslavement of women, and I have been much influenced by having feminist arguments brought to bear in my own family. When my daughter was sixteen I remember she put up notices all over the house saying: 'End sexism in the Benn family.' That altered my attitude quite substantially.

As someone who has suffered from relentless press intrusion into your own private life and that of your family, what view do you take of the proposed reforms of the press?

I've had a very hard time which I don't generally speak about. To give just one example, my rubbish was once collected in a fast car every day. My son made a bell so that when they lifted the sack the bell rang and we looked out and saw the Rover taking it away. They also rented a flat opposite, and they harassed my children. It was worse for my family than for myself. It has placed a terrible burden on the children, and I daresay there have been ill effects, though not in terms of breaking up the closeness of the family. I

The Rt. Hon. Tony Benn

would never take a libel action, because all the money goes to the lawyers, and anyway, if you win, what does it amount to? You have to recognize that a press intrusion is designed to intimidate you, and you just have to survive it though it is very unpleasant. I'm not in favour of any state control of the media at all because I think it would be used against the left. The government wanted to stop the Peter Wright book being published and to stop Gerry Adams talking on the radio, so I'm never going to believe the Government is an instrument of freedom.

You have always been sensitive to comments about private wealth and trust funds for your family, and so on. Is that because these things sit so uneasily with left-wing politics?

My father had a pension of £500 a year from a publishing house and my wife's father was a lawyer in Cincinatti, but otherwise most of what was published was completely untrue. I just have to live with that lie. I mustn't pretend I've ever been short of cash, but this sort of millionaire stuff that has been put about is just part of the lie. The newspapers have five lines about me: he's mad, he's dangerous, he's a hypocrite, he's incompetent, he's ill, and they have run them all, and when they get very excited they run them all at once. I've got to know them now.

Khrushchev once said: 'Politicians are the same the world over – they promise to build a bridge even when there is no river.' Would you agree?

[Laughs] I've come to the conclusion that you should not make promises of what you will do for people; rather you should invite them to join you in doing things together. If I knock at a door and say, 'Vote for me and I'll solve your problem,' people don't believe it and neither do I. I favour a manifesto which asks people to help, not a manifesto of promises. It's a different approach to the political process.

Despite your energy, your vision, your tireless campaigning for social justice, it's difficult not to sense that your story is marked by disappointment. Are you ever in the still watches of the night overcome by feelings of failure or self-doubt?

The Rt. Hon. Tony Benn

The one thing I do conceal are moments of despair, because if you spread your anxieties then other people won't make the effort. I don't think of personal failure; my life has been rewarded beyond any reasonable dreams, and I've had the most marvellous family and political career. At the moment I'm very optimistic because I think the whole tide is turning politically. I am sustained by letters of support and what people say to me in ordinary daily life – that's worth a million leading articles by Bill Deedes or Peter Riddell. But of course I am human and yes, there are moments of terrible despair. I find the National Executive of the Labour Party the most painful thing in my monthly calendar; I dread going, I feel unhappy when I'm there, and I come away and lie down afterwards. The best discussions I attend are the ones in the Chesterfield constituency party; they are brilliant, clear, principled and knowledgeable, but the National Executive I find terribly distressing.

How has it been possible in the dirty business of politics to avoid bitterness and cynicism?

Cynicism is a very destructive thing. I would say I have been guided by certain things I was taught by my parents. They used to say, 'Never let the sun go down on your wrath' and 'Dare to be a Daniel, dare to stand alone', and so on. All these little sayings lodge, and when you get older you realize the whole of human wisdom is summed up in seven little phrases. I am genuinely not a bitter man, and I am not cynical because cynicism would destroy me.

Jad Adams writes at the conclusion of your biography: 'He was always true to himself and no sacrifice made a stone of his heart.' Would you be happy to have that as your eventual epitaph?

It was very generous of him to write that. I've made a million mistakes, many of which are published in my diaries, and there are many things I wish I had done differently, but I have been blessed with lovely parents, and a marvellous wife, children and grandchildren. I have been so richly endowed that it's impossible to express the gratitude I feel.

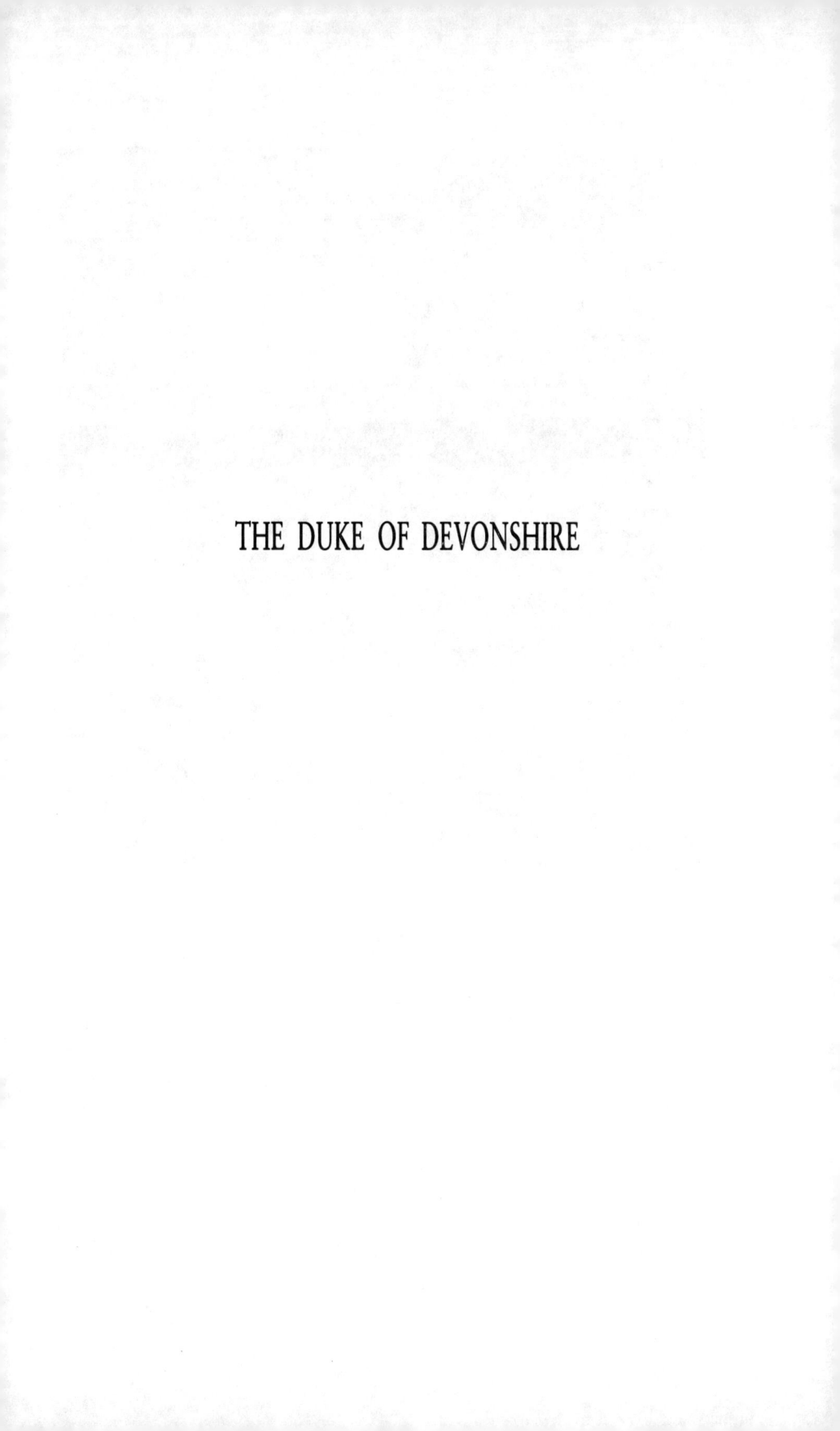

THE DUKE OF DEVONSHIRE

DUKE OF DEVONSHIRE

Andrew Cavendish was born in 1920, son of the 10th Duke of Devonshire and Lady Mary Cecil. He was educated at Eton and Trinity College, Cambridge, and was then commissioned in the Coldstream Guards. He was awarded the Military Cross for gallantry on the Italian front in 1944, and the same year became heir to the dukedom when his brother was killed in action. He married Deborah Mitford in 1941 and they have one son and two daughters. After his father's sudden death in 1950 he devoted himself to securing the future of Chatsworth, the family estate in Derbyshire. From 1962–4 he was Minister of State at the Commonwealth Relations Office and from 1965–86 he was chancellor of Manchester University.

The Duke of Devonshire

Your family can be traced back to feudal times, to the famous Bess of Hardwicke... has the sense of your own history affected your outlook on life very much?

Yes. I'm proud of my forebears. Bess was a very remarkable woman who married four men of property; fortunately she only had children by her Cavendish husband, so we inherited the lot. She was the first lady who put us on the way to fortune.

Have you felt an immense responsbility as a member of one of the important aristocratic families of England?

My years as head of my family have coincided with the decline of the influence of the aristocracy. Nowadays they have no power and virtually no influence.

Do you regret that decline?

No, it is right. Mr Major is a man for his times, but I sometimes wonder whether it is just coincidence that the decline of Britain as a world power has also coincided with the decline of the power and influence of the aristocracy.

You were born just after the First World War. During your childhood were you aware of the huge legacy of grief and horror which resulted from that war, or were you completely sheltered from it?

Two things brought it home to me as a child: one was the vast crowds that used to walk on the pavements on either side of military bands, no doubt largely composed of ex-servicemen; and the other was that we lived in Belgravia and used to walk to Hyde Park to see the construction of those great memorials, particularly the Royal Artillery one at Hyde Park Corner. And I remember my mother saying that all her dancing partners had been killed.

How do you look back on your schooldays at Eton?

The Duke of Devonshire

I enjoyed being there, but I was a horrible boy, and I'm not being falsely modest about this. I was dirty, I was lazy, and I have lived long enough to regret deeply my wasted opportunities. I could have had a marvellous education and yet I did so little.

Did you ever question your privileged status in those days, or did you regard education at Eton as part of your birthright?

I wouldn't have used the word birthright, but I did accept it. And of course although my mother and father took great care in our schooldays not to differentiate in any way between my elder brother and myself, I was becoming aware of the principle of primogeniture. My father would talk to me about it, making clear that it would ensure the survival of the estate. He knew it was unfair but he said, 'I accept the unfairness, and you must also accept the unfairness.'

Those who were sent away as children to boarding school often say that it distanced them in every way from their parents and family. Did you experience anything of that?

Yes. I didn't like it when I went back to school, but it's right, and it's got to be done sooner or later. When I had the honour and privilege of being Chancellor of Manchester University, I saw undergraduates in their late teens or early twenties away from home for the first time, and many of them found it very difficult to cope. It's a brutal system but you've got to be thrown in at the deep end, and it works.

Did you send your children to public school?

I did indeed. One of the worst things I've ever experienced was the first time I deposited my son at his private school; it was dreadful. I felt the pain, and so did he.

How did you meet Deborah Mitford . . . was it love at first sight?

I first saw her at Eton, when she was fifteen or sixteen and strikingly

The Duke of Devonshire

beautiful. Then we met at a dinner party in 1938, and if it wasn't love at first sight it was certainly attraction at first sight.

The Mitford girls were a legend in their own time. How did you feel about becoming part of that legend?

I was mildly jealous at being an addendum to the Mitford sisters.

Debo was involved in helping Unity travel back from Germany after she had shot herself . . . do you remember that time and the emotion it aroused?

I remember it vividly. My wife was very courageous during what was a dreadful and searing experience for her, and I had great admiration for Unity also in what she did. Rightly or wrongly she had a deep feeling for Nazi Germany, and when it came to war, she couldn't face the clash of loyalties between the two countries. One shouldn't condone suicide or attempted suicide, but it was, I thought, an heroic gesture.

You were married in London in 1941 as the bombs fell. Did the fact of war lend a heightened sense of emotion to the occasion?

Yes, I suppose it did. The Blitz was very exciting – I loved it. I was in the army, stationed in London, and there was a terrible raid the night before we got married, but we went to the wedding as if nothing was happening.

You were commissioned in the Coldstream Guards and your first child was born in 1943. Did you ever think that normal family life would be impossible because of the war, or did you always manage to keep the faith?

I think we managed to keep the faith . . . you see, it never crossed our minds that we were going to lose the war; it just never occurred to people of my generation. The war was just something that had to be got through.

The Duke of Devonshire

Your brother was killed in action shortly after D-Day. You must have been shattered by his death . . .

Yes I was. I felt terribly inadequate because I wasn't there – I was in Italy. Of course it was awful for my father and mother. And my brother had only just married Kathleen Kennedy who might well have been expecting his child, and it was perhaps only human to be curious to know.

Your father was a minister in Churchill's government. Was Churchill supportive, compassionate at that time?

My father was only a junior minister, and he and my mother were friends of Sir Winston's, but not very close friends. I'm sure Sir Winston would have been supportive, but he wouldn't have played a role in my family's grief.

Did you ever meet Churchill?

Not as a child, but when I was in the army in this country we did guard duty at Chequers and Sir Winston used to ask me up to dinner sometimes. He was very kind; he thought we never had enough to eat in the army, and pressed me with food. I was at Chequers the night the *Bismarck* was sunk. Churchill was getting all the radio messages, and it was one of the most thrilling nights of my life.

Your brother only had a few weeks of marriage before his death. That must surely have made you and Debo very aware of the fragility of family life . . .

It was worse, much worse for Debo. I actually enjoyed the war in Italy. I liked my fellow men, the camaraderie, and we were doing something; but for the wives here it must have been terrible.

Later in the same year you were decorated for gallantry on the Italian front. Did you brother's death make you all the more determined to defeat the enemy?

The Duke of Devonshire

Yes, it did. I hated the Germans – I think I still do. Yes, it brought a sense of personal resentment.

Your brother's wife, Kathleen Kennedy, died in an air crash in 1948, one of a succession of tragedies in the Kennedy family. Were you closely involved with the Kennedys?

Yes, we kept up the connection, and still do, and when they come to England, they nearly always visit Chatsworth. My sister-in-law was one of the most delightful ladies I've ever met. She wasn't exactly beautiful but she had a great vitality. We all loved her. And Jack Kennedy was the most marvellous man. My wife and I went to his inauguration which was very exciting and thrilling. I went to his funeral also, which was terrible.

Both your families were touched by the terrible effects of the war. Debo's brother Tom and also Unity were casualties of the war. Did you feel at the time that you had been singled out for particularly harsh treatment, or was there a kind of universal loss and grief?

It was very sad that Tom was killed so late in the war. He could have had a distinguished career in politics if he'd wanted to. But we all lost a lot of our close friends and family, and though it wasn't anything like the First World War, it wasn't a scythe right through society, it was universal. But Tom's death in Burma when the war was really over was particularly hard.

Your brother's death altered the course of your life in that you became successor to your father, the Duke. Were you a reluctant heir?

My brother had been killed in action, so it wasn't right, was it? It wasn't my fault, but it certainly made me uneasy.

Apropos your father's sudden death in 1950 your wife has written, 'Not only did Andrew lose his father; he also lost his friend and wise counsellor.' Does that describe how you felt?

Exactly. He was marvellous. My father wasn't a mean man, but he spent

The Duke of Devonshire

very little money on himself, whereas I've always been very extravagant, and my father vicariously enjoyed these extravagances. He didn't like horseracing at all, but he was only too delighted to find the funds for me to buy horses, nearly always bad ones.

In addition to the title, you inherited enormous problems in the form of death duties which it took over twenty years to clear. How did you face up to this colossal task?

There again I was singularly lucky. First of all at thirty I was young and resilient. Secondly and more importantly, I had the most brilliant financial and legal adviser, a man called W.D. Macpherson, now dead. If we'd panicked, I wouldn't be sitting here now. We had to pay eighty per cent of everything but thanks to the way it was handled, a great deal survived on the art side which was perhaps what mattered most to me. We had to lose the ten best things we had, and they went – perhaps rightly – to our national institutions, the V.& A., the National Gallery, and so on. I had to take the decision whether to lose the very best and keep the bulk of the contents of Chatsworth, or to sell a tremendous lot and keep the very best. Rightly or wrongly I settled for the very best to go, but we've still got a very nice collection.

But do you feel any sense of bitterness about it?

No. The Lord gives and the Lord takes away. I'm one of the luckiest men in the world, and most people would give the eyes in their head for what's in Chatsworth. I'm philosophical about it, though I do sometimes think that but for that German sniper's bullet none of Chatsworth would have been lost.

You must surely at times have felt defeated by the enormity of the problem. What was it that kept you going?

My wife, my relative youth, and my advisers.

It must have given you great satisfaction to secure the future of Chatsworth and moreover to make it completely self-financing.

I've achieved virtually nothing in life, but that is certainly what I am most proud of. It was due to my advisers more than to me, and my wife has been a pillar, but to keep Chatsworth going is my overwhelming ambition, as it was my father's; and I would guess it will be my son's.

Do you get on well with your son?

I get on very well with my son. I'm proud of him, and I put him very high on my list of good fortune. He also gets on well his mother and stands up to her too, more than I do.

She is a strong character?

That would be an understatement.

During the 1960s you held various political posts which you say yourself you would never have held but for Harold Macmillan's nepotism. Is that a false modesty or something you genuinely believe?

Oh, it's true. It was gross nepotism. I had made a few speeches about the reorganization of betting in this country, but I hadn't been very active in the House of Lords, so there was no justification. But Harold obviously thought I could do it. I imagine he thought, 'I can risk him, he won't make too much of an ass of himself.'

Harold Macmillan is a very controversial figure; the historians disagree about him. What was your view?

To begin with, unlike many politicians, he was a clever man. He was also an extremely astute politician – 'wily' is an apt description. My judgement of him is biased because he was so good to me that I can never repay the debt I owe him. Not only did he give me a job which I enjoyed very much but it led to other things. For example, I became chancellor of Manchester

University which was one of the great experiences of my life. He also had the best manners of any man I ever met.

But was he trustworthy?

I was too junior in government to have political dealings with him so I never had any reason not to trust him. It would be presumptuous of me to sit in judgement on him.

You say that you left the Conservative Party and joined the Social Democrats 'largely for sentimental reasons'. What exactly did you mean by that?

We were Whigs and then we were Liberals, and we left the Liberal Party over Home Rule for Ireland. We were wrong about Home Rule for Ireland, wrong for good reasons. We thought that the Irish would suffer materially from independence, and indeed they have, but I'm a fervent believer in the political nostrum: 'It is better to govern yourself badly than to be well governed by others.' I like to think I am still a good Whig.

You have an impressive record of public service. Is that area of your life as important as sitting on the cross benches in the Lords?

Sitting on the cross benches in the Lords is not important. You've been kind about my record of public service which is very modest, and what I'm going to say now sounds extremely priggish. I'm aware of how lucky I am, and if I can help people or do anything in the way of charitable work, well, God knows, that's the least I can do. Also I really like people, and if I come away from meeting someone and I've been bored, I regard that as my failure.

Some time ago you hosted at Chatsworth a gathering to promote peace in the Middle East. Is that a special area of interest for you?

Yes, it is one of my great interests. Through my father I've always had a great affinity with the Jewish community. My father was a friend of

The Duke of Devonshire

Weizmann and I can remember the excitement in our house in London when we was coming to lunch. My father much regretted that he himself had no Jewish blood, and occasionally after dinner he could be seen looking through the Peerage and when asked what he was doing, he would say, 'Surely somewhere there must be some Jewish blood . . .' There is a large Jewish community in Manchester and when I became chancellor to Manchester University, that's where I strengthened my links. I've been to Israel six times now.

You were formerly president of the Conservative Friends of Israel, but now you support the neutral Next Century Foundation. Why did you change?

I ceased to be a Tory so I couldn't go on being president of the Friends of Israel, and the Next Century Foundation is trying to build bridges between the Palestinian and Jewish communities.

Are you optimistic that eventually a solution will be found?

I cannot say I am, and I regret that very much. I used to endorse the Jewish cause without question, but last April I went to the West Bank, and I was horrified by what I saw; the army was everywhere. Israel's got a lot to answer for, but of course there are a great many people in that part of the world who want to see Israel driven into the sea, so I think it is not quite fair to judge them by ordinary standards. Nevertheless, however simplistic it may sound, if the Jewish people are justified in having their own state, are not the Palestinians? Forgive me for talking vulgarly, but what is sauce for the goose is sauce for the gander.

I sense in you a certain discomfort with your aristocratic status. Would you have preferred to live your life in comparative obscurity perhaps?

No, I can't say that. It has great advantages, but there are also disadvantages. I dislike being called Your Grace, for example, and ninety-nine per cent of the population of this country think dukes are freaks, and they may well be right. People will not accept that you can have perfectly ordinary interests – for example, I really care about professional football, it interests me a great deal, but when I talk about it most people think I'm putting it on.

You once said that the trouble with being a duke was that people thought you were a blithering idiot. Do you care very much about what other people think?

Too much. It is an attractive quality not to give a damn what people think of you, but I haven't got it.

Debo once said of the late Duke of Beaufort that he was the most pointless man she had ever met.

I'm very sorry to hear that.

Do you think perhaps that in the late twentieth century pointlessness is a sad feature of much of the aristocracy?

I suppose we've only got ourselves to blame, but our power's been taken away. The caravan moves on, the days of the aristocracy are over. I wouldn't exactly use the word pointless, but we've had our day. We had a good long run.

Would you be upset if a future government were to disband the House of Lords?

I should be very sorry if there wasn't a second chamber, although I wouldn't in the least mind losing my title and being called Andrew Cavendish, but all the newspapers would add to it 'formerly the Duke of Devonshire', so it wouldn't make much difference. I'd mind very much if my wealth and possessions were taken away, but my title, no.

Do you think the House of Lords makes a valuable contribution to the political system?

The Duke of Devonshire

Yes, I do. The standard of debate is extremely high and I think the House of Commons has got a great deal to learn from it. One of the problems in this country is our over-adversarial attitude in the Commons as exemplified by Prime Minister's Question Time; I can only describe it as extreme disagreeableness which sets a bad example to the rest of the country.

Your image was rather tarnished a few years ago when in the Old Bailey witness box you revealed what many people would consider the rather disreputable side of your private life at the time. Was that a difficult period for you?

Very. It was very disagreeable. Being in the witness box and speaking on oath is a salutary experience, and it was very painful for my family. The only consolation was that I didn't attempt to lie. My private life isn't all it might be, but it would only make it worse to lie about it.

Do you resent the way that dukes and duchesses are public property in the sense that they are thought to be accountable to the nation – in much the same way as the royal family are under constant scrutiny?

I don't know that we are; we don't count any more. As I say, we're regarded as freaks, and we're totally marginalized now.

Infidelity has been the breaking point of a great many marriages and yet yours seem to very stable and solid. To what do you owe its success, do you think?

I'm not sure that's a fair question. You're going too deeply into my private life. The essential ingredient of marriage is tolerance, but I really can't go any further than that.

Do you believe that men are not naturally monogamous and that perhaps too much significance is given to one or other partner straying from the path?

The Duke of Devonshire

Those marriages where neither partner has been unfaithful are relatively few and astonishingly lucky.

I think it would be fair to say that the Cavendish line has had something of a reputation for philandering, right back to the first duke in the seventeenth century. Is this something you would prefer not to be the case, or is it more of a badge of honour?

It is certainly not a badge of honour. Philandering is nothing to be proud of; it's a weakness.

Have you yourself repented?

I find repentance very difficult, particularly if you are aware that you may do the same thing again . . . one has to be very careful of repentance.

Do you think the Establishment is under serious threat and if so, are you dismayed by that?

I don't know what the Establishment is, but I'm certainly not part of it. I don't think it exists any more. In this country the civil service has much more power than the politicians. I was never more than a middle-ranking minister but it was enough to know just how powerful the civil servants are. I long for someone to define to me what the Establishment is. Is there a group of people in this country who can fix things? I don't know.

Do you think that politicians today are less powerful than they once were?

The economic conditions prevailing in the country limit the power of the politicians. If the Labour Party had got in at the last election, and it is a great pity they didn't, Black Wednesday would have happened just the same. I have my own views on political matters but the downside of privilege is that there are great constraints on what you may speak about. If I were to express my views on the Welfare State, for example, people would say, 'How dare he?', and they'd be quite right to say that. When I was on the opposition front bench I was No. 2 to Peter Carrington on foreign affairs, and after about eighteen months I was moved to transport which was rather absurd because I must have been the only member of the House of Lords who can't drive. But transport was the only thing which a duke could speak about. Privilege prohibits you from commenting on a vast swathe of national issues.

Are you a religious man?

I can't make up my mind. I can't believe in another world, although I shall certainly go to hell if there is one. The Sermon on the Mount is absolutely right, as are Christian values; I have no doubt about that; but I envy those with real faith.

Would you consider yourself to have been a good man?

No, I'm afraid not. Even with money I'm not really a generous man. I only give to charity what I can afford, and not enough to affect my standard of living. The truly generous man gives a sacrifice of himself. I've never done that.

Does death worry you?

No. I look forward to it really. Wonderful things have happened to me in my life; I've had too much good fortune. It's time my son had his turn. When I was young I used to like casinos, fast women, and God knows what; now my idea of heaven, apart from being at Chatsworth, is to sit in the hall of Brooke's having China tea. I can't think of a greater pleasure than that . . . that's what comes of being old.

… MARY ELLIS

MARY ELLIS

Mary Ellis was born in New York in 1900. In 1918 she made her début opposite Caruso at the Metropolitan Opera House where she remained for four years. She was the original Rose Marie in the musical by Hammerstein (1924). She starred in a number of theatrical roles on Broadway and in 1926 appeared in Dostoevsky's *Crime and Punishment* with the English actor Basil Sydney who became her third husband. In 1929 they travelled to England and she made her London stage début in 1930. She remained in London and starred in *The Dancing Years* and *Glamorous Night* which Ivor Novello wrote especially for her. After the war she resumed her stage career and made many appearances at Drury Lane, the Old Vic, Stratford-upon-Avon and the Lyceum, Edinburgh. Her autobiography, *Those Dancing Years*, was published in 1982.

Mary Ellis

I have the impression from your autobiography that your mother was a kind but rather remote, even unhelpful presence in your life. Yet presumably it was her interest in music which sowed the seeds of your own career.

She was a very talented musician who had given everything up to marry my father, and when she saw I had talent she put all her unfinished ambition into me. Usually Americans are overflowing with affection and warmth, whether it's honest or not, but she wasn't demonstrative at all. I can't remember any cosiness or anything maternal, and I had no real childhood. I am more of a child now than I was then in the sense that I have reactions now which I should have had when I was ten or eleven.

You say you learned the rudiments of morality, optimism and compassion from your nurse, and yet she was despatched from your life when you were only six, leaving you desolate. Can you still recall that feeling of being abandoned, what you call your 'great dark grief'?

Yes. It is moderated in my mature life but I have a theory that everybody has a typical experience; no matter how people try to change their reactions and what happens to them, somehow it becomes a recurring leitmotif. I have had a continual feeling of abandonment in my personal life, and even though I am ninety-three I still fear it. Maybe I expect too much of people, but I know it's going to end badly.

Did this feeling of being abandoned have repercussions in later life, do you think?

I was brought up in the Edwardian way of thinking; everything had to be terribly contained, there was none of this permissive feeling at the time, and if you thought you were in love with somebody you had to marry, even though mature thinking would have dictated otherwise. Consequently I had a very unsuccessful and unhappy first marriage. I don't blame fate or life because it has been wonderful to me in other respects. There's just something in me that has always invited emotional distress or disaster.

Were you close to your father?

Mary Ellis

I absolutely worshipped him, and to displease him was the most awful thing in the world to me. It was he who helped out in all my unhappiness, and he who nursed me when I was ill. He also taught me my first music and I remember sitting on his knee and he'd sing all the Viennese waltzes with the result that I always moved in three-quarters time. He died in 1937 and I missed him dreadfully.

Your mother was quite indulgent towards you in the sense that 'she condoned too much without understanding enough', as you put it. Do you think you would have benefited from stricter guidelines?

Indeed, yes, but my parents were so Edwardian that it was taken for granted that girls didn't do certain things. There's a sense of safety in obeying authority, whether it's parents or teachers, and that sense is absent nowadays in young people who would consider our way of life to have been very austere, but in fact it built a wonderful foundation.

You wrote in your book: 'Never once, even in the emotional crises of my life when I needed her help, did she explain anything to me.' Did you ever manage to come to terms with this feeling of disappointment in your mother?

As I grew up it became more amusement than disappointment. I was an afterthought in my parents' lives – I came ten years after my sister. My mother was a most amazing woman, very talented, suppressed, flirtatious and beautiful – full of contradiction. I imagine she must have been very passionate, because my father never looked at another woman all his life. In the eighteenth century she might have been a marvellous courtesan.

You fell in love at a very tender age, but the boy you loved was killed in the Battle of the Somme. Did that early shock, that linking of love and death, make its mark on the rest of your life, do you think?

Emphatically, yes. First love is the greatest experience one can have, and it wasn't a silly, baby love, because we had been more or less brought up together. But when I look back on my life, I was very lucky, because if, poor boy, he hadn't been killed, I think I would have ended up in Manchester, without a career, the mother of a great many children.

Looking back on your youth, you say that in terms of maturity, you were really the same as today's young people, only more self-conscious and less sex-conscious. Do you think that being less sex-conscious made it an easier or more difficult time for you?

Oh heavens, sex didn't enter into it. I confess that I suffered from innocence, and I can say absolutely truthfully that I still do. Although I know everything with my brain, I cannot see how people behave as they do. Innocence is a quality, not a physical thing, so that someone can have been through the mill, indeed several mills, and still retain a quality of innocence that has nothing to do with what's happened. I don't envy today's youth at all; they have mistaken sex for love. I have never in my life slept with a man I didn't love.

You have managed to retain your innocence?

Yes, though that has been unfortunate in some ways. I would have behaved quite differently if I had had a sophisticated approach to life. I would certainly have been more sensible. I'm a hopeless romantic, and romantics have the worst time of it because they persist in translating the happenings of life into miracles and fairy tales.

You describe singing with Caruso in L'Elisir d'Amore *as the pinnacle for you. Did it also seem so at the time, or did it become imbued with such significance only later?*

I hardly ever realized anything important was happening to me at the time. The most astonishing things musically and professionally took place, yet I never knew. My dream of living a life over again would be to know the value of things as they take place. In my late years I have been more able to appreciate moments of happiness when they happen, but when you're young the peaks pass you by.

Mary Ellis

Before you were twenty-five you had already sung with Caruso and Chaliapin, and you describe the thrill of Chaliapin 'dying' in your arms in Boris Godunov. Did you become aware of Caruso's legendary status only afterwards?

No, that was something I knew then. I remember almost fainting during the first rehearsal. It was a physical thing, really. I was small and slender, and I had to kneel on the floor and hold this great heavy hulk, and when he started to sing and it was like embracing a church bell – the vibrations and sound filled all one's cavities and senses. But all this was so long ago and such a small small part of my life that I've practically forgotten it; I don't live with it at all, and can only remember the effect of it.

You don't live in the past?

No. I remember the past like a marvellous book I've read. Life is the most important thing, it's the only thing we have, so we have to make something of every minute, even if it's tragic.

You write movingly of Caruso's last performance and his subsequent death. You describe the shock you felt when the manager at the Met said, 'Persona e indispensabile', which made you realize 'how every moment of living in an instant becomes the past'. Has that been a recurrent shock throughout your life, or is it something you have come to accept as one of life's truths?

I shall never accept it, but it happens all the time. Every word that you and I utter now is consigned to memory in a second.

Your first marriage was unhappy and shortlived, ending in divorce after a year. In those days divorce must have been a comparatively rare phenomenon . . . was that a very difficult time?

No, it wasn't at all. My father just took me by the nape of the neck and we boarded a train for California. I stood before a judge for three minutes while my father told the story, and I was divorced.

Mary Ellis

Was there any stigma attached to divorcees in those days?

Oh no, there never has been in America. Money is the only thing that counts over there.

Your second marriage to Edwin Knopf seems to have been motivated by a mixture of guilt and pity, and you say you have always felt sorry and ashamed of the way you behaved. What were your feelings after that marriage broke up?

Guilt. Guilt, for my letting it happen, not for what I did. I can't explain it any better than that. I had refused to marry him in the first place, whereupon he went to Europe to get over it in the way young men did in those days. He had a terrible accident in which his left arm was blasted off by some kind of a snow bomb, and his parents came to me and begged me to help by giving him some hope when he got back. Like a fool I sent him a very emotional and encouraging cable. He came home full of joy, and I had to marry him. I helped him a lot and taught him to use his right hand for everything, but he knew I didn't love him in the complete sense. The next bit sounds like a terrible Barbara Cartland novel: I knew that my best friend from school had always been in love with him, and so, taking strength from that, I let things happen that broke the marriage. She married him, and they lived happily ever after.

In 1925 after starring in Rose Marie, *you gave up singing to concentrate on acting, which was an unpopular decision with the public. The fact that you had to sign an agreement with Hammerstein meant that you never sang in the US again. Would you still have signed if you had known that would be the consequence?*

No, although I was absolutely passionate about the theatre and had no regrets. But to this day I miss the physical exhilaration of singing. I don't miss the operettas or the opera, rather the actual experience of singing, the thinking of a note, hearing it come out, sending it into the auditorium and knowing they've got it.

What about the thrill of the audience standing to applaud you?

Mary Ellis

I suppose I never thought I had done anything as well as I should, so the acknowledgement was always shaded for me by a lack of belief in myself.

At one point in the book you say: 'All through my life I've missed opportunities because of human relationships, and I've tried very hard not to regret anything.' Have you succeeded in being philosophical about missed opportunities?

Yes. If I hadn't I'd be a dire mess.

Your marriage to Basil Sidney was one which he dominated completely, although you loved him deeply. Was his betrayal perhaps the most difficult thing you have had to bear in your life?

It was the most surprising thing certainly, I'm not sure I can say it was the most difficult. I lost my voice for ten days through nervous shock; I just didn't believe it. Of course, I was a fool. I should have known, but I didn't.

I was struck by your words, 'I have never been able to unlove someone I have loved.' Has that been an added cross to bear in life?

No, it's been something delightful. In any case, how can you unlove someone you've loved? It would imply a total lack of self-respect. If you've loved someone intensely, there must be something in that person you found worth loving. If that person does something terribly disappointing and hurtful, well that's that. I'm extremely philosophical in these matters; I never would try to keep anyone who didn't want to be with me. I'm much too vain for that.

In 1935 you went off to Hollywood for a couple of years to star in three films. One imagines it must have been a very glamorous place at a very romantic time, but it struck you as being rather sad. Why was that?

Because it was so artificial. People had no lives of their own outside the pictures. I imagine it's changed now because so many people I admire managed to go back and enjoy it, and even made second homes there, but at that time there was only work, there was no real living.

You met many famous people during that time, and struck up a warm friendship with Fritz Lang who had fled from Germany. Did that develop into a special friendship?

Well, isn't every friendship special?

I mean, were you romantically involved?

No. We went on Sunday motor trips together, and I'm pleased to feel that I helped him over a terribly hard time. He was an amazing and wonderful man, inspiring and very clever. It was so awful to see him crushed. I was also friendly with Charles Boyer, a charming man. He gave a marvellous party for me when I first went over there. Mrs Patrick Campbell was an honoured guest and she sat at the head of his staircase in a chair, greeting the guests before he did. Marlene Dietrich arrived, looking absolutely wonderful in black tulle, with diamonds tinkling, and she made a deep curtsey in front of her, whereupon Mrs Patrick Campbell said, 'Oh you are so pretty. Are you in pictures too, dear?' I thought Marlene would fall down the stairs backwards.

Did you know Marlene well?

Yes, she had the dressing room opposite mine. She used to knock at my door while I was being made up, and would come in without any make-up, freckles on her nose, pale eyelashes and a towel around her head, looking much prettier than when she was all made up. And she'd say, 'Sing me a little German folk song', so I'd sing some little thing I sang on my father's knee, and she'd go away quite happy.

After America you returned to England to work with Ivor Novello, with whom you were very close until his death. Were you ever in love with him?

No. He was very romantic man, but I don't think he thought about marriage or anything like that. His musicals meant nothing to me intellectually or emotionally, but I know if I hadn't done them I wouldn't have had the thrill of singing at Drury Lane which looks bigger from the stage than the Metropolitan Opera House. To feel that you are filling the auditorium even with a whisper or a soft note, that is an amazing experience.

You write in your autobiography: 'The working relationship with Ivor developed into a very good kind of loving. To my mother it was incomprehensible that it did not entail a romantic ending.' Was it also a sadness for you?

No. He was a delightful and intelligent man, a wonderful musician and an enchanting companion, but he was totally of the theatre and had no life apart from that. He was a wonderful friend, and for all the years afterwards until he died, he came to everything I did and offered me sound advice. He had his own entourage, the faithful, but I was very unsophisticated, and believe it or not, until I came to London when I was thirty-one years old, I didn't know about any of those intricacies of life at all, although I soon learned to live with them.

Apropos your close friend, Tim Brook, you write: 'The men I've known who had loving natures, but who could not love women completely, I have found comforting friends. My unhappy experiences with the total male made such relationships a relief.' Were you ever made happy in a complete sense with any man?

Oh yes, but of course, I wouldn't be a complete woman if I hadn't. But people are people to me; I don't question their religion, their politics or their emotional habits. If they are fine people, intelligent or artistic, or they give something to their friends and the world, it's all right by me. I have no set prejudices at all. In classical times it didn't matter so much; I don't see why it should matter now.

After your third marriage ended in divorce, there seemed to follow a period of despair during which love seemed to be beyond your reach. How did you manage to come to terms with this feeling?

I don't know exactly. I think I worked very hard. Although I've been disappointed, I'm not the kind of person to allow desperation to enter into my consciousness. I know when I've done wrong, and I'm very sorry for it, but I try my best either to fix it or to live with it. One has to be a realist without losing one's dreams, if that's possible.

During this time when love seemed beyond your reach, you even sought comfort in Catholicism, but that was not to prove to be the answer. Do you consider yourself to be religious now?

I certainly believe in God, something greater than self, and I've said my prayers since I was a child. There is something which in our wildest moments either pulls us back or pushes us forward. We think we are free to do as we like, but I'm sure that the whole cosmos of being is arranged by something far greater than anything we know.

But do you believe in heaven or hell?

Not pictorially, not as a place where the angels fly, or the devils have horns, but I feel very seriously that this can't be the end. All you have to do is to look at nature: a tree dies every autumn, but it flowers again the next year.

Do you find that you have that serenity which is supposed to come with old age?

Yes, but I hate to call it serenity. The compensation for growing old is that there seems now to be a reason for everything. And it's completely untrue that the senses become dimmed as you grow older; as your physicality slips away, your senses get sharper and more intense.

Just before the war, you met your next husband, Jock Roberts, in Edinburgh, the day after you had news of your father's death. Do you think the two events were in any way connected . . . did you fall in love partly because it was an emotionally vulnerable time for you?

Mary Ellis

I didn't fall in love with him when I first met him. But it was the strangest thing, just as though a male element had been sent into my life at precisely the time I had lost the one I respected most. It was also unexpected because by then I had become philosophical about life and imagined it was going to be just my own work and friends from then on.

Your husband had fallen in love with you on the stage, and was determined to keep you behind the footlights. Did this not strike you as an uncertain basis for marriage?

I made the great mistake that I made all my life in personal relationships, and I blame myself for it. I tried to become what the person who cared for me wanted me to be instead of being myself and letting him see all my faults. For example, I had never climbed mountains, I had never skied, but I gave up the theatre for several years to be a companion to Jock doing these things, and it almost killed me. I hated it, every minute of it, but I was determined to be that companion. Of course that wasn't what he had fallen in love with, but I wasn't sensible enough even to see that.

Your husband's view of lovemaking was the rather Victorian one that 'nice' women should not enjoy it – an attitude you persauded him to overcome. Do you think that was an unusual achievement for the 1930s?

The whole thing was very unusual for the 1930s. It never occurred to me that a grown-up male could be that way. But of course all British men had been told from childhood that they mustn't show their emotions, and in Victorian days, young gentlemen were sent away to Paris for three weeks to learn all about it when they came out of university, but they weren't allowed to practise it in Britain, and certainly not with the lovely creatures they married. Well, you see, having been born a free soul, this was absolutely amazing to me.

During the war you chose not to remain in the theatre but 'to fight the war the hardest way I could find', as you put it. What kind of feelings impelled you to do this?

There were many people in the theatre who bravely entertained the troops, but that to me wasn't doing enough. Men were having to leave the things they loved, and so I felt that like them I had to do something opposite from what I enjoyed – something far away from the theatre, the make-believe and the glamour; that way I could really feel part of the war. I wouldn't have given up that experience for anything. I worked in emergency hospitals, I looked after children who had been bombed in Glasgow, and later I learned to do occupational therapy which taught me something for life. I experienced an entirely different kind of consciousness and it's lived with me ever since. I can never think of people just as what they seem to be; I always look for their wounds, because everybody has wounds inside them that haven't quite healed, or that ache occasionally.

The war years placed a great strain on your relationship, and your husband seemed to have been changed by war. Do you think that was inevitable?

It was quite inevitable that it should have happened to him. He was so enclosed in that Scottish world of habits and beliefs that he didn't know about the other world. He hadn't realized that other people had to live a different way. However, it didn't change my love for him at all. I got very interested in what was happening to him and thought he'd come out of it, and if he hadn't been killed, I expect he would have come out of it.

His politics changed during the war period . . .

Yes, because he had contact with something he'd never seen or heard before, and lived with men who changed his mind about all sorts of things. I don't blame him in a way. Before the war he had never seen the black side of life, or never chosen to see it. Everything he had done and stood for before the war had vanished when he came back. He had become very interested in the Communist movement, though I never knew whether he signed any papers or not. He gave up a lucrative position in his father's business, and came to London and took a job for six pounds a week at Camberwell Art School. He broke his father's heart. He didn't succeed in breaking mine because I tried to look at it romantically, and until he was killed I kept leaping ahead in years, believing he would change back. But even if he hadn't, I suppose I would have accepted it. I loved him enough. Still do.

Mary Ellis

Everything seemed to have a heightened significance during the war. You write in your memoirs: 'The war was salting life through with partings and reunions, but when I was able to be with my husband nothing else mattered.' Had you by then found the love you had been searching for?

I thought so, I thought so. But since all that has happened, I know it wasn't. I wasn't truthfully myself.

Your time with Jock was cut tragically short when he was killed in a climbing accident, something you describe as a new low in your life. It must have seemed as if the world had collapsed...

Yes, but doesn't it to everyone? I just made myself work harder, and the theatre became everything to me till the 1970s.

Did you ever manage to love again in the way you loved Jock?

Nobody ever loves again in the same way. Every love is new.

But did you come to love someone else?

Not as I loved Jock, no. I have loved lots of people, and I feel I know now what love should mean, but I'm too old. Heavens, at ninety somebody doesn't come into your life, and even if someone did one would be too old ... The point about growing old is that one sees everything one should do, one would know exactly how to behave, but one is too old to put it to the practice.

That's the tragedy you mean?

There's no tragedy. It's very amusing.

You never had any children. Have you felt that as a loss?

I had one very bad miscarriage and then I couldn't have children. I carried a child to seven months, so I had the experience of that wonderful foretaste. I also had two stepdaughters, Jock's children, and that was very satisfactory.

After all these years in England, do you feel thoroughly English yourself, or is there part of you which longs to be in the land of your birth?

I have never longed for the land of my birth. I visited Britain from the time I was four years old and all my relations and friends seemed to be here, so I always felt thoroughly at home here. I also know France very well, and I must say I miss the atmosphere of France and the way they care for their older people. What appals me about this country more than anything else is the way old people are treated. In France they would think it absolutely disgraceful if Grandmère didn't live at home with her son or her daughter, and the same applies in almost every other European country.

You have had a fascinating life which spans the whole of the century to date. You watched Sarah Bernhardt perform, you saw Pavlova dance, you sang with Caruso – you are linked with so many magical figures from the past. Does the present now seem very tame to you by comparison?

No. All those people you mention are in the distant past, whereas I tend to think of myself from 1932 onwards, when my life was the theatre, the Old Vic and the season at Stratford – all that seems more important and much closer to me. I don't want to be put into a box labelled The Past, I don't like that at all. I know I may pop off at any minute, but for the moment I'm still here.

If you were to live your life over again would you do it differently?

I wouldn't live my life differently, but I'd behave differently. I would be braver, kinder, because sometimes we think we have done the kind thing, and we haven't. I missed out on life on account of carelessness, on account of being afraid of being unloved, and those things I would change.

Mary Ellis

Do you fear death?

I'm as full of curiosity about death as I am about life, so I cannot be uncheerful. It's going to be something new, another adventure.

LORD FORTE

LORD FORTE

Charles Forte was born in Monforte in Italy in 1908. At the age of five he came to Scotland with his parents and he was educated in Alloa and Dumfries before attending Mamiani College in Rome. He opened his first milk bar in London in 1935. Within twenty-five years he had acquired the Criterion Restaurant, the Monico, the Café Royal, the Waldorf Hotel and Fuller's Ltd. In 1970 the Trust House Forte Group was formed and his empire gradually expanded to include over 800 hotels and several hundred restaurants. He was created a life peer in 1982.

Lord Forte

You didn't have an entirely settled upbringing in the sense that it was divided between Scotland and Italy, and you were often separated from your parents and siblings. Do you think this worked to your advantage in the end?

It's a question I can't really answer except to say that I never felt uprooted. I spent a lot of time with my family and I was always very close to my parents. I still own my childhood home in Monforte, and I go back there regularly. I've never lost my feeling for Italy and whenever I go back to the tiny little village up in the hills, I get that prickly feeling of knowing I am back where my ancestors came from. I have a similar feeling of excitement if I go to Alloa in Scotland. The strange thing is, although I have been all over the world, and I suppose at my age I could live anywhere, I do regard Britain as home. Whenever my wife and I fly into Heathrow, even though it's raining and cold and miserable, we always look at each other and say, 'Ah, thank God, we're back, back home.'

Your childhood seems to have been a mixture of over-protectiveness from your parents and a large degree of independence. Was this an ideal combination, would you say?

I don't think my parents ever gave me the freedom I needed, but they were lovely people, God bless them, and I hope there's another world so that I may see them again. Although they didn't encourage independence, I took it anyway, and managed to remain close to them. They needed my affection because they were away from home, my father spoke English very badly, and they had no friends beyond their family. They never really assimilated.

You did not take to boarding school in Scotland and persuaded your parents to take you away, and yet the alternative was boarding school in Italy. Why was the one acceptable and the other not?

They were both unacceptable. The difference was that one was nearer home and I was able to escape from it, and the other was in Rome and since I was isolated I had to stay. My father was determined I should have some discipline so he consulted a relative who was a monk at the Mamiani College in Rome, took me there and told me to stay.

Lord Forte

You decided at a very young age that you were going to be the most successful member of your family . . . where did this driving ambition come from?

The Fortes have always been very competitive. They've been in the village of Monforte for generations, and they've always been keen to try and do better than one another. I just knew I was going to be successful. I had it in my bones. I was cut out for the job and I always had the idea that the more persistent I was, the more successful I would be. I always remember Gary Player, the great golfer, playing a shot out of the bunker, and it dropped two inches from the hole, and a lady from the crowd said, 'Oh Mr Player, how lucky!', and he looked up and said, 'Madam, the more I practise the luckier I get.'

When the war broke out, did you have any sense of divided loyalties? I know you wanted the Allies to win but you must have feared for your family and friends back in Italy . . .

When war broke out I went to the Home Office and volunteered for the Air Force. I didn't want to fight against people who were my own countrymen, so I asked to serve in the catering corps. A few days later I was interned – maybe because I had made myself too prominent, I don't know. It was one of the big disappointments of my life because I was waiting for my naturalization to come through. And this was my country, this has always been my country.

What were your feelings when you were interned?

For the first three or four days I really couldn't get used to it. I was angry at the treatment, the idea of being thrown behind barbed wire. Within a few days I was offered a job by Captain Myers who was the head of the camp. Since I spoke English, he wanted me to be a kind of liaison officer. He explained that some people needed help with applications and so on. After I had agreed, he then asked me – in his very nice manner – to identify any fascists in the camp. I said to him, 'Captain Myers, I am only too pleased to be your personal assistant, but if you want me to be a spy, you must get somebody else for the job. I won't do it.'

Lord Forte

Did your internment affect your attitude towards life, did it change you?

No, I wasn't there long enough. After two and a half months I was released. At the tribunal I was asked all kinds of questions: who did I want to win the war, did I have a cousin in the Italian Air Force, and so on, until I stood up and told them I had had enough and was not prepared to answer any more questions. I turned around and walked to the door where there was a Scots soldier barring my way with a rifle. I shouted at him: 'What's the matter with you? Get out of the bloody way! I'm one of you for God's sake!' The chairman of the tribunal told him to let me through. I thought I had really blown it, but two days later Captain Myers called me to his office and I was released.

Did you feel any bitterness or anger towards the British government for giving the order to intern?

No, I knew there was a war on, I knew that London was being bombed. I have never felt any bitterness whatsoever. I just thought what a lucky fellow I was compared to all those poor buggers in the army being shot at in the desert. I'm not given to bitterness, and I love this country, then as now.

Your father seems to have been a model of propriety in business and in his personal life, and you appear to have adopted his values wholesale. Did you never feel the need for rebellion at any point?

We had several ups and downs, and even when I left Brighton to come to London we had a row. He told me I was mad and that I should stay and work with him. But when he saw I had made up my mind he took £500 in cash out of the drawer and gave it to me.

Your son Rocco has carried on the business. Isn't a working relationship within the family a very delicate thing?

Yes, it's probably more difficult, and I'm sure Rocco would say the same, but if you observe certain principles, it can be done. He's been working with me for twenty-nine years, and for twenty of those years he had to do what I told him. It isn't easy, but it isn't impossible.

Your meeting with Irene seems to have been love at first sight. Was she the first women you really loved?

There was another woman I was to marry when I was about twenty, a distant relative, a third or fourth cousin. We fell in love, but her parents, who considered themselves to be superior in all ways, strongly objected to the marriage. Eventually she went to America where she became ill and died.

Tell me about your first meeting with Irene.

I first saw her in her mother's *charcuterie* in Old Compton Street where she was being very patient with an elderly Italian man, translating a letter for him from English to Italian. I immediately thought, what a nice girl. I asked her for dinner the following evening but she said she already had an engagement. 'Well, put it off,' I said. And she did. That's how it all started. I proposed to her after only one week, and we were engaged to be married after two or three weeks.

That was surely a departure from the normal caution you exercised in business deals . . . were you conscious of any element of risk?

I had no hesitation. She was British Italian and I knew she was the woman for me. I was absolutely certain of what I was doing, because at thirty-four years old, I had met many girls. Irene was exactly right, and by God it's the best deal I've ever done.

You describe your marriage as the happiest and most fortunate thing that has ever happened to you. Do you regard a successful marriage mainly as a result of good fortune, a matter of luck?

Yes, in the sense that I might not have met her – there are millions of people in London after all. But it also involved good judgement. I knew I could make her a damned good husband – I'd had a few girls, I wasn't too bad looking, I had a bit of money and I used to dress nicely. I wasn't short of girlfriends, but I knew this was the woman I wanted to marry. It wasn't entirely straightforward because once again the parents objected. Her mother didn't want her to marry me because she thought I was a womanizer.

And were you?

Not really. Of course I went out with girls, and certainly I slept with them, but they had to be certain types and of a certain quality. I never yet paid a woman to go to bed with her. In any case the importance of sex is often exaggerated – I could certainly be without a woman for a year or so.

After the war you gradually built up your business until in 1954 you bought the Café Royale which you say gave you more pleasure than almost anything else you have ever done. Did the purchase have perhaps as much symbolic significance as actual, that is to say you were buying something which symbolized British grandeur and style, and that was the start of the golden road?

Yes, it was. The Café Royale was a very big move upwards. I used to go there and look at the wonderful grill room and see all the famous people, and I'd think, by golly, what a place this is. I'd always wanted to improve my social station – I had been a young tally wally in Scotland and had had to use my fists quite a lot – and it was in my make-up to want to improve, to be part of the Establishment in this country. I think I've succeeded. The Café Royale was a first step; my first hotel, the Waldorf, was another.

At the end of the fifties you were offered a peerage by Hugh Gaitskell, then leader of the opposition, but despite wanting to be established and honoured, you turned it down because of your rejection of Socialism. Did you ever have moments when you regretted that decision?

Never. Hugh Gaitskell was a great friend of mine and one of the nicest and most honest men I have known. But I believe you have to have certain ideals. It's not that I'm anti-Labour; we are a democracy and the Labour

Lord Forte

Party has a right to exist, but I'm not a Labour man. I believe that free enterprise is good for the country, and that everyone is better off under the Conservatives. Years later I accepted the knighthood from Harold Wilson because it came as a result of financial help I had given to Oxford University to build a gallery. A peerage would have meant that I couldn't go and vote Conservative, but a knighthood was fine.

You had to wait until 1981 to be made a life peer by Margaret Thatcher. What were your feelings then?

Well, it was the Conservative Party who asked me, but I'm fairly sure it was Margaret who recommended me. I accepted immediately. It meant a great deal to me. I'm the only person of Italian origin who has ever received a peerage in the history of this country.

In 1986 you wrote that you had a special liking for Margaret Thatcher and felt she was leading the country back to greatness. Do you think her Party made a mistake in getting rid of her?

Yes. And the way they did it was so nasty... but then we Conservatives are always good at stabbing our leaders in the back. We're doing it now with Major. A country needs strong leadership. If Margaret came back we'd see the difference immediately. I admit that she is a friend of mine, but she is an outstanding person, and the admiration I have for her is unbounded. She ran the country like a small grocer's shop in the high street, and she ran it damned well. When she was here we were all doing all right, and she would do all right again. I'm not a great feminist, far from it, but by God Margaret Thatcher has what it takes.

The merger between Forte and Trust Houses, although it looked very attractive initially, was beset with difficulties and friction. It involved you in a prolonged boardroom battle which you admit drained you of energy and money in defence of your position and that of the shareholders. Looking back, was it all worth it?

It was a very difficult time, largely because people didn't keep their word. When we amalgamated, I was supposed to be chairman, but in the event

Lord Crowther refused to resign. We had a terrible row during which I started banging the desk hard. He told me to stop banging and I said, 'I'll bang your head in a minute!' That's the state I'd got to, and by God I would have done it if I hadn't walked out of the room to calm down. I slammed the door so hard that the handle came away in my hand. Lord Crowther's secretary was sitting outside and she wore an expression of terror as if this mad Italian were going to bludgeon her. I said to her, 'I'm very sorry, my dear, for making all that noise. Please give this to your boss with my compliments.' I laid the handle on her desk and the following day I sent her a nice big box of chocolates.

But was it worth the struggle?

Yes, because it was a matter of principle, and it was also essential for the amalgamation of these two companies. I'd put my hotels and restaurants in the hands of these people, and I knew they were inefficient; they simply did not know what they were doing. The Grosvenor House Hotel, that wonderful place, now making millions, was making nothing at all. The wages were about 40% of the turnover instead of 23% maximum. Even now, with all our turnover, our marginal profit is only 8 per cent. It is not an easy business to run. You have to be dropped on your head as a child to go into the hotel business, and that was something these people did not understand.

Your struggle for control of the Savoy has been your bitterest battle, and it still seems to be going on, although a five-year truce has been declared. Did it develop more into a personal war than a business battle?

Yes, in a way, but it's not been my bitterest battle. The Savoy is by far the best deal I've ever done, and I haven't had one sleepless night over it.

But the voting is not with you . . .

It will come. They always say I have only 42 per cent of the votes, but I paid 36 million for 70 per cent of the Savoy equity, and that's the part that matters. The Savoy is valued now at 260 million, and we bought 70 per

Lord Forte

cent for 36 million. People call it a bad deal; I wish I could do a deal like that every day.

You always dreamed of owning the Savoy which has a special significance for you – your father's first café in Scotland was named the Savoy and you proposed to your wife at the Savoy. Do you think you let this significance on a personal level cloud your commercial judgement at any stage?

There is an element of sentiment, but anything I do in business has to make a profit. My function is not just to give people comfortable beds and good service and beautiful views; my job is to run a business profitably, and if I don't do that I'm no longer worthy of being chairman, or president, or anything else. My responsibility is to my shareholders, and the day I don't give a good dividend, I let my shareholders down.

The row between you and Sir Hugh Wontner seems to have its basis in old-fashioned English snobbery, the idea that a grand old institution like the Savoy would be ruined by a reduction in standards. Did this aspect of things make you all the more outraged and determined to succeed?

I would have been determined anyway, but that aspect probably inspired me more. What he said about lowering standards was nonsense. Did he ever visit our hotels? Unlike his, they were always full because people liked the food, the accommodation, the décor and everything else. What's wrong with that? What's wrong with the Hyde Park Hotel, Grosvenor House, the Westbury in New York? What's wrong with having your hotels full? What's the fun in having hotels that lose money? Hugh Wontner used Claridges as his private house; he had a flat on the top and a custom-built lift direct from the kitchen to his flat so that he could have his coffee sent up quickly in the morning, and he didn't even hold a bloody share . . . well, he had some shares eventually, but they were more or less taken and given. He also had a string of call girls – that's how he ran the great Savoy, and yet he looked down on me because we had Little Chefs on the motorways.

You believed that you could double the profits at the Savoy, but manager Peter Crone said that you would do this by using half the cream and half the wine. Did you resent that remark?

Lord Forte

Peter Crone doesn't know what he's talking about. They call themselves hoteliers, but none of these people knows the first thing.

You say in your book that Hugh Wontner has a great gift for supercilious indifference, and that this attitude might have been excusable but for the dismal profit record. Was this the main reason for your aggressive bid in 1981?

Yes. If they had been profitable I wouldn't have bothered. I couldn't bear to see these lovely hotels losing money.

In 1988 you launched a virulent attack on Hugh Wontner claiming 'a breach of duty' in an allotment of high voting shares, and you also made other serious allegations. Did you ever consider taking legal steps to establish this in court?

There was no use in trying because he had the thing in his hands, and he had the votes. We approached the tax commissioners, but I felt they were biased in his favour.

But wasn't Wontner simply using every legitimate means available to preserve the independence of a public company, something you yourself might have done in similar circumstances?

I wouldn't have run a company like that. He went for years and years without making a profit, never paying a dividend, while he himself lived like the lord of the manor. The man was dishonest. I'm not the sort of person who has evil intentions towards people, and I'm sorry that he's dead, but the man was a humbug, no doubt about that.

An article in the Sunday Times *in 1992 stated: 'In the ten years since he became chief executive, Rocco has failed to live up to the legend of his father.' Do you think perhaps yours was an impossible act to follow?*

It's so unfair to write that when the father has had sixty years to make a reputation. My son is doing a bloody good job. I'm delighted that he's there, and I do everything possible to keep him there. I wish I'd known what he knows at his age.

But if he hadn't been your son would you have chosen him as chief executive, do you think?

Yes. There's nobody better I could choose.

Family solidarity has been the constant theme of the Forte story. Would you say that sometimes that has been as much of a weakness as a strength?

It's always been a great strength and it still is.

You say that nowadays your son, and not you, is accountable to the shareholders, but there is a widespread perception that he is still accountable to you. Is that true?

It's not true. Of course I am still here and occasionally he asks my advice, but he makes his own decisions. He is the chairman and chief executive, and I made him so. If I hadn't trusted him, I never would have put him there; there's too much at stake.

Do you expect the same loyalty from your own children as you extended to your parents?

Absolutely. And so far I have had it.

It is said that you kept a very tight rein on your daughters, and that you were a very strict father. Is that true?

Yes. I have given my daughters everything but I have also been very strict with them as regards morals. Rocco did what he liked, and I couldn't have cared less, as long as he looked after his health. With my daughters it was different. But they love me, all of them.

You went to Roman Catholic schools, as did your children. Is Catholicism something you have always accepted without question – I have the impression that you have never really had to wrestle with your faith.

I have no doubts. I'm a Roman Catholic, and that's that. I don't want to be anything else, I don't aspire to be anything else. I go to church every Sunday, and I'm enthralled by it.

Do you have the feeling that you are being guided by God in your life?

I wouldn't be telling the truth if I said yes. But I always think there's a protecting angel somewhere.

Some years ago you met Pope John Paul II who is seen by many Catholics and non-Catholics as being one of the most reactionary popes this century. What is your view?

Things that have worked for centuries and centuries should not just be overturned by one man. I think one must go quietly about it. Catholicism has been a good religion and the papacy has acted properly over two thousand years – why change everything now?

Yours is not exactly a rags-to-riches story in the sense that your own background was not impoverished. Nevertheless, you have risen far above the way of life you were born to . . . have you ever wished that you could return to the simpler way of life?

No. I haven't noticed much difference in the way I live. I've always been properly dressed, I've always been clean, I've always had enough to eat. Of course I have a different social level, but it's not as if I suffered before.

You have said that self-doubt is every man's worst enemy. You seem to have succeeded in keeping that particular fiend at bay . . .

Yes. I don't try and do the impossible, but I never have doubt in myself. I know I'm an honest man, and that is a very good sleeping pill. If I ever think I have done something wrong I apologize immediately, as soon as I have the opportunity. Some time ago, for example, I was very rude to one of my co-directors, a man who has been with me a long time. He criticized me about something and I took objection and called him fat and lazy. He looked at me and then he got up and walked out. That night I couldn't sleep. The next day I asked to see him. He thought I was going to repeat my insults but instead I made amends and told him how much I admired him. If I am in the wrong I do not hesitate to apologize.

You have lived by old-fashioned values which you have taught to your children and grandchildren. Have they taught you anything in return?

They have taught me patience at times. They have also put me in touch with the modern generation, which I sometimes find difficult to understand. It's a very valuable contribution.

You have been married to Irene for fifty years. To what do you attribute the success of your long and happy marriage?

We have a deep mutual respect for one another. Irene is a wonderful woman, a marvellous wife, a good mother. I think of her in everything I do.

My wife always says to me there isn't a rich man who is unattractive to women . . . in other words when we become successful and have power and influence and money, we can easily be flattered by the attention women pay us. Were you ever tempted . . . ?

Well, yes, but I'm not going to tell you any details . . .

No, of course not, I didn't expect you to . . . You have become a legend in your own lifetime. How would you like to be remembered?

If they write on my tombstone in fifty years' time: 'This was an honest man. He lived an honest life', I should be happy.

LORD HARTWELL

LORD HARTWELL

Michael Berry was born in 1911 and educated at Eton and Christ Church, Oxford. He served as captain and major in the army and was twice Mentioned in Despatches. His career in newspapers started in 1934 when he edited the *Sunday Mail* in Glasgow for a year. From 1937–9 he was managing editor at the *Financial Times* and in 1954 he became chairman of Amalgamated Press Ltd, a post he held for five years. When his father, Lord Camrose, died in 1954 he became chairman and editor-in-chief of the *Daily Telegraph* and some years later of the *Sunday Telegraph* which he founded in 1961. Lord Hartwell retired in 1987 when the Telegraph Group was acquired by the Canadian businessman Conrad Black. His biography of his father, *William Camrose: Giant of Fleet Street*, was published in 1993.

Lord Hartwell

Did you feel that education at Eton and Christ Church equipped you well for your subsequent life in newspapers?

Education at those two places depended really upon the application of the boy. I can't say I worked very hard at Eton, but I didn't do badly. In my last year I had a great deal of responsibility. The trouble was you had so much freedom at Eton that you didn't feel the extra freedom most boys from other types of schools felt when they went to university. The consequence was that you really rather let go. The examination wasn't until the end of the third year which seemed an aeon of time away, and you didn't take it very seriously until the last year by which time it was a bit late to catch up.

Were you very much in awe of your father Lord Camrose? Did the fact that he was a press baron, along with people like Beaverbrook and Northcliff, lend him a certain eminence and remoteness as a father figure?

Certainly not. He was in no way remote, and he was very good with his children. He treated them like young adults and discussed all his problems with them, so although I had the deepest respect for him I was not in awe of him. He was very supportive of us, particularly when we got into trouble. I can't say I had very many troubles myself but I saw it with the rest of my family, and I now know he did even more for his children than I had realized before.

Your father knew Churchill well. What was your impression of Churchill?

I only saw him towards the end of his life when he was already a national hero. My father didn't really trust him at all at the beginning. He first came across him in the early 1920s and until about two years before the war he regarded Churchill as a fascinating mountebank, as indeed most of the nation did; he was thought of as somebody not to be trusted, always out for office and his own self, and for the massage of his own ego. I saw him only after the war when he was already established in his own right as being the great of the greats. I had some professional dealings with him because when my father died I took over Churchill's war memoirs which the *Telegraph* had bought. In fact I think I must have been one of the few people ever to have given a sizeable tip, twenty thousand pounds, to

Lord Hartwell

Winston Churchill. Like all authors he over-wrote his memoirs and although he had sold them on the basis of five volumes, he wanted to write a sixth. Most of the international publishers wouldn't pay extra but my father had agreed to pay for another volume though there was nothing in writing about it. Churchill asked me to lunch and was very much relieved to hear that I was going to honour my father's unwritten promise.

You have suggested that Churchill would have made your father Minister of Information in 1943 but for the fact that Beaverbrook was jealous and told Churchill that your father was too ill to take the post. What is the evidence for that?

The suggestion that he should be made Minister of Information came from Oliver Harvey, later Lord Harvey, who was principal private secretary to Eden when he was Foreign Secretary. Churchill had agreed to my father being Minister of Information until Beaverbrook – who had been falsely promised leadership of the House of Lords – heard about it and told Churchill that my father, who had had a serious illness five years before, was likely to break down if given any responsibility. The source of that information was Churchill's scientific guru, Lord Charwell, who was a great friend, very close to Churchill and also close to my father.

What was the origin of the jealousy between your father and Beaverbrook?

Just that they were the same age, exactly the same age, and both newspaper proprietors. Beaverbrook, by virtue of his Canadian fortune, had started at the top while my father was still working his way up, and he didn't particularly like the idea of a man of his own age becoming as important, if not more important, than himself in the journalistic world. There were several manifestations of this which I have detailed in my book.

In 1954 you became chairman and editor-in-chief of the Daily Telegraph. *What were your feelings as you stepped into your father's shoes?*

My feelings were that I wished to continue his traditions, and to maintain the *Daily Telegraph* as an institution in such a way that for anyone who really wanted to know what was going on, not only in this country but in the whole world, it would be difficult to be without the *Telegraph*. My father had already deputed a good deal of the running of the paper to me in any case. In fact he had already nominated me two years before as deputy editor-in-chief, believing it would be a mistake for him to linger too long. We got on very well indeed and he was such a tolerant man, although he did say when he put me in charge that he did not want a new broom, in other words he didn't want me to start throwing my weight about and trying to change everything and everyone; rather he wanted the paper to continue to evolve. That was his great feeling about the *Telegraph* itself, because when he bought it in 1927, it had been a very great paper in the previous century but it was definitely in decline. It wasn't actually losing money but it wasn't making any and it might not have lasted another ten years. He permeated it with his own ideas, and although he did bring in a few people, he got rid of very few indeed, and he congratulated himself afterwards since he didn't think a paper had ever been revived in quite that manner, so apparently effortlessly. That was an achievement he particularly prided himself on, and he didn't want me to start making mistakes he hadn't made.

But by all accounts your father ran the Daily Telegraph *as if it were a feudal institution; in the words of one observer, 'he ruled as well as reigned'. Were you at all critical of this autocratic approach?*

It was centralized to a certain extent and he wasn't prepared to let everybody do their own thing; he preferred always to know what they were doing. Lord Burnham, the managing director, said he wasn't very good at what in the army they call staff duties, which means apportioning duties to everybody down the chain and making them responsible only to those directly above them. For example, he was continually ringing up the newsroom to talk to people who were running a particular story without going through the news editor. My father interfered in everything if he wanted to.

Was it filial devotion and respect which kept you from altering much at the Daily Telegraph *or was it the fact that the newspaper was doing well and there was little point in changing a winning formula?*

The last proposition is always a good idea, but there were one or two

Lord Hartwell

things that he would never have let me do, which I did do in the end, but nothing of any importance – the masthead, for example. He took over the *Morning Post* in 1937 or 1938, and he always insisted on including the *Morning Post* in the masthead, which I thought rather an anachronism after the war. He wouldn't allow me to take it off, because he thought there was still some goodwill left in these ageing *Morning Post* readers, but when he died I did take it off. Apart from appearances I think I also made the paper less stuffy; concentrated on more good writing and introduced more humour.

You have been described as a journalist through and through. Do you see yourself as a journalist by nature, and if so, what does that entail?

I think a journalist principally is a person who is interested in people and who is immensely curious about affairs and wonders why things happen and why people do what they do. I suppose it's a form of busybodyness. Everything is grist to the mill.

Although in your capacity as editor-in-chief of the Telegraph, *you always defended your journalists loyalty, some people have detected that you are a little uneasy with journalists as a breed, and that you are particularly suspicious of columnists and leader writers . . . is there any truth in that?*

As a generalization, none whatever. I do think a leader column ought to be consistent, and if it pronounces once a fortnight on some subject, it ought, on the second occasion, to remember what it said on the first. You shouldn't contradict in your leader something you said in the previous one unless you draw attention to it and do it gently and for apparent good reason. If you have to box the compass, admit to it.

In the quality newspapers there is a tendency nowadays for the intellectuals to rule the roost; newspapers have become platforms for opinion. How do you view this trend in journalism?

Certain journalists have their hobby horses and one should simply not employ hobby horses because they can't move anywhere, and then they become a bore. They plug the same line and use their column for their own personal purpose and not for the purpose of the newspaper, which should be a different thing every day.

Richard Ingrams once said to me that journalists who take themselves seriously or believe they have influence are bad journalists. Would you agree with that?

No, I would say they have to be very good at their job, otherwise they're bad journalists. Journalists would do well to remember that they hold no position of responsibility in the running of the country, and bearing that in my mind, they should acquire a little humility which is quite a rare quality in Fleet Street.

There is, however, a great deal of talk nowadays about 'opinion makers' in newspapers. Politicians obviously believe newspapers hold great sway over the way people think . . . what is your view?

I don't know that they do. Because of the rise of television they have far less influence than before. Newspapers tend to provide the public with information, the facts, which television can't do, because it's trying to do too many things at once. Television is rather like opera for a beginner; it's very difficult for an untrained person at an opera to appreciate the décor, the singing and the music, let alone the words which don't matter. The same thing applies when people watch television – they are so obsessed with whether a man's tie is straight or his eyes rotating to hear what he's saying. But what they are able to do is to get an idea of the genuineness or the non-genuineness of the man talking, and therefore the opinion to a certain extent is made by watching television. In short, people get their information from the newspapers and their prejudices from television. People say that such and such a man is a very poor performer and conclude that he must be a very bad administrator, and form their opinions in that way. It's not the way that public opinion is supposed to be directed but that is what happens.

You have always upheld editorial independence. People often recall how the Daily Telegraph *criticized Anthony Eden just before Suez and how*

Lord Hartwell

protests on the Prime Minister's behalf failed to move you. Did you have any qualms about that at the time?

Not at all. We'd all thought that Eden was faltering a bit in so far as he was trying to be like Churchill, or how he thought Churchill was, always interfering in every department without going through Cabinet. I well remember a story told to me by Jim Thomas who was First Lord of the Admirality when Churchill was Prime Minister. Churchill used to ring him up early in the morning, about 7.30 – he of course had been called with a large whisky at about 7 o'clock – and Thomas was always very much annoyed to be wakened at this hour. One morning he rang up: 'Is that you, First Lord?' 'Oh yes, good morning Prime Minister, how nice to hear your voice.' Then Churchill said, 'I'm very worried about that submarine, you know,' and Thomas hadn't any idea what he was talking about. It turned out that some submarine had brushed a sandbank in Portsmouth; Churchill had read about it in the first editions of the papers, but by the time the final edition came out the submarine had come off again, so it wasn't news any more. Anyway, that was the sort of thing that Churchill used to do, but he did it just to keep his ministers on their toes, whereas Eden got the impression that he really was trying to interfere in all their business, and he tried to do likewise, only in a rather schoolmistress sort of way, thereby making himself very unpopular. It was Donald MacLachlan our deputy editor who wrote that the government under Eden lacked the smack of firm government, a phrase that put Eden very much on edge. But we weren't highly critical of him, we just said that things seemed rather a shambles and there was no firm direction. We did criticize him on one or two other things, as one has every right to do, and he took this very much amiss. I remember Lord Salisbury and Butler came to see me at my home and asked if there was anything personal about it, and I assured them there wasn't, but that the paper wasn't going to give unthinking support to the government. This was discussed some time before Suez on which we were generally supportive of him; we were only critical of his having stopped it midway, and having no plan as to what to do next.

Is it perhaps not surprising, given your uncompromising stands on critical independence, that your life peerage came from a Labour Prime Minister, Harold Wilson? Were you conscious of a certain irony in that – after all, you were editor-in-chief of the Telegraph, *a widely perceived Tory stronghold.*

Lord Hartwell

I certainly wouldn't have accepted a peerage from a Tory government because it would have looked as if it was payment for services rendered – not that I was offered one.

But all the editors do that now.

Well, that's no business of mine.

But would you have turned down a peerage from a Tory government?

Most certainly.

Why do you think Harold Wilson gave you the peerage?

I think it arose because Cecil King, a very strong Labour supporter, also a man of immense self-importance, wanted to be placed in Wilson's Cabinet and to be given an earldom. Wilson turned this down but offered him an under-secretaryship and a simple barony which made him furious, and so in order to stop the *Daily Mirror* turning against him altogether – that being the way politicians think – he gave a peerage to Hugh Cudlipp, and I think I was pulled in to balance him. Wilson never told me this, but that's what I assume.

But tell me, of all the former Prime Ministers, Harold Wilson is perhaps the least talked about, the least respected. Why do you think that is?

During his government there was so much backbiting and backstabbing, and everyone seemed to act so much out of self-interest, and then he retired for supposedly mysterious reasons. I didn't think them mysterious at all; he was getting past it, even though he was only sixty. Callaghan who took over from him was a much rougher man, made of much tougher moral fibre than Wilson. Wilson was much more like Lloyd George, a tremendous wheeler-dealer but without the same skills.

Did you know him well?

Lord Hartwell

I knew him quite a bit, yes. When he was Prime Minister I saw him often at Chequers because we had a house nearby. He was always extremely agreeable and could be very funny, but one couldn't really respect him much.

It is sometimes said that your late wife, Lady Pamela Berry, persuaded Wilson to confer the peerage. Is there any truth in it?

She hardly knew him.

Your wife was very sociable, gregarious and someone who loved meeting people and giving parties. By contrast you always preferred to remain in the background socially. Was this ever a source of tension between you?

Not at all. She gave quite a few small lunch parties but she resented being called a political hostess. A lot of her friends were middle-ranking politicians and perhaps quite a few left-wing journalists, but she really invited them for their conversation. She found them much better company than the more respectable lot. But she was not interested in politics, she was interested in people.

You have a thinly disguised distaste for social life – how on earth did you cope with your wife's enthusiasm for entertaining politicians, people from the arts and other dignitaries?

I found them interesting on the whole. But the difficulty for a man in his own house is that he is usually put next to a wife . . . and although many wives are often very interesting, very often they aren't. People tend to marry young and when the husband has achieved something in life the wife may have got stuck in her early rut. My wife quite rightly thought that general conversation made the most interesting party. Sometimes one of 'my wives' – the ones sitting next to me – couldn't keep up and kept turning to talk to me. One could not but answer and my wife used to frown at me angrily. I once suggested to her jokingly that I should give her a silver bell which she could ring when she wanted general conversation – as did a Parisian hostess described by the Goncourt brothers. But this of course would have seemed arrogant in her and rude in me.

Lord Hartwell

Most Englishmen seem to prefer the company of other men, is that because of the public-school background, do you think?

No, it's because men are usually doing something, and as a journalist I like talking to other people about what they do, not about things at large.

Lord Weidenfeld said of your wife, 'She had a respect approaching reverence for her husband's profession', but he added that she did not exercise influence over the contents of your newspapers. Would you agree with that?

Yes. Actually she never tried to, and I would certainly not have approved of it. She'd advise me on certain things, but she was never able to persuade me unless I also thought it a good idea. She was a great influence on my life personally I suppose, because of our mutual confidence, but she wasn't an influence so much on what I did as what I was.

Weidenfeld also said that she 'humanized' you. What do you think he meant by that?

I suppose he meant that without her I was inhuman, but I plead not guilty.

The Hartwell house was often regarded as the last private political and intellectual salon *in the classical tradition. Were you conscious of that at the time, and do you mourn its passing?*

I wasn't conscious of it at the time, nor was she, and therefore it's nothing to mourn. She didn't regard herself as a centre of political discussion; she only asked people who amused her, and it so happened that some of her left-wing friends she found more amusing than the right-wingers, perhaps because they were more indiscreet which helps conversation. The thing she really hated was to be called a Lady Londonderry type who had vast parties of only one political persuasion – that was what a political *salon* was really about.

Peregrine Worsthorne, referring to your keen sense of duty, wrote that

Lord Hartwell

newspaper proprietorship for you was 'a high public trust to which all private and family life must be subordinate'. Did you ever come to regret that scheme of priorities?

Certainly running the *Telegraph* dominated my life, and I daresay I should have been at home more than I was. But I don't feel any guilt about it. If you've got a rather important job, you must devote everything you've got to it. I don't think my family suffered as a result. My wife would have liked to have travelled more, but other than that I don't think so, and certainly my children did not suffer at all.

Would you consider yourself to have been a good father to your children?

I'm the wrong person to answer that, but I was a good father according to my own lights, and I hope they would agree. Now that they have all made their own way in life we all seem to get on very well together.

Lady Pamela was often the subject of severe criticism in the press. To what did you attribute these attacks?

Spite more than anything else. She attracted a certain amount of publicity because she associated with the people I describe, and I suppose those who didn't like her thought she was becoming too big for her boots.

In 1980 Lord Lambton wrote a disparaging article for Now *magazine about Lady Pamela. Why did you take such exception to that?*

It made me very angry because it was highly offensive to her. It was written as if she were already dead, and as she was suffering from a disease which killed her two years later she found that particularly damaging and hurtful. I daresay Lambton didn't know it at the time. There was a long story behind it involving Sir James Goldsmith who had been attacked three times in the *Daily Telegraph*, on three separate occasions about three different things by three different people. Being a very sensitive chap, he got it into his head that I had organized and coordinated a campaign against him, and having started *Now* magazine he decided to hit back at me. His editor commissioned Alan Brien, who could wield a vicious pen and had been on the *Sunday Telegraph*, to write an article attacking me, but Alan Brien said he couldn't do it because he couldn't find anything to attack me on. Then Goldsmith had the idea that if he couldn't get at me, he would get at my wife instead, and so he hired Lambton, who had been a friend of ours, to do it.

But why did Lambton do it?

He has a great deal of money but he liked notoriety, and thought it a rather jolly thing to do. He was a sort of acolyte of Randolph Churchill who regarded all personal attacks as jolly jokes – that's what he called them – and this was one of those jolly jokes. We didn't find it at all jolly; in fact it was astonishingly offensive, so I wrote a letter, and had great difficulty getting it published because it was thought to be libellous. But I offered to guarantee it personally and financially against libel, though later I discovered that is illegal.

Did you ever regret having the letter published?

No. I was rather pleased with it. My wife was unmollified. She had put so much enthusiasm into working for the great museums that she deeply resented her efforts being rubbished.

Lady Pamela appeared to have been singled out for attack by Evelyn Waugh in letters he wrote in 1962, including one to the Sunday Telegraph. *She was accused of being a 'Judas' and 'a Sneakhostess'. The recent publication of Auberon Waugh's autobiography reveals that it was in fact he who had passed on information to the* Telegraph, *not Lady Pamela, though he never confessed to his father. Did you suspect the provenance of the diary story at that time?*

Not at all. In fact I quoted to him Auberon Waugh, who was working on the *Telegraph*, as evidence that that was not the way we did things. I had no idea that he'd done it.

What are your views on the current libel laws in this country?

I think it quite ridiculous for juries to deal in sums of money which mean nothing to them. They know perhaps what money means up to about two or three thousand pounds, but beyond that nothing. I can give you an example. We were sued by a real rogue called Lewis who was chairman of a rubber company, the biggest manufacturer of french letters in the country. Without going into the details of the case we reported that he was being investigated by the Fraud Squad. We were given damages of a hundred thousand pounds against us. Afterwards our solicitor's clerk went into the jury room and examined the contents of the wastepaper basket only to find that each member of the jury had written down what he thought damages should be; it ranged from five thousand to a hundred and fifty thousand, so they settled on a hundred. That's the way libel damages are decided – the people who do it have no idea what it means. What does an assistant in a grocer's shop know about sums over ten or twenty thousand pounds?

What do you think is the duty of a newspaper man, editor or proprietor, when faced with the problem of whether or not to publish potentially scandalous material?

It's a question of whether we restrain people who say it's in the public interest, which means absolutely nothing, since they do it for obviously moneygrubbing purposes.

Yes, I agree. It's becoming a dangerous weapon in the sense that anyone can threaten your livelihood or position for personal gain.

I certainly don't approve of that trend. I can give you a good example from my father's day when he personally refused to do something like this, even though it would have been a great journalistic coup. After the war the Duke of Windsor was determined to make himself whiter than white over the abdication crisis and he wrote, or rather had ghosted, *A King's Story*, which his solicitors brought to my father. The Duke wanted it published in the *Daily Telegraph* which he thought influenced respectable opinion, and not in the *Daily Express*, even though Lord Beaverbrook had supported him during his crisis. My father said he wouldn't even see it, and he certainly wouldn't publish it. He advised the solicitor to tell the Duke not to publish as it would only reopen old wounds. But the Duke did publish it; he took it to Lord Beaverbrook who printed it in the *Sunday Express* which put on an extra three quarters of a million copies. I tell you this to

Lord Hartwell

illustrate the *Telegraph*'s attitude, which would be the same now I think. Certainly we wouldn't have published Morton's book.

Are you in favour of the French privacy law which forbids newspapers to pry into people's personal lives?

The trouble is the French don't find the law very satisfactory. It is an extremely difficult problem, but if we instigate censorship, then it has to apply to everybody, and censorship is a very big and undiscriminating club; it may hit the sort of thing we deplore now, but it will hit a lot of other things as well and make freedom of the press very much more restricted in ways unthought of, unexpected and not desired. There are two different sorts: there is the Andrew Morton book about the Princess of Wales which doesn't involve privacy so much – it may involve indiscretions of 'friends' and possibly the encouragement of the Princess herself but one doesn't know whether that's true or not; the bugged telephone conversation is quite a different matter – that really is Peeping Tom stuff. And I think there should be some way of stopping that by law. In America you're not allowed to tape anybody's conversation, even if he's a friend, without telling him you are doing it.

Don't you think that in Britain we are rather hypocritical about sex? Someone in public life who is a womanizer is a hero among his friends as long as he's not caught; once caught he becomes ostracized.

Do you know the famous story about Disraeli and Palmerston? Just before a general election in this country when Disraeli was leader of his party, his aides came to him and said they had a wonderful story about Palmerston – that although over seventy he had made some lady pregnant. Naturally his aides wanted to publicize it; but Disraeli said, 'Are you out of your minds? If this gets out Palmerston will sweep the country.'

In 1979 there was a public row between you and the Attorney General, Sir Michael Havers, over the Jeremy Thorpe affair and the Sunday Telegraph*'s offer to buy the memoirs of Mr Peter Bessell, the chief prosecuting witness. Do you think with hindsight it was right for the* Sunday Telegraph *to offer Bessell a financial incentive for a Thorpe conviction?*

Lord Hartwell

We were advised that it was perfectly safe. We bought his memoirs quite a long time before the case came up; he'd already given his evidence to the prosecution, and it had been circulated to the defence, so there was nothing more he could say other than what was already in his evidence which he was going to give to the court. Some bright spark, I don't know who it was, put it in the contract that we would pay him double if a conviction was secured. That's what got us into trouble with Mr Justice Cantley. I was attacked afterwards in the House of Lords by Lord Wigoden, who is a friend of mine, and Lord Elwyn Jones. I replied at some length and Wigoden congratulated me on my speech; he said it was like a speech where an attorney had no case but puts up a very good one.

But with hindsight, would you do it again?

Certainly not. Principally because Bessell's story was so frightfully boring – just a repetition of what he'd said in court – and certainly I wouldn't give double money.

1985 was a very difficult year for you, perhaps the most difficult in your career, when you were unable to prevent financial control of the newspaper slipping out of your hands. The financial disaster seems to have been rooted in two things: your commitment to the £100 million modernization package, and an overwhelmingly generous redundancy agreement with the unions. Would you agree with that analysis?

No. It was generous, but it wasn't overwhelmingly generous. The modernization programme was rather complicated but I'll try to make it simple. It had two components – electronic composing and banks of new-style printing machinery (more modern than anybody else's), the horse and the cart. Unfortunately there was a definite date when the cart had to start so that the time the horse had to be schooled in (a long process) was far too short for comfort. The experts said that eighteen months was the right period to allow for training our own compositors to work electronic composing as distinct from the old Linotypes using hot metal. The compositors' union (the NGA) saw here a wonderful weapon for extracting the maximum concessions from the management: it would not allow electronic machines into the Fleet Street building until about Christmas '84, and even then we didn't start training until May or June

'85, barely six months before the deadline for the cart. The latter date had been determined by the unexpected action of our Manchester Contract printers throwing us out of their works, so that we had to provide not just our new building housing new printing machines in London but a second one in Manchester, most of whose composing would be done in London. The result in the composing room was chaos. We had to have two composing rooms – one old technology, one new technology – running in tandem. The paper was always late, always filthy with misprints, the malaise spread to other departments, trains were missed, hundreds of thousands of copies remained unprinted, management set a nightly limit on the number of columns that could be set, readers gave up in droves. All this began to happen just as we were finalizing our funding plans. The effect on profits was profound. What's more, it was just the time when unemployment was reaching its peak and the revenue from job advertising, in which we always led the field, fell right away. To cap it all, the Chancellor in the March budget of '85, put VAT on advertising which had a tremendous effect on us. So all told, our revenue was slipping away and our costs, instead of going down, were going up. The cost-saving new machinery had not yet come into use.

Max Hastings has said: 'The great enigma remains the readiness with which Hartwell, without seriously trying to find a more sympathetic investor, sold fourteen per cent of the newspaper to a Canadian he met only once in a New York airport hotel.' What comment would you make on that?

In about 1975 we started to look for a new building site, and eventually we found it in the new enterprise zone which had great financial advantages. The question was one of how we were going to finance the new plant. First of all, we tried to raise money on loan from our banks but the banks said our capital base was too restricted. Then our merchant bankers said we had to raise thirty millions in ordinary shares, and the syndicate of banks decided they'd put up the money. We came on the market in May and the first twenty millions went immediately. Then there was a long interval, and the last ten millions could not be raised. At that point our advisers found Conrad Black of whom I'd never heard. I had to do something fast since we had the machinery ordered. Conrad Black was unable to come over to London for another week, and since our advisers said they couldn't wait that long, I decided to go and see him. I got into a Concorde with the

Lord Hartwell

managing director (the finance director could not get a visa on Bank Holiday Monday), and we saw Conrad Black in New York where he agreed to back us. But he did not want always to be a minority shareholder and he insisted that should we need more financing he should be able to increase his proportionate stake. I did not see how I could avoid agreeing to his terms. We had been advised we'd get by quite all right, and that's when the trouble started, because when we did need more money Black had my rights. I didn't sell out to him; he bought in, so to speak.

It is of course easy to be wise after the event, but looking back, is there one crucial thing which you wish you had done differently? Would you for example have allowed Black the option of increasing his stake to the point of taking control?

We had been advised that we'd got plenty of money there. I took great trouble going through the prospectus for the investors, but I didn't take any trouble at all in going through the covenants we were signing with the bankers who stipulate various levels of profits at various stages. I remember that on 30 June, which was the financial deadline, I was made to sign a dozen documents which had been thrashed out by ten lawyers who had been arguing about them for a month. For instance, the saving we expected to make in our costs should have covered the interest on our loans. Of course it didn't. In the end it turned out that our wonderful new Manchester site actually cost more to run. What was planned is what is called a leasing arrangement. Banks agree to put up large capital sums to pay for equipment which you don't have to start to repay until the equipment is installed and running. In return for their patience they expect to see your plan of how you will provide the profits in stages so as eventually to repay in total. When you borrow in this fashion you covenant at least to reach the level of profitability in the plan. If you fail at any stage, the deal is off, or has to be renegotiated. Thus when in a far bigger scheme like the Channel Tunnel you see that the banks have promised £8 billion or whatever it is but are refusing to advance more than six, it means that the covenant has been broken.

There are those who have suggested that the tragedy might have been averted if you had been more willing to take advice. Is that something you found difficult to do?

Lord Hartwell

I didn't get the advice. Perhaps I should have asked for advice. I should have had more detail about whether we would ever require any more money. I didn't. I was told it was going to be all right so I didn't question it. I didn't ever reject any advice; it's advice I didn't get which I regret not having.

But before the sell-out you dismissed reports of a crisis . . .

It wasn't a sell out . . . I didn't sell out.

But you dismissed speculation that you would be forced to lose control. You even wrote an open letter to readers of the Telegraph *explaining developments in the paper, a letter full of hope for the future. It must have been all the more painful when events took the turn they did. Did you suffer a personal sense of having let people down?*

No, I didn't. I had a sense of personal humiliation. I don't think I let anybody down. I personally assisted those who weren't to continue in the new regime where I thought them rather shabbily treated. So I don't think I would say I let people down.

I understand that Andreas Whittam Smith, at the time a journalist with the Telegraph, *offered you financial advice along the lines of selling shares to* Telegraph *readers. People say that you were deeply offended by his advice. Was that true?*

Quite untrue. I wasn't offended by it. In fact I took it on board, but the trouble was we were already in the middle of this issue and it would have been swapping horses in midstream. If I had stopped then, God knows what would have happened. Anyway, you can't raise thirty million pounds from your readers. I didn't think it was a very practical idea, but I didn't take the decision to turn it down myself. I think I referred it to our financial advisers and I was told it wasn't on.

Shortly afterwards Whittam Smith's decision to start his own newspaper and take two Telegraph *journalists with him was leaked. With*

111

characteristic good manners you wished them well, but it is said that privately you felt a deep sense of betrayal. Is that true?

No. It's true that I did wish him well, but I didn't feel a sense of betrayal. I didn't think the paper would fall to pieces because he'd gone. I didn't particularly like his taking the two journalists; one I was delighted to lose, and the other one I much regretted. I won't say which.

You are accused of never having stood up to the unions in the way that Murdoch, for example, did. It is said that you looked upon all your employees as friends, that there was no 'them and us' situation at the Telegraph. Is this an accurate portrayal, and if so is it something you feel proud of or embarrassed about?

I did go on a bit about there being no 'them or us'. Till 1979 my brother and I owned all the ordinary shares; then we decided to make them all over into a trust. We didn't want to pay big dividends, but if we didn't pay dividends commensurate with our profits, the surtax people would have taken about ninety-eight per cent, money which should have been left in the company. One of the ways of getting out of their clutches was to put it all into a trust, and the rules of trust were that the income was to be used for either the paper or for the employees, all at our discretion. (When it came to the crunch I did lend £3 million to the company to sustain the company's cash. The trust didn't have any money so I had to borrow it from my family.) When appealing to staff to try to behave like human beings, I said there was no more them and us, that was the context of it.

But did you regret the stand you took? Would you have done a Murdoch if you had had a second chance?

You couldn't do a Murdoch unless you had a separate plant. And Murdoch never intended to do what he ended up doing. His companies were weaker with the unions than practically everybody else, and we were really as tough as anybody. When he put up the plant, an old-fashioned letterpress plant, he told me it was for the *News of the World* and the *Sun*, and if it worked happily then later he would add to the plant in order to accommodate the *Sunday Times* and *The Times*. That building stuck there for six years after it had been finished, rusting up, and nothing happening.

Eventually he made a proposition to the *Sun* and the *News of the World* people to move down there, but the unions wouldn't wear it. He lost his temper and was advised that the only way to get people out was to so manoeuvre them that they would all go on strike at once; and that's what they managed to do. Unlike an ordinary strike where one union is out and you have to pay all the other ones, they all went out at once and they had dismissed themselves. It was a great stroke doing it, and very clever organization, but it wasn't a thing that anybody else could do because they didn't have a plant to move to. Eventually when our plant was ready much later, the new management did give new contracts, and if the staff wouldn't accept them, then they were out. Wapping was a great blessing for everybody else, because you were then able to do this kind of thing, and the unions became like Samson without his hair.

In 1986 you experienced yet more difficulties when effectively you lost editorial control over the newspaper. Was that even more painful for you than the loss of financial control?

I should have resigned straightaway. Black said he wanted me to remain as editor-in-chief, but he also authorized Andrew Knight, who appointed editors over my head, to report not to me but to him.

You didn't know Max Hastings but you said of Peregrine Worsthorne, 'He couldn't edit a school magazine, let alone a national newspaper.' On what did you base this low opinion?

My experience of him. I used my judgement of him.

Your own son Adrian, though loyal to you, spoke out in Worsthorne's defence and though he wouldn't vote against you, he decided to abstain. You must have regretted that the troubles at the Telegraph *divided the family in this way.*

I did, but because I had lost the vote so handsomely his abstention didn't make any difference.

Lord Hartwell

You have been reluctant to offer any judgement on the new breed of newspaper tycoon. Does silence conceal contempt in this instance?

No. Reticence forbids it, though that sounds very condescending. Most of them are not journalists, you see, and I don't think non-journalists ought to run newspapers. It's like hiring a jockey who has never ridden a horse.

Are you saying that the old traditional proprietor was basically a journalist?

Yes. Even Beaverbrook was a marvellous journalist, a natural journalist, and even though he wasn't trained as one, he quickly became one. He is reported to have said when he appointed Beverly Baxter editor after Blumenfeld retired in the 1920s: 'I'm appointing you editor of the *Daily Express* because you know even less about journalism than I do.' I wouldn't say he was a very nice man, but he did put sophistication into a popular paper, so that it was read by all sections of the public.

How do you view Murdoch?

He's become purely a financier. He's very good at tabloids, but he's never had a success with a serious paper anywhere, here or Australia. The success of the *Sunday Times* is not his at all. Anyway, I don't like the way it's going at all, quite apart from the scandals.

How do you view the Telegraph *now?*

I don't want to discuss my successors at all. I think they're producing a very good paper on the whole. Naturally they're not doing it exactly the way I would, but maybe I'm out of date.

This year you wrote a letter to the Telegraph *which spelt out your own anti-federalist, anti-ERM view of Europe. Do you align yourself with Lady Thatcher in this regard?*

That's something of a poisoned chalice, but I personally thought the

Lord Hartwell

Bruges speech very sound, though not over-burdened with tact. What ERM means is fixed rates of exchange, and that is always disastrous. Rates of exchange to my mind depend on purchasing power parity, and our purchasing power is not at all the same as it was. That's why I do agree wholeheartedly with Lady Thatcher who says you can't buck the market. That's what we tried to do, with disastrous results. We are striving, it seems, to be at the heart of Europe. The heart of Europe, under ERM rules, is either in Herr Kohl's waiting room or in Carey Street.

Why do you think the government is sacrificing everything for the sake of a strong pound?

Why indeed? The exchange rate is the answer to the equation; it's not a constant.

What is it you are proudest of having done – was it founding the Sunday Telegraph *in 1961? Was that the high point of your career, do you think?*

No, it was an obvious thing to do. I preserved the integrity, the popularity and the eventual prosperity of the *Daily Telegraph*, and the fact that I wasn't there to see it happen doesn't matter. The whole thing was planned by my team, and if things had worked out right, we should have succeeded. The costing was right to within two per cent.

So what do you see as your proudest moment?

My first job on a newspaper was on the sports pages of the *Aberdeen Evening Express* and after my first day subbing, the chief sub said to me almost angrily, 'Why didn't you tell me you'd done this before?'

You were perhaps the last great gentleman proprietor and when you left it was in some sense the end of an era. When you look back on your life, do you think mainly of your great achievements, or are they now overlaid with a sense of loss and perhaps failure?

They are overlaid with a sense of failure; certainly loss, and of failure in so

Lord Hartwell

far as I didn't see it through. But I think it has worked out for the best in the end. It has certainly benefited my family, because in the last two years we have made quite a lot of money out of the *Telegraph*, and it's gone not to my brother and myself, but to our nephews and nieces and their children. It has been more to their financial advantage than if I had soldiered on with no intention of selling anything.

How have you coped during the last ten years since the death of your wife?

Certainly it has made me a much lonelier figure. I also feel that she would have been greatly upset at my losing control of the newspaper. She was terribly loyal to me and she realized that I was bound up in this thing with my whole life, and she would have been deeply shocked to see the present regime, or me out of it. She would have been much more conscious of my failure than I am. That she was not there to see it is my only consolation at our parting.

PATRICIA HIGHSMITH

PATRICIA HIGHSMITH

Patricia Highsmith was born in Texas in 1921. After attending Columbia University in New York she worked as a freelance journalist until the publication of her first novel *Strangers on a Train* (1950) which was filmed by Alfred Hitchcock. Her numerous psychological thrillers include *The Blunderer* (1955), *This Sweet Sickness* (1960, filmed 1979), *Those Who Walk Away* (1976), *A Dog's Ransom* (1972) and *People Who Knock on the Door* (1983). *The Talented Mr Ripley*, the first of the Ripley series, was awarded the Edgar Allan Poe Scroll. The world she creates was described by Graham Greene as claustrophobic and irrational, 'one we enter each time with a sense of personal danger'. Patricia Highsmith lives in Switzerland.

Patricia Highsmith

Your parents separated before you were born, at a time when separation and divorce were not as common as they are now. Did you feel different from other children?

Frankly, no. I was born in my grandmother's house in Texas. It was a very warm, friendly atmosphere, and I was very happy until I was six years old when I was taken up to New York, but even there it wasn't bad. It was suddenly different to be amidst all those people, but I remember getting along very well with the blacks in my school because they seemed to have the same accent. And New York is always interesting.

You seem to have had a highly unusual childhood . . . do you remember it as an unhappy time, or did you just accept your circumstances?

I had to accept them. My mother remarried when I was three or four, and she was rather a neurotic type to say the least, always picking quarrels with my stepfather, so life was a little bit difficult.

Do you believe that childhood influences and environment shape and mould the pattern of our adult lives?

I believe very much what the Roman Catholics say about a child up to the age of seven. Moral training has taken place by then, and my grandmother was rather strict on those things. She was not severe, but she knew what was right and wrong, and nobody ever tried to cross her. I'm quite sure that left its mark on me.

Did you ever regret being an only child?

No. I never missed having brothers and sisters. Even now, although I very much like people, I am happy to live alone. The main point is that I can't work with anybody else in the house, so if I lived with somebody I'd have to give up my work, or else somehow create a small house on the lawn and just take myself off there.

Patricia Highsmith

You didn't meet your real father until you were twelve years old. Can you recall your feelings at that time?

I was shy and also curious. It was in my grandmother's house and I saw him for only five or ten minutes – we didn't even sit down. He took a look at my hand, as if to say, yes, you're my child, but he was almost a stranger, rather brusque and formal.

Did you see him later on in life?

Yes. After the first encounter, he walked me to school and back a couple of times. Later between high school and college I went to Texas again to visit my grandmother, and I saw a great deal of him then. We went out to dinner and I met a lot of his friends.

And did you begin to like him?

In my opinion, there was nothing to dislike about him.

Your novels are often concerned with anxiety, confused relationships and loss of identity, which would seem to be the outstanding features of your own childhood . . . would you agree?

I don't see the loss of identity. I took the name Highsmith which was my stepfather's name, but that is not a loss of identity. In any case, fiction writers tend to write about problems, not about happy families. I write about murders, but I never wanted to murder anybody.

How would you describe your relationship with your stepfather? Was he to all intents and purposes your father, or were there barriers?

He was not what you would call a strong father figure, or indeed a strong anything. He was a man of very good character, a mild man whom my mother bossed around. I was about sixteen when I began to realize that it was my mother who was causing the difficulties. But I don't feel his influence. I had to make my own character.

Patricia Highsmith

It seems that your mother explained family circumstances to you when you were ten years old, but that you had worked things out for yourself before then. Did you feel betrayed by that, or angry that she hadn't told you before?

No. I did not feel angry at all. She had simply been evading the issue, putting it off.

I read somewhere about your mother losing one of your manuscripts which you interpreted as an act of terrible indifference. You must have felt very hurt and disappointed.

Not really. By then I was already thirty-four years old – I know because it was the time of my grandmother's death. My mother did not take care of things and she lost the manuscript along with a lot of other papers, my letters to my grandmother, my college exam results, and so on. But I did not think it malicious. She was simply disorganized.

Do you think that your experience, or perhaps lack of experience of men during your formative years – absent father, stepfather, etc. – led to a mistrust of men in later life?

No, because I had boyfriends from the age of sixteen. And, as a matter of fact, I regarded my stepfather as being very trustworthy.

The heroes of your books are invariably men. The women are less interesting – they are often sluttish or have disagreeable habits. Do you have a kind of contempt for your own gender?

No. *Edith's Diary*, for instance, is entirely about a woman and her struggles, a woman who tried to do her best. She failed in the end, but I think I wrote about her with considerable respect.

Your Little Tales of Misogyny, *in the words of the blurb, shows 'the generic awfulness of the female sex'. Were they written tongue-in-cheek, or with an underlying conviction?*

Patricia Highsmith

With a conviction about certain aspects of women, such as a kind of phoniness and trying to be oh-so-correct, but one could do the same kind of book about men, a similar exaggeration of masculine traits.

Do you feel a sense of solidarity with your fellow women?

No. I've never been in that position. I can be in favour of women's causes, but I don't join them. If it's a matter of donating a little money, or signing something, I might, but not extra work.

You have been independent all your life, you are successful, your own woman, all of which would seem to make you a shining example of the feminist movement. Have you ever felt strongly about women's liberation?

Not strongly, no, but I'm not in a job that discriminates against women. I might have become angry if I'd been working in an office all my life.

Your book Carol, *published under a pseudonym, describes the love which develops between two women. Why did the subject interest you?*

Because society was more against love between women in those days, and I thought it was a good story, especially with the ex-husband in pursuit, making things as difficult as possible. I wasn't consciously trying to convey a particular message, but I wanted to give it a happy ending.

Why did you write it under a pseudonym?

I was already labelled as a mystery writer, even though *Strangers on a Train* was not a mystery, and I didn't want to be labelled as a gay writer. My publishers wanted another book like *Strangers on a Train*, but as usual I wrote what I wanted to.

It was unusual in those days to give a positive portrayal of homosexuality.

Patricia Highsmith

Were you trying to shock, or make people examine their prejudices, or what?

Neither. I was trying to tell a story which I thought was interesting.

Your heroine Carol has to face the choice of losing her daughter or losing her lover, but there is no attempt to portray the situation from the child's point of view, or to engage the reader's sympathy with the child. I wonder if you perhaps lack a natural sympathy with children . . .

The child is only ten and I don't think a ten-year-old would have been able to understand the situation then, or the feelings of society towards lesbianism. Besides, I don't know much about children because I haven't been around children since I was a child myself. Frankly I'm not particularly interested in children.

Have you ever wanted to have children?

No. Absolutely not. I think it's very difficult to raise children properly, and I cannot live with people round me.

You live quite a reclusive existence. Is that how you planned it, or did it just happen that way?

To say I am a recluse is journalistic nonsense, as though I made an effort to stay alone, which is not the case. I like talking to people on the phone, I like people to drop by for a coffee. I do not consider myself a recluse.

You have always avoided literary circles or discussions with other writers. Do you think they might be too incestuous or is it perhaps a fear of boredom?

I'm not inclined to talk about my work before it is finished – I think it is very dangerous to do so – and then when a book is finished, why talk about it? To me another writer it not enough of a change mentally. I very much

Patricia Highsmith

prefer painters and sculptors and photographers; they have a different way of seeing life.

In your books violence seems to take place almost as much in the head as in any overt way. Do you think this is a true reflection of the way it is, that most violence is cerebral, and seldom actually manifests itself?

I'm not interested in brute force, which is what prevails in the world today. The kind of people I write about debate with themselves beforehand – should they do it or not? This makes for more thinking about violence in my books than doing it.

You have said that you find the public passion for justice boring and artificial because 'neither life nor nature cares if justice is done or not'. What exactly do you mean by that?

It's a rather extreme remark, but even justice frequently goes wrong. There are cases of men and women falsely accused of murder. Also, only eleven per cent of murders are discovered now. Some people don't count for very much so the police don't try very hard to find out who killed them. In the majority of cases nobody cares enough to catch the murderer, especially in America where the jails are full and the police are very busy.

The world you portray is a very cynical one, full of emotional cripples. Is this for you a totally imaginary world, or does it reflect your experience of life?

The world is certainly full of very strange people. It's a matter of degree. Sometimes people are just quirky which makes them interesting and funny, but sometimes their quirks are terribly serious.

In 1965 you said that you were sick of violence and butchery and psychopaths . . . yet psychopaths have followed you into the 90s.

Well, I made a mistake in 1965 then.

Patricia Highsmith

Graham Greene once described you as 'the poet of apprehension rather than fear'. Is that a description you're pleased with?

Yes, I regard it as a compliment. Apprehension implies that my books leave something to the imagination. The reader is made curious about what is going to happen.

He also said that your world is one 'without moral endings', in other words justice is often not done and the villains are free to carry on their evil doings. Do you see yourself as seriously challenging the normal moral scheme of things, or is it purely a game, an entertainment.

It's more of a game. I'm principally interested in telling a good story.

But your novels often invite discussions of morality, fuelled by characters like Ripley who murder without conscience and get away with it. What message are you aiming to give to people?

None. I'm simply trying to create an interesting story. Some people might say Ripley's attitude is impossible but I think his lack of conscience is entirely believable. My books are written to entertain. I don't consider myself a deep thinker; I'm much more an intuitive kind of person.

Your book People Who Knock on the Door *was dedicated to, 'The courage of the Palestinian people and their leaders in the struggle to regain a part of their homeland.' Why did you make that political gesture?*

Because I thought it was right that I should. I blame my own country to some extent for what is going on now. I know people blame England for the mandate which led to all this, but America finances it now to a great degree. They also have the press under control and people are more or less told to shut up. Well, I don't feel like shutting up. I think statements about injustice should be made. It's shocking the way people sit in Long Island saying that the Palestinians should get their act together. When Hitler used the gun and the boots on the Jews nobody told them to get their act together. Nobody is able to face up to the gun. The Palestinians can't even form small collectives to grow vegetables in poor soil on their own West Bank and Gaza without the Israelis breaking them up.

But what first brought the Palestinian cause to your attention?

The atrocity of it, the absolute injustice of the situation.

I understand you won't allow your books to be published in Israel. Do you think gestures like that have any effect?

No, only in a very small way. I'm sure the world couldn't care less, but it shows that not every American refuses to see what's happening. That is what the Israelis want, and that's frankly what they get round the New York area. From a humane point of view America turns too much of a blind eye to what Israel is doing there.

Do you feel as you grow older that your writing gets better and better?

That's very tough. Unfortunately, I feel a tremendous slowing up; everybody does at my age, I think. Also life becomes more complicated as one grows older. There's more paperwork, income-tax returns for two countries – all this has become burdensome somehow.

You have described the criminal as a free spirit. Can you tell me what you mean by that?

It's not very flattering to the criminal because he just does anything he wants. It's not something that I admire, but he's definitely free in that respect. The rest of us have certain constraints, which is normal. For example, there are one or two people in my life whom I absolutely detest, but to murder them is out of the question.

Your heroes are usually unscrupulous, amoral and sometimes schizoid. Is it simply that they are more dramatically interesting figures to write about, or does your attraction to them run deeper than that?

It's not so much attraction. I find them interesting, puzzling. Nobody questions why somebody is good, but most people are curious about a murderer – they want to know why. Also there is entertainment value in somebody getting away with something. One may disapprove, but it's still fascinating.

Ripley differs from your other heroes in that he appears to have no conscience. Other characters are much more concerned with their own guilt. Is Ripley the exception . . . in art as in life?

Ripley is abnormal in the sense that he doesn't feel the same amount of guilt as other people. He feels guilty for the first murder and then is reconciled to the others. I have to say that he's exceptional.

It has sometimes been said that you are in love with Ripley, the rather likeable psychopath. Does this strike you as an absurd suggestion?

It's just an exaggeration. I like to write about him, yes, but that's all. It's a silly phrase, 'in love'.

Have you ever been love with a man?

In a way, yes. When I was around twenty-one . . .

What happened?

Nothing happened. It turned into friendship, and we were friends until he died.

Have you ever regretted not marrying?

No.

Lucretia Stewart who interviewed you for the Telegraph *wrote as follows:*

Patricia Highsmith

'Her manner, which is at once diffident and disdainful, precludes intrusive questioning. It is not a secret that she is or has been a lesbian, but it would have been impossible to ask her about her private life.' How do you react to that?

It's better than some things I've read. If she wants to put that, it's OK by me.

What about the suggestion that you are a lesbian?

OK. Fine. But I don't talk about it.

Have you been a lesbian?

Yes.

One concludes from reading your books that happiness is a frail commodity, touched by anxiety and often guilt. Has that been your own experience perhaps?

Very often with regard to people, yes, but it does not apply to happiness in general. Many people of course want to say that I'm unhappy, that I'm reclusive, but I'm not going to be unhappy just because somebody tells me I am.

In all the attention given to death in your books, do you ever contemplate your own?

No, although I would really like to be sure about my will. I have made a will, actually written it in holograph which is what the Swiss want, but I have a feeling it isn't finalized yet. The most important thing is to have everything well organized before one's death; that is more important than the phenomenon of dying.

Patricia Highsmith

Do you see the world as a friendly place?

In principle, yes. I have an optimistic attitude. When I get up in the morning, I first of all make the coffee and then I say to my cat, we're going to have a great day . . .

P. D. JAMES

P.D. JAMES

Phyllis Dorothy James was born in Oxford in 1920 and educated at Cambridge Girls' High School. During the war she was a Red Cross nurse and later she was employed in hospital administration before working in the Home Office, first with the forensic science service and then in the criminal law department. Her first novel, *Cover Her Face*, was published in 1962 and in 1979 she retired from the Home Office to concentrate on her writing. Many of her novels feature the detective Adam Dalgliesh, most popularly in *A Taste for Death* (1986) which enjoyed an international vogue. In 1987 she was awarded the Crime Writers' Association Diamond Dagger. She serves on the Arts Council, is a governor of the BBC, and in 1991 was made a life peer, Baroness James of Holland Park.

P. D. James

You describe your childhood as having been a time of considerable anxiety: Do you think this was primarily nature or nurture?

Probably a little of both. My parents were not very well matched, so I think it was a house where there was considerable tension. I was quite frightened of my father. I loved him very much, and I remember him with great respect and affection, but the qualities that I admired in him – his fortitude, intelligence and a certain sardonic humour – are aspects you come to appreciate only when you're older. A child wants a father to be loving and kind and rather more affectionate than mine was able to be.

It is often said that to have a great deal of trauma in childhood is an excellent preparation for the creative writer. In that sense would you say that you served a good apprenticeship?

I have to be very careful here because, although this may seem platitudinous, I'm always aware of the fact that three quarters of the human race go hungry. I didn't go hungry, so it's very difficult to feel I had a less happy childhood than I should have done when in fact I had a roof over my head, I had enough to eat, I had an education. But it was a time of some trauma; that is certainly true. It is good for a creative artist to have this, but I'm not so sure it's good for a human being. Perhaps that is why some creative artists aren't very easy people.

You seem always to have regretted the fact that you did not go to university. Is this a straightforward sadness at missed opportunity, or is it overlaid with resentment towards your parents for not making it possible?

It would have been very difficult for them to have made it possible, although if I had been a boy my father would have made a greater effort. As it was I was born in 1920, and there were no grants before the war. You had to be clever enough to get a scholarship, and you didn't get an awful lot of money even then. I wasn't bright enough for a scholarship so I didn't get the chance. I don't think I can altogether blame my father who was only a middle-grade civil servant, but I would have loved to have gone to university instead of leaving school at sixteen. It had been my childhood dream – I had always thought of university as being a very beautiful place, somewhere full of learning and books and conversation and intelligent people, much brighter than myself. Whether it would have made me a better writer, I don't know; it may have been lucky for me not to go.

Are you one of those people who believe that all our adult virtues and failings can be explained in terms of childhood influences, or can this delving into the past be overdone, do you think?

It can be overdone. I tend to think heredity is more important. The first Queen Elizabeth said, 'I am endued with such qualities that if I were turned out of the Realm in my petticoat I were able to live in any place in Christome.' And one feels she would; she would have survived. Certain people are born with such qualities of character and intellect that they are survivors, and even if they're born into bad environments or deprived families, they're going to make their way all right, because it's in them to do it. Having said that, I do accept that early environment and childhood experiences are immensely important.

You yourself have made the connection between your literary interest in death and your childhood experience of seeing a drowned boy retrieved from a river. That seems to have been a psychologically significant moment . . .

I didn't actually see the body, though I do remember being immensely interested in it, and I wouldn't have minded seeing him. As it was, the children were herded together on one side and then taken away, but just *knowing* a body had been found was fascinating. I didn't really understand this interest, but from early childhood I certainly was aware of the fact of death in a very strange way. For example, if we were talking about what we were going to do in the summer, even as a small child I would think, 'Well, if we are still alive that's what we'll do.' Of course I do that now all the time, I always have at the back of my mind the thought 'if I'm still here' – that is because I recognize the inevitability of death and the knowledge that it can come at any time; but it's odd for a child to think in those terms.

Your mother seems to have provided the warmth and security in your life, and although later you came to respect and admire your father's qualities, you have often said that you feared your father. Was this a rational fear? What exactly were you afraid of?

Just afraid of his displeasure; of him as an authority figure. My parents were mismatched. He was very intelligent, very musical, but he didn't have many opportunities in life. He had to earn his living from the age of sixteen, so I think in many ways he was a disappointed man. My mother was sentimental and warm and not very bright. She would have been a good wife for a country parson with eight children. My mother was slightly afraid of him and that communicated itself to me.

When you became a mother yourself, were you conscious of trying to reverse this rather unhappy experience of childhood for your own children? Was it very important to convey a sense of love and approval to your children?

Oh yes. All that is tremendously important, especially a sense of approval. It was difficult of course because my husband was very ill, and obviously I had to support the family by myself. The children lived with their grandparents, so they didn't see me as much as children normally do, but certainly I was a very affectionate mother. Whether I would have been as good a mother had they been difficult children, I don't know. I'm not very fond of children as children, but I did like my own. They were very easy to love; they were themselves loving and bright, and our interests coincided, so we always had something to talk about as they grew up. But I might have been a poor mother of a stupid, irritating child.

Many people who married during the war have described how the fact of war gave their marriage a sense of urgency or fatalism – it was a defiantly optimistic act in time of uncertainty. Was it so for you?

It was. In some ways it was such a happy time, which is a curious thing to say, but I think there was a great sense of comradeship; and during the bombing there was a great sense of excitement. It was a romantic time really, and one didn't think about things so very deeply.

You were to have three happy years before your husband's tragic illness.

P. D. James

Are you still able to recall those years, how they felt, or was that something that was lost in the stressful times which followed?

Oh I can recall them . . . I can recall them. They haven't been really lost. I was so young then, and when you're young, you've got all that optimism, that enthusiasm for life.

It seems that you coped with the difficulties of supporting two children and your sick husband in an entirely pragmatic and unself-pitying way. Were your strength and resourcefulness innate qualities, do you think, or were they born of your immensely difficult situation?

They were probably innate. Throughout life my attitude to problems has been to find a solution and to survive, and I was helped by the fact that by nature I am more suited to having a career and a job than I would have been to being a doctor's wife and staying at home. On the whole I enjoyed the jobs I did; not all of them and not all of the time, but I had no reason to feel terribly aggrieved that I was having to work. Once I realized my husband was unlikely to get well, I went to evening classes and qualified in hospital administration so that I could get a reasonably senior job. After he died I took an examination for a senior post in the civil service; so there was a lot of ambition there really.

Was your husband your first love?

More or less. There were various experimentations . . . but yes, he was my first real love. I still miss him. We were very well suited; I was the dominant partner, but that didn't worry him; he was quite happy for me to be the one who arranged things in his life. He was eccentric, clever, Anglo-Irish; a strange race, the Protestant Anglo-Irish. He loved books and pictures, he had a wonderful sense of humour, and very great charm. He adored his daughters, and he would have loved his grandchildren. And since he was totally without envy, he would not have minded a wife who was more successful in worldly terms than himself. I miss him very much. We were very happy.

And after he died you never fell in love again?

No, never. I didn't meet a man whom I could really love, and the men who proposed marriage to me after Connor died, I didn't want to marry. I would also have been wary of falling in love. I do believe that as one gets older one looks at marriage in rather a different light. When you're young you are forced by sexual desire and youth and romance, while underneath it all the genes are wanting to perpetuate themselves, but when you get past childbearing you begin to think, do I really want to wake up every morning and see this face at breakfast? I would have been happy to marry again if I'd met someone for whom I had a great respect and affection, but it's very easy to get quite selfish after a bit when you live alone, especially if you're a writer; you do things in your own time and in your own way.

You have an impressive record of public appointments – you were on the board of the Arts Council, you chair the literature panel, and you are a governor of the BBC. Being a woman seems to have been no impediment in this area . . .

Not at all. When I was appointed to the BBC there weren't enough women on the board, so a woman can have a slight advantage in that way. Not always of course, and there are still not enough women in public life. In the Health Service I had to be much better than the men if I was going to get a job over their heads, but otherwise I've never felt disadvantaged as a woman, and I never felt that I was sexually harassed. Perhaps I've been lucky.

Is it attributable to luck, or do you think sexual harassment is a bit exaggerated?

It's been overdone. Men have always flirted, and why shouldn't they? I'm quite prepared to flirt with a man if he's attractive. And a woman always knows the difference between a man who is flirting with her because she is a woman, and a man who is really sexually unpleasant. If women have lost the art of knowing that, I'm very sorry for them. If a man opens a door for you nowadays it's regarded as an insult, and I think that's dreadful and also rather sad.

You have done a great deal in your own career to advance the cause of

P. D. James

women, but am I right in thinking you might share Doris Lessing's view on feminism – you support its aims but you dislike its shrill voice?

I share her view entirely. I also suspect that many of the extreme feminists are so because they envy men and dislike being women. I don't dislike being a woman. I have many men friends, and I admire men, but I've never wanted to be one, and I sometimes suspect that the shrillness comes from a huge resentment that they haven't been born male. I very much dislike the suggestion that all men are by nature rapists. It just is not true. There are some very unpleasant men about, one knows, but to look at the entire male population and castigate them as anti-female, uncaring, sexually harassing and potential rapists, is nonsense, complete nonsense.

In your public life you are very much an Establishment figure, an Anglican, a Conservative, a former magistrate and high-ranking civil servant. Do you see any link between the Establishment and the rather murky lower depths you explore in your novels?

No, I don't think so. I suppose I am an Establishment figure – I'm certainly an Anglican, though not a very good one in the sense that I'm not a regular churchgoer. I am also on the liturgical commission of the Church of England, but I think I sit there more because of my interest in the language of the liturgy. I'm not a member of the Conservative Party but that's the way I vote; I am a natural conservative, no doubt about that. And I am an ex-magistrate, so yes, I do qualify as an Establishment figure. There is in my character a natural love of order, and a real fear of violence and disorder, which may account for the kind of fiction I write. I'm very frightened of emotional and psychological violence as well as physical violence, and I think good order is important to any country. All the old certainties are just being swept away, that's the trouble nowadays. I think one needs the central certainties, just as most people need a religion, whatever form it takes. In the modern detective story, order may be restored in the sense that the crime is solved, but the crime is so contaminating that all the characters are in some way touched by it. In the 1930s when the detective stories were set in a village, the crime was solved, and the little village went back to what it was before. We don't write like that now, but it is still about restoring order. It is also about affirming the belief that we live in a moral universe and one that we're capable of understanding. All this is very reassuring, yet with part of my mind I wonder if we're not living in a universe that is not moral, a universe with chaos underneath.

As a governor of the BBC where do you stand on the business of violence on television? Do you have any sympathy with the Mary Whitehouse view that violence on our screens is corrupting and ought to be censored?

There is no proof that it does harm but I do think that from a common-sense point of view, for young people to be perpetually exposed to images of violence cannot be good. Of course people are apt to say there is nothing but violence on our screens, but when you ask for some examples it's not so easy. I don't honestly think it's the BBC we have to worry about, it's the videos which children can buy nowadays. These videos are really quite appallingly violent, and that, I think, has to be bad.

What about violence in books?

In books I hate scenes of torture, but I don't worry so much about violence in the detective story, because it is such a moral form. The villain always gets found out. What worries me more is that books are becoming increasingly pornographic, and when that happens they cease to be erotic. It's the same with films. I saw *Basic Instinct*, which is supposed to be a thriller, on video and every time the main characters were near a bed we had another ten minutes of reeling and writhing. All this heaving and loud breathing and acrobatics... oh dear, oh dear... it's just not subtle enough to be erotic. Perhaps it's my age, but I do believe that some of the most erotic things are the most subtle; you can have the most erotic scenes where the couple don't in fact touch each other, you can have a huge sexual charge without having people rolling around naked on beds.

You have sometimes said that you're not a professional writer in the sense that you never have actually had to earn your living from writing. Is that something you have regarded as a liberation or a constraint?

A liberation. This is part of my innate caution. Without the writing I would have been quite poor, but we wouldn't have starved. When I worked in the Home Office it was a good wage and it paid the mortgage. I didn't expect the writing to make me rich, although it has; I had ambitions to be highly regarded, and I set out to be a good and serious writer. I certainly don't despise the money – it's totally dishonest to pretend that you're not happier if you've got money, by and large. But I've never taken a penny in advance for any book until it was completed. Some people work better if they are given a huge advance to write the next book, but I can't stand that anxiety, I never wanted that. Don't misunderstand me; I'm not making any judgement here or any moral point – it just happens to be right for me. I do remember the depression of the 1920s and being constantly told by my mother how lucky I was that my father was a civil servant. People were hungry then and I grew up with this great need for security.

I wonder if you are conscious of your readership as you write. Do you feel the need to justify the particular moral scheme within which you operate, or is it something you take very much for granted?

I don't think about the readership. I think about what is going to satisfy me. If I have an idea for a book I do the very best I can with that idea. It's a matter of total artistic pride, not to publish a book until it's as good as I can make it, and I suppose I feel that if I can satisfy myself then I shall satisfy my readers. There is a moral climate in which I write, but my characters don't always share it. My characters can make powerful arguments in favour of a world in which there is no God, for example, and I understand those arguments absolutely, so in that sense I'm not a didactic writer.

Would you increase the sexual interest in order to sell more books?

I've never done that, and I've never been tempted. But I can't imagine a book without sex, because love, including sexual love, is such an important part of human life and it controls so much of what men and women do. In detective novels where you have motives, where you have people driven by compulsions, where there is moral conflict, almost certainly you are going to have strong sexual motives. It would seem a very bloodless book if it had no sex in it, whether it's heterosexual or homosexual sex, and I've had both. In one of my books Dalgliesh remembers a constable saying to him, 'People will tell you that the most dangerous emotion in the world is hatred, but don't you believe it; the most dangerous emotion in the world is love.'

P. D. James

Are there any passages in your books which you would mind your daughters reading?

No. I've never written anything of which I'm ashamed, or that I'd mind them reading. With regard to my descriptions of dead bodies I sometimes think they will say, 'Oh Mummy, really, this is a bit much', but I've never written anything which I feel I couldn't justify artistically. When a body is found I want the description to be absolutely realistic, what it would look like and smell like. That's important.

Do you believe novelists have a moral responsibility towards their readers?

They have a moral responsibility to do the very best they can with their talent, without considering what is going to earn the most money, without twisting it to suit a particular market, without inserting gratuitous sex or pornography in order to increase sales. It's artistic honesty that counts.

Your books are as remote from the comfortable middle-class world of Agatha Christie as it is possible to be. It seems to me that your concern is more with the ethical problems of murder and the consequences of crime, something which allows you to probe deeper into the complexities of human nature. Is this the real area of interest to you?

Yes, it is. What I'm interested in are the people, their motives, the characters' compulsions and the moral choices. That's why there are no psychopaths in my detective stories. A psychopath murders because he just happens to enjoy murder; he has no moral choice, and therefore he is of no interest to me.

Do you perhaps rather disapprove of Agatha Christie and her Poirot and Miss Marple? Has part of your purpose been to explode the cosy class-ridden snobbish world she portrays?

Sometimes people say that I am Agatha Christie's crown princess and successor, and that always seems to me to be nonsense because I think we're very different writers. I don't think she's a good novelist; I have to say that, although I feel it's very unbecoming of any writer to deride her because she has given immense pleasure to millions of people all over the world. Some people say she's done harm to the crime novel, but I don't see that. She's a kind of literary conjuror. Every time most of us are surprised – I'm not because I now see through the trick – but if we think about it afterwards we realize it could not have happened in real life. She puts down a character as pasteboard, and we get the same ones in each book; she shifts them around, and we think ah, that's the murderer; it never is. I wouldn't be too unkind about her, but I don't think I am at all like her. The accusation of snobbery in connection with a classical detective story arises from the fact that you are really hoping to provide an intelligent murderer who knows the difference between right and wrong, makes the moral choice, and is out to commit a very clever murder; and that being so, he is very unlikely to be a stupid, professional villain. The horror of the deed is greatly enhanced if there is contrast, as W.H. Auden knew when in an essay called 'The Guilty Vicarage' he said that the single body on the drawing-room floor is a great deal more horrible than the dozen bullet-ridden bodies down Raymond Chandler's mean streets. You need contrast, and it's a good thing to have it in a fairly prosperous, orderly society. If I were to set a detective story among professional criminals in the worst areas of inner-city violence, it would not be very interesting. Murder has to be set among people to whom murder really is an appalling crime if you're going to get that contrast, and I suppose Agatha Christie felt that to an extent, even though she produced prosperous middle-class books set in cosy little villages.

You have described the detective novel as essentially an unsentimental form. Does sentiment hold many terrors for you?

I'm very wary of sentimentality and I don't think it's the same as compassion. Sentimentality is a very easy and agreeable emotion which doesn't often find its outlet in effective action; compassion does.

I imagine you are wary of conclusions about art imitating life, but at the same time your hero Dalgliesh is intelligent, self-sufficient, unsentimental, wary of relationships – is he not created in your own image?

Yes, he is a bit. If you have one character who goes through a succession of books this tends to happen.

P. D. James

You have used Graham Greene's words of Dalgliesh, saying that there is a splinter of ice in his heart. Is there also a splinter in yours?

Yes, there is. It's difficult to explain why because it involves something which happened to me, and telling it could be much too painful for my children. Let me just say that even when appalling things have been happening to me, part of my mind has been observing my own reaction to them; I have known myself to do that in many quite terrible situations. I know I couldn't do it if one of my children died. If that happened I wouldn't be able to watch my own grief or record it or watch myself grieving; it would consume me, absolutely. But in most other situations, when I've been in a condition of great trauma, and sometimes if I've been comforting friends in great distress, I'm still observing the manifestations of the distress.

You have a fascination with the bridges we construct over the chaos of personal and psychological disorder, the bridges of law and order and religion. Murder, the ultimate crime, blows away these bridges and reveals how people behave under stress. Are you attracted to writing about the chaos in the knowledge that you are able to put it right?

Yes, I'm sure that's so. In life you aren't able to, but in books you are. Of course you don't put it totally right. In *A Taste for Death* in which the bodies are found in the church vestry by poor Miss Wharton and the little boy she befriends, we know at the end how the murder was done and we know who's guilty, but nearly all the characters in that book had their lives changed because in some way they came in contact with the two butchered bodies in that church. And yet it is controlled, and this profound sense of imposing order on disorder is highly agreeable to me. It's psychologically satisfying, especially in a world where there is so much disorder.

Albert Camus believed that the evil in the world almost always comes from ignorance and that 'good intentions may do as much harm as malevolence, if they lack understanding'. Is that something you agree with?

I could agree with it in certain circumstances, but I don't think evil is just the absence of education and the absence of knowledge. It's true that good intentions on their own are not enough; well-intentioned people who lack wisdom and knowledge and intelligence can do a great deal of harm, but it doesn't follow that these qualities when present make for an absence of evil.

But do you think that without evil there can be no goodness?

I don't think goodness depends on evil, but it depends on the possibility of evil.

Despite the fixation on death in your books there emerges a distinct sense of the sancitity of life. Is that an intended effect, one you're pleased with?

Yes, it is intended and I am pleased with it.

Do you ever apply your mind to the abortion issue?

Yes. It's extremely difficult because here my reason is at war with my instinct. If the child is going to be grossly deformed, mentally or physically, then abortion is justified, but I find it abhorrent when abortion is used as a method of birth control or for the convenience of the mother. Of course one can argue logically that if the woman is to have a choice, then the choice includes abortion, and who am I to judge whether her motives are selfish or not. Yet it is abhorrent, it is abhorrent.

Are you saying that the sanctity of life depends on the quality of life?

Yes, I am, though I don't think that's very logical. The easy answer is to take the extreme view that abortion is never justified; or to say that it is always justified, and no child should come into the world unwanted. It is far more difficult for human beings to have to apply their minds to this essentially moral question: are there circumstances in which the destruction of the embryo is justifiable? I would say there are, when it's a question of preserving the life of a mother, or if the foetus is so abnormal that its chances of having any kind of life worth living are virtually none. But it's a very slippery slope.

P. D. James

You are fond of quoting the psychologist Anthony Storr who said, 'All creativity is the successful resolution of internal conflict.' How would you describe your own internal conflict?

What he said is profoundly true for me. My fear of violence and disorder reveals a basic insecurity which likes this ordered form, because in the end, although I can't put it right in the real world, I can put it right between the covers of my books.

You are generally dismissive of psychological theorizing about yourself, and tend to promote the image of a respectable, sensible grandmother figure. Is this to keep intruders at bay, to keep yourself private, or is it perhaps an unwillingness to delve too deeply into your own psyche?

It's a bit of all three. I do delve quite deeply into my psyche, as deeply as I would want to delve, but I don't like other people doing it, and I don't feel much good comes of it. The old idea that if you can understand things then somehow you put them right is not necessarily so. I can see that my insecurity might well have come from a childhood trauma, that my need for religion, my belief in a God is perhaps the need to have a better father figure than I had; but I don't think I gain much by knowing, or by somebody else expecting me to lie on a couch and pay a great deal of good money in order to reach that same conclusion.

You fear violence a great deal, which is perhaps a natural condition of women. But in your case it seems a rather heightened, almost irrational fear – keys always kept round your neck, doors locked, truncheon under the pillow, and so on. Would you agree it borders on the pathological?

Borders perhaps. But it's very difficult in this modern world not to feel that it's really quite sensible. The keys round the neck are simply because I have a fairly big house and if I require to open the door, if only for the postman, it's just maddening chasing up and down for keys. I am meticulous about locking up, but I think that is no more than common sense. The house was never locked throughout my childhood, and people who had cars could leave them unlocked in the street, but it's a different world now.

P. D. James

Do you believe that we are all potential murderers?

I believe we're all capable of homicide but I don't think we're all capable of murder. I would make a distinction between killing to save other people, to protect one's children or grandchildren, to protect oneself if assaulted, but the legal definition of murder involves premeditation: 'causing the death of a living creature under the Queen's Peace with malice aforethought, death occurring within a year and a day'. And I don't think we're all of us capable of that. I would not plan to kill someone, but if I woke up in the middle of the night and found a rapist in my bedroom, I wouldn't give much for his chances; and it wouldn't worry me, not in the slightest.

Would it be overstating it to say that your novels perhaps offer a catharis of the natural state of guilt, your own included?

I think the detective story does that, for my own guilt and the reader's. If people don't look back on their life and feel guilty there's something wrong with them. Guilt is almost inseparable from being a human being. I certainly think I could have been a better daughter, a better wife to my husband, a better mother to my children, and there are those to whom I could have been a better friend. At the same time we shouldn't let guilt master us. If we don't learn to forgive ourselves we never learn to forgive other people, so guilt can be very destructive, and that's why religions make a provision for coping with it.

The subtext of much of your writing seems to be a deep disapproval of the present world and its moral climate. Is there something of the old morality play in your fiction, do you think?

Not intentionally, but it tends to be so. Auden certainly thought that a detective story was the equivalent of the old morality play. Its moral stance is unambiguous: murder is wrong, and it should be discovered and punished. There should be an attempt to understand the murderer and what the temptation was, but my books would never say that what was done was right.

P. D. James

Do you believe in punishment as a deterrent to crime?

Yes, I'm sure it is. I remember a conference where people were saying that punishment was never a deterrent, and the speaker stood up and said, 'If the penalty for illegal parking was a public flogging very few would have left their cars where they are standing now.' And she was absolutely right. It's a common-sense thing – it would deter me. I don't know how far, if we had the death penalty, it would deter potential murderers, but by and large human beings are deterred by the thought of punishment.

Do you agree with Muriel Spark that although novels are fiction, there emerges from them a kind of truth, a moral or metaphorical truth perhaps, but none the less truth?

Yes, she is right. The truth which emerges is the truth about human beings. I don't think that one can make a universal application from a particular novel; one can only say this tells us something about how human beings would behave in certain circumstances, and the consequences of that behaviour.

I have noticed that in your earlier books there is almost a complete absence of cruelty, or description of pain; the reader was protected in a sense. In later books, such as A Taste for Death *and* Devices and Desires, *this is not so. Why do you think your writing developed in this way?*

I think it had to do with becoming increasingly aware of the pain and the violence of life. If only our moral progress could match our scienfitic progress. I remain an optimist, but that is a state which is very difficult to justify intellectually.

Your new book The Children of Men *describes a futuristic world stricken by universal infertility. Your hero Theodore recounts the fact that people's interest in sex is waning, and that 'romantic and idealized love' has replaced 'crude carnal satisfaction'. Do you think sex is dangerous when it is separated from love?*

Dangerous is perhaps rather a strong word. It can lead to the dangers of being promiscuous and that in the end is not satisfactory to human beings. When sex is divorced from love it's a sterile business. Women find it extremely difficult; men find it much easier.

Is it something you would be able to do?

I think I could. I can quite see that I could have a sexual relationship simply because the man was very attractive and I was sexually drawn to him, but I don't think I'd find it very satisfying. The highest satisfaction from sex is through love.

Your detective books are concerned with the judgement of men, but your new book is more to do with the judgement of God. This is surely difficult ground for any writer . . .

Very difficult, yes. The idea for this book came to me from reading about the extraordinary reduction in fertility of Western man. The sperm rate is down by about forty per cent in thirty years, and there seems to be no reason why the same thing shouldn't happen to homo sapiens as has happened to virtually every one of the millions of living forms that have inherited our planet. In the nature of things we should die out, and dying out in one year spectacularly is not impossible, but a bit unlikely, so to that extent the book is a fable. It was a slightly worrying book to write, rather traumatic.

The book tells us that much of the sinister, bleak picture you paint can be traced back to the preoccupations of the early 1990s – 'Pornography and sexual violence on film, on television, in books, in life, had increased and become more explicit, but less and less in the West we made love and bred children.' That sounds like a terrible indictment of modern times and morals. Is it meant to be?

There's quite a lot of truth in it, but that's what Theo says – it isn't necessarily what I believe, although I can see some evidence for his views. For example, he says somewhere that we know more and more about sex and less and less about love, and I think that's probably true. Even St

Valentine's Day has been reduced to commercial nonsense about sex rather than a celebration of love.

The fact that you describe The Children of Men *as a moral fable rather than science fiction seems to place it within the possibility of human experience . . .*

Once infertility had taken hold, it would not be reversed in the way I describe, but the rest of it is well within human experience. We would start storing sperm, and then there would be all sorts of interesting questions, such as, from whom do you get the sperm, and who has access to it? People would be screened for their suitability to breed, and a great many ethical and philosophical issues would arise.

Isn't the nightmare scenario you depict in which sex, in so far as it takes place at all, has become 'meaninglessly acrobatic' and women experience what they describe as 'painful orgasms – the spasm achieved without the pleasure' – isn't this getting dangerously close to the idea of the wrath of God being unleashed, the extremist view of the Aids epidemic?

Yes. In this new world people discover that if there is not the possibility of breeding children, sex loses its point and therefore more and more they're striving after a sensation which isn't coming to them naturally. I don't know whether that would happen or not, but it seems to me it's very possible it could.

Happy sexual relationships tend not to be a feature of your novels. Is that because you regard them as a rare feature of real life?

It's rather the result of the kind of fiction I write. The detective story is an artificial form, and though all fiction is a rearrangement of the artist's view of reality, a detective story is highly stylized in its conventions in order to form a coherent entity: there is a central mysterious death, a number of clues and a close circle of suspects who are all – the reader must believe – capable of this particular murder. One of the strongest motives is the sexual motive, so the novel is not likely to be full of very happily married, jolly people, but rather people whose lives are full of tension and unhappiness and misery of some kind. As my dear mother, God rest her, used to say, why can't you write a nice book about nice people? But you're not likely to get an awful lot of nice people in a detective story; it's inherent in the situation that people aren't living very happy or stable lives.

The ending of The Children of Men, *although ambivalent, suggests that the future of mankind is not entirely beyond redemption, and that ultimately the power of good can overcome moral depravity and corruption. Do you see this as essentially a Christian message, the triumph of good over evil . . .*

The triumph of good over evil and the triumph of love over hatred is essentially a Christian message; and it is central probably to the great religions of the world. There is a lovely story which has always amused me about a man who appeared in court for some kind of public disorder, and when asked how he pleaded, he said, 'I plead for hope against despair, I plead for good against evil, I plead for peace against war, for sympathy against unkindness', and the judge said, 'That will be recorded as not guilty, and if we hear any more from you I shall order a psychiatric report' [laughs].

But do you yourself believe that good triumphs over evil?

Yes, I think I do. I have a fairly simple view of these things. I think of life in terms of a mountain with God at the top, and those of us who are religious or have any aspirations are slowly working our way up. I am a practising Christian because that's the tradition in which I was brought up. We start life according to where we're born – I know if I had been born a Roman Catholic I wouldn't have changed; I would have remained in the religion of my fathers and my people. I'm a very strong traditionalist, although that does not mean that I assent intellectually to all the articles of the Church of England, with which I am sometimes disenchanted. For example, I really can't accept the idea of a God whose notion of justice was to send his only son to be tortured on earth to atone for the sins of the world. I believe that death on the cross had a universal significance, but I can't quite see it in those crude terms. I don't conceive of God as being less merciful than an earthly father would be, and an earthly father wouldn't do that. So certain aspects of the Christian religion present me with some problems, but within that basic view of religion, I am certainly a deist. If one thinks of God as being the Father, the Son and the Holy Spirit, I like the idea of the Holy Spirit moving through the whole of creation, but it is to the Father I actually pray. God as Father is my concept.

Another possibility which you might be reluctant to consider about the ending of The Children of Men *is that there is an element of romanticism in the denouement, the idea that the world can be saved through an act of love . . .*

The Christian religion said the world could be saved through an act of love; what I was saying was that Theo could find his salvation by learning to love, and at the end of the book he has learned that only through love will he find redemption. I don't think that's romantic; I think it's true. E.M. Forster wrote that we must learn to love or we will destroy ourselves.

Isn't there an element of tendentiousness in The Children of Men, *the idea of divine punishment and retribution hanging over the world, and our agnostic hero ending up making the sign of the cross?*

I don't think the book ever specifically says that what happens is divine justice. God is not saying, 'I'll teach this lot, I've lost my patience with them.' The God of the Old Testament might have felt that, but I didn't see it in those terms. Theo makes the sign of the cross as a kind of impulse. He is not saying that the world is thereby redeemed; it's more a natural instinct for him to do it, an affirmation of love, the sign of redemptive love on the child.

Last year you preached the university sermon in Oxford. What was the subject of your sermon?

Faith in the modern world, and people's attitude to God and to faith. It was also a sermon about doubt, how one copes with doubt. I talked about different kinds of faith: the faith of people who, like the poet Gerard Manley Hopkins, strive with God and argue with him; the very simple faith of people who, however sophisticated they may be in other aspects of their life, have absolute certainty from the day they're born till the day they die. I talked about people who have never felt the need of faith, people who believe that man is born of the absolute chance fusion of one sperm with one ovum; that when they die they will go into annihiliation and they face that without particular fear, believing that it is not among the most ignoble ways to live or die. And then I spoke about others who work towards faith, for whom life is a kind of pilgrimage, of which group I consider myself to be one.

You once said, 'When people are maimed, or sad, or die for no reason, it isn't anything you can cure by means of justice in this world, so it's important to hope there might be justice in the next.' Is that hope a tentative one, or is it central to your faith?

If you believe that God is just, and I do believe that God is just, it's rather more than tentative. There must surely be an eternal justice. Men and women have a huge need for justice; it's born in us to hate injustice, so there is a natural wish to believe that if things are terribly unjust in this world, if God exists at all, they'll certainly be put right in the next. There's a little poem about a disabled man who lives all his life in pain, who has nothing but misery and pain from the day he's born, and it ends: 'God of Heaven, God of Hell, see you recompense him well.' And I think there's a need to feel that.

You have been scrupulously careful never to use your husband's illness or the more traumatic parts of your own life in your fiction. One senses, however, that your characters are infused with your pain and suffering. Would you perhaps allow that this is the case?

I would allow that if the writer hasn't actually suffered it must be very difficult to write about suffering. No doubt some of the pain gets into the fiction; I think that's inevitable.

You have sometimes remarked that the passage of time has not helped ease the pain of loss and bereavement. Has this surprised you?

Yes it has, although you do somehow come to terms with it. You either lie down and die, or you adapt, so after a few years somehow you're coping. But time doesn't heal everything.

Do you believe in an afterlife? Do you expect to see your husband again?

I don't know, I really don't. I don't believe in the traditional old-fashioned Christian view of heaven, that's for certain. I don't think we're all going to go up there into eternal bliss with pearly gates and everlasting feasting, but I think something does survive. I suppose one would call it the soul, but in what form, I have no idea.

Do you ever feel a sense of loneliness?

No. I don't feel lonely. But I can see the possibility of feeling it. And I don't think I'd like it at all.

You are anxious not to be a burden on others. Is that partly because you yourself have borne great burdens in life?

It's not a very noble thing; it's more a matter of pride. Partly it's just not wanting to be a nuisance to one's dearly loved children, but it's also that one doesn't want to be poor old gran who has to be visited and supported, poor old gran who's got to be found a nice place in the nursing home. I don't much like old age . . .

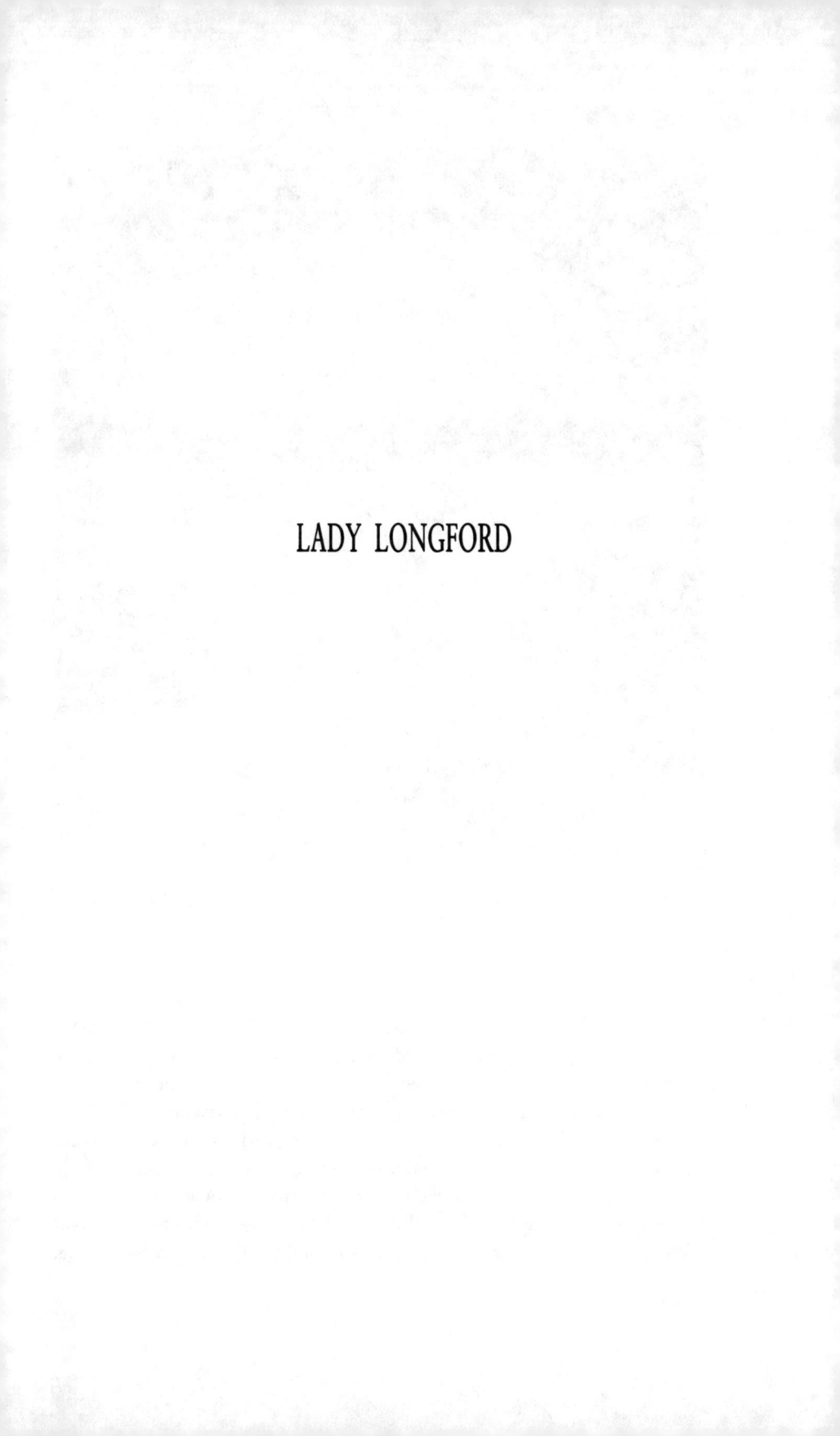

LADY LONGFORD

LADY LONGFORD

Elizabeth Pakenham was born in 1906 and educated at Headington School and Lady Margaret Hall, Oxford, where she took a degree in Literae Humaniores and was one of the few women to be accepted into the intellectual circle led by Maurice Bowra and Hugh Gaitskell. In 1931 she married Frank Pakenham, the 7th Earl of Longford. She twice stood for Parliament as a Labour candidate, but laid aside her political career in favour of looking after her eight children. Her publications include a two-volume biography of Wellington, *The Queen Mother*, *Eminent Victorian Women*, *Elizabeth R* and her autobiography, *The Pebbled Shore*.

Lady Longford

Lady Longford, in your autobiography you describe your childhood as containing the conflicting ingredients of puritanism along with middle-class comforts, affection with restraint, and your father's insistence on Victorian standards of obedience and sobriety. Did you regard it at the time as a perfectly normal childhood?

Absolutely, yes, although I did sometimes question his ruling of moderation in all things. For example, when my brother and I wanted to take a gramophone on a picnic on the River Medway in Kent, my father forbade us, and I realized then that he thought it was bad for children to be too happy, to have everything they wanted. It was good to be moderately happy, but not absolutely happy, and I must say that did make me begin to wonder about his standards which certainly differed from those of my friends' fathers.

Before you were born your parents had had a religious battle which your father lost – the Baptist faith was surrendered to Unitarianism. Presumably you knew nothing of this at that time. Did it help clarify some of the mysteries of your childhood once you learned the family history?

It certainly did. At the time I didn't understand why my father was such a keen lay preacher, or why he liked getting into the pulpit. That was something else my friends' fathers didn't do, and it was years before I understood that he'd given up his religious beliefs to his wife's, and that since his own beliefs had been much stronger than hers, he had to do something to make up for them, to keep them fresh and lively; and so he became a Unitarian preacher.

Your father comes across as a very sober puritan figure and not altogether stable, and it took a great many years before you yourself could make what you called 'a dent in that austere emotional legacy'. Was that something that you held against him?

I held it against him when I was a child, but luckily I had the support of my eldest brother to whom I was very close. I didn't go on resenting it when I was grown up; somehow or other it just seemed to be a fact which I accepted.

Lady Longford

It was only a year or two before his death that he made any effort to be affectionate, something you say he had not thought of doing when you were young. Has that been a source of sadness and regret in your life?

My only regret now is that I didn't show him more affection, because I realize with hindsight that he was shy and difficult and that if I had taken the lead, he would have responded.

You belonged to an extraordinary generation at Oxford – John Betjeman, Maurice Bowra, Osbert Lancaster, and so on. From the outside it seemed as if it must have been intellectually thrilling and in all ways stimulating. Were you aware of that feeling at the time, that you were part of a very special and talented group of people?

I certainly thought life very thrilling and intellectually interesting. Before I got my scholarship, I very nearly became engaged to a charming young doctor, but when I knew I was going to Oxford, that was consigned to the past. I remember as I got into the taxi at the station to go to my college, a voice, my own voice, said to me, 'This is going to be a new life and it's going to make a difference to everything.' I was tremendously stimulated and influenced by my contemporaries, particularly John Betjeman who was the first person to show me that you could laugh at something and at the same time be devoted to it, and that the same is true with people. Maurice Bowra influenced me academically more than anybody, and led me to read Classics. I had gone up to read English, but my college showed imagination and let me change. Osbert Lancaster was more of a friend than an influence, I would say. I loved him and his wife deeply. Of course I was influenced in a sense by being in Osbert's company. He was a genius and it's wonderful to be in contact with genius.

At Oxford you were friendly with Hugh Gaitskell, who even proposed marriage. Do you ever think how differently things might have turned out if you had accepted?

Yes, they would have been very different. But it wasn't one of those *grandes passions* where you can never see the person again if it doesn't work out. We always remained friends. Hugh had a very happy marriage and I've had a very happy marriage, so obviously we did the right thing. Hugh influenced me politically more than anybody while I was at Oxford.

Lady Longford

I wasn't interested in politics at the beginning of my time at Oxford, only in poetry and literature, but Hugh really took me in hand. He was a born teacher and whoever came to know him would be changed and improved by him. He was a most remarkable character.

Gaitskell talked later of 'the heavenly freedom of Oxford', where the happiness of the individual was 'the only acceptable social aim'. Was that an ideology you shared?

I didn't think about it in those terms. He had an analytical mind, and he would see things in terms of principles for which he made many sacrifices. My mind, I'm afraid, works differently, and I judge everything by individual actions. After I'd gone down from Oxford his training must have had some effect, however, because I became, and still am, a very enthusiastic member of the Labour Party. But I began to realize you can't just think of the happiness of the individual; there are other important factors.

You were one of the very first and very few women to be admitted to the male intellectual enclave of Oxford. Were you aware of that at the time? Did you feel privileged, or did you regard it as your right?

I certainly didn't regard it as my right. It was more a feeling of being tolerated than having rights in that particular society. I knew perfectly well that a great number of them were what we used to call queers or pansies – we didn't have the word gay in those days. But I was very fond of them and enjoyed their brilliance and their literary and artistic lives.

What was your attitude to homosexuality in those days?

It was of course still a criminal offence to be gay. I remember when Hugh Gaitskell was vetting me, so to speak, before he passed me as fit to be introduced into the holy of holies, namely Maurice Bowra's rooms, the question he asked was what I thought of Oscar Wilde and all that. I knew exactly what he meant though I don't think I knew a single homosexual; it was all just through reading, or intuition. Luckily I gave the right answer, otherwise it would have been no good; he wouldn't have introduced me, and quite rightly. I must say, however, that at Oxford they were mostly ambivalent, because they nearly all married afterwards, except Maurice. But even he made several proposals, not only to me, though I was the first, but also to two others. His friends thought he was right to have failed, that it wouldn't have worked. The others led perfectly normal happy family lives with children, so their apparent homosexual leanings were partly to do with the Oxford spirit.

Why do you think that religion and politics were of little importance to you at Oxford? Was it because Oxford was too much of an ivory tower protected from the outside world?

I would say that was true for perhaps three quarters of my time there. But after the Wall Street Crash in 1929, and then the slump, people began to change, in the way of being more serious and more connected to the real world. The heyday of homosexuality went at the same time. Quite a lot of people began having girlfriends in my last year, who hadn't before, and gradually the outside world began to sweep in.

But you were not influenced by religion in your student days?

Not at all. I had quite a number of dear friends at Balliol College who happened to be Roman Catholics, and had been to Ampleforth or Downside. I knew they were Catholics, but that's as far as my knowledge went. I wasn't the slightest bit interested or influenced by them. I can tell you a rather ridiculous story to illustrate the point. I don't think I had ever met a Roman Catholic priest until I went to some lunch party at Balliol with these undergraduates. They had invited a very famous Catholic priest called Father Martin D'Arcy. He was extremely brilliant, charming, and right-wing, and I remember thinking, with rather a tremor, of childhood stories like *Westward Ho* by Charles Kingsley, where the Catholic Church is the scarlet woman. Father D'Arcy was very good looking with crimpy hair, a faintly hooked nose, and very fine features. I decided he was Mephistopheles and that I must beware. When we got up from lunch he helped me on with my coat, and to my amazement I noticed that he handed it the wrong way round, so that the sleeves were hanging down inside. This gave me a sudden new intuition that he couldn't after all be Mephistopheles, who was a very polished courtier-type gentleman who would never hand a lady's coat the wrong way round. I concluded that he must indeed be a priest, and I took a great interest in him from then on.

You were related to Chamberlain, so politics were in your blood, but it was Frank Pakenham who awakened political interest in you. Do you think the fact that you were drawn to the left was ever a serious threat to your relationship?

We had tremendous arguments about it. He was a professional in politics while I was an absolute baby. I put up very silly arguments, but I believed in them all the same. In any case, being half Irish there was a kind of leftward vein in him which remained at peace until he met me, and then I stirred it up. He had his revenge on me by getting rid of my rational humanism.

You say that Frank was deadly serious and intellectual about politics, whereas you were emotional. Did you remain that way or did your different attitudes rub off on one another?

Frank's rational attitude certainly rubbed off on me. I had never read a political book in my life until I met him, but I then began reading the famous bibles of the Labour Party, like R.H. Tawney and different writers of that generation. Did I rub off on Frank? I suppose he must have thought, 'If I love this girl, there must be some sense in what she's saying,' and he set about trying to find it.

When you first met him, did you fall madly in love with him?

To begin with I didn't know who 'him' was. All I had seen was this figure, two nights running, at college balls, but each time he was alone, detached from the world, fast asleep. The first time he was sleeping in a chair and as I stood admiring his very handsome, wonderfully classical features, I wondered whose partner he was and thought how strange that she should have let him spend the evening asleep instead of dancing the happy hours away. Next evening at a New College ball he was fast asleep on his friend's sofa. Hugh Gaitskell had taken me up to his room, and I recognized the same lyrically handsome, classical features; so I planted a kiss on his innocent forehead. This woke him up and that was the beginning of our romance.

I had the impression that although you contested two elections, your heart was not really in politics and the pull of motherhood was stronger. Is that a fair assessment?

It's true that the pull of motherhood was stronger because I did make a choice at one particular point in my life. There was a time when I was very ambitious and was encouraged by some of the dear old boys in the Labour Party – I remember Ernest Bevin telling me I ought to stand for the women's section of the Executive – and this rather fanned my ambition. However, it was just a temporary blaze, and when I was forced to choose, I chose the family. I did not have too many regrets because I suffered also from a common disability, migraine, and if I had been elected to Parliament, I might easily have had an attack in the middle of a speech, which wouldn't have been a very good show.

As you describe it, Frank's diffidence and complete lack of confidence in himself as a future husband all but wrecked the marriage plans. You were obviously affected deeply by his despair. Did you manage to keep faith, or were you seriously worried that you might lose him?

I knew we would get married, that we would get over all these things, and that it would be a success. It never crossed my mind that it would break up, and I was right. Although I wasn't in the least bit superstitious and I didn't believe in Providence or anything like that, the coincidence of our first meeting did seem to me a most extraordinary thing. Afterwards Frank discovered that he had actually seen me, without my having seen him, when he was sharing digs in Oxford with Hugh Gaitskell. I was visiting Hugh for tea one day and Frank asked the landlady who I was. The landlady said she thought I was a French lady, the greatest compliment that's ever been paid to me. Nobody could have been less French looking, though I longed to be.

Your husband's conversion to Catholicism which he kept secret from you shocked and distressed you and although you say you knew that 'even the rustling curtain of priests would never separate us' you must have felt very angry, betrayed even . . .

I wouldn't say betrayed exactly. I certainly felt indignant and angry that he should have taken this step without consulting me and certainly without my consent or any discussion. I realized, however, that it was better for me to have been faced with a *fait accompli* than to have an argument that went on forever; I would have felt bound to keep my end up and to have thought of all the arguments against it, even to have created some in order to keep the battle going. So in a way, although I didn't agree with the principle, in practice it worked out better.

But did it take you a long time to get over the shock?

No, not very long. I began to think it was one of God's mysterious moves. Frank had done this to annoy me, and he had annoyed me so much that the Holy Spirit entered into this angry person, me, and before I knew it I was reading books about religion which I'd never looked at since I was a small child.

Evelyn Waugh had greatly influenced your husband in his conversion. Given that Waugh had already opposed your marriage and offered the opinion that Frank had married beneath himself, you must have felt outraged by his interference?

I was more amused than outraged, because I was very fond of him and I didn't know at that stage that he had opposed our marriage. In fact, all the evidence was that he'd pushed it forward. On one occasion before we were married Evelyn came to stay with us at Frank's brother's house in Ireland. He was very friendly and we were all fond of each other, and I remember when the party was breaking up one evening and Frank and I were going off in slightly different directions but in the same wing of the house, Evelyn suddenly gave me a push and said, 'Go on, follow him, go after him', which I did. Nothing happened, I may say, except that we had a very nice conversation sitting on the edge of his bed, but I would never have been brave enough to go up into his quarters if Evelyn hadn't given me that push. So Evelyn's attitude was totally contradictory.

Lady Longford

Were you angry when you heard about his remarks regarding your marriage?

I knew that he was extremely reactionary, and that he liked to make fun of women as well as falling in love with them. The way in which he liked to poke fun at me was by making out that I was a great hockey player who loved the games fields and women's netball teams and all that kind of thing, which was pure invention. It didn't make me angry because if you're basically very fond of a person, which I was of him, those kind of aberrations don't really matter. They didn't do me any harm; they didn't make Frank suddenly say, 'My God, I'm married to a blue stocking who galumphs about a hockey field.' It was only years afterwards when his letters were published and sent to me in manuscript that I realized he had taken this extremely class-ridden snobby line; with no effect, I'm glad to say.

How much do you think the fact of war influenced your husband in his decision to convert?

A great deal. It was Evelyn who actually said to him, 'You're going out with your regiment; who knows what will happen? You've got to make up your mind now. You've dallied long enough on the edge.'

Your own response to the war was to have another baby. Was that a way of making a hopeful statement in time of uncertainty?

That was the abstract reason, but the personal reason was that I already had children, and I couldn't go away and have a wartime career and leave them with somebody else; I had to be at home. Frank came home on leave now and again, and afterwards he became Beveridge's personal assistant, so he was around at weekends, which made some sort of family life possible. I also believed in the family and in children, and in those days the country was worried about the fall in the birthrate, so everything seemed to come together for good.

Some years later, you also converted to Catholicism, though I have the impression that your approach was far more pragmatic. There was no

Lady Longford

Road to Damascus vision, it was much more that you felt an awkward division in the family vis-à-vis churchgoing, and that your own father had died so that you would not have to contend with his disapproval, and so on. I didn't sense any of the agony which one expects to accompany such decisions.

No. There was no agony. As you rightly say it took several years, six in fact, and I had spent time gradually reading more about Catholicism. One book in particular by a French Catholic interested me, because it was the first Catholic book I had ever read which took a left-wing point of view, something I hadn't thought possible. I was really entranced by this wonderful revelation. There were one or two setbacks, however, such as when Frank became Sir William Beveridge's personal assistant over the Beveridge Welfare State report. Frank had been invalided out of the army, and this became his war work and he put everything into it. The very first Sunday after it was published we went to church together in Oxford, and the subject of the sermon was 'The no-good Beveridge Report'. This was a cold douche for something that we were both absolutely devoted to, but we couldn't help laughing – Frank's greeting by Mother Church was to say his work was of no use.

Evelyn Waugh, after your conversion, wrote to Nancy Mitford, 'Lady Pakenham is my great new friend', and this made you feel that you had been received, and not only into the Church. Did you ever feel that you had capitulated in a sense, that it would have been better if Waugh had been able to accept you on your own terms, Catholic or not?

One couldn't say no to a question put in that way, but I don't really think I minded. I can remember asking myself why he now liked me so much, what had changed. Although I was not as close to him as Nancy, because temperamentally I wasn't his cup of tea, he was always writing to me, and we met a lot. Before that there had been all those insults about the hockey field, but now I was in the family of the Church and he seemed to have a kind of supernatural feeling that my having been baptized with holy water had literally changed me, not only in myself, but to him; that it had been a real physical change.

One of your worries about Catholicism before you converted was that it

Lady Longford

would prejudice the children in their careers and in life generally. Did you ever have occasion to feel that afterwards?

Never. It was one of the most fallacious predictions or feelings that I've ever had. In fact I often think now how wonderfully lucky we were that we were able to bring up all our children successfully. I often think of other parents and wish they'd had the same good fortune.

There is also some evidence that the Establishment is anti-Catholic although this is always very difficult to prove. What is your view?

I've heard so many conflicting views on that subject. I don't think I know the Establishment well enough to judge, but I do know when I was young, long before I had any connection with the Church, people used to say that the Foreign Office was biased in favour of Catholic candidates, which was exactly the opposite of what I later feared. Two people in the Oxford Labour Party objected when Frank became a Catholic, because they had the same feeling that I did, that he would be under the influence of an outside power, namely Rome, but I myself never came across anything of that sort. In a way I'm sorry, because I think religion doesn't mean as much to people as it used to when I was young, and therefore although you have fewer of the bad effects you also have fewer of the good. Certainly my father would have made a tremendous to-do. He would have thought it was condemning our children to inferior treatment, but he would simply have been wrong.

You have written a great deal on the monarchy and are obviously a royalist. Catholicism has no place in the royal family – for example, if Prince Charles were to convert to Catholicism, he would not be able to accede to the throne. How do you feel about that?

The Act of Settlement and the Royal Marriages Act should be repealed as quickly as possible. They might have done a little good in the reign of George III but they are totally outdated now and positively harmful. The world of princes and princesses is naturally a very small one and to shut out a whole section of European and other nationalities or other populations from any kind of real friendship or inter-marriage with the royal family is the most colossal mistake nowadays.

Lady Longford

Your new book on the future of the monarchy was commissioned before there was any serious doubt about its future. You yourself are still a firm believer in its survival. How far did you take into account recent events and upsets within the royal family?

My dear, I can't tell you, it was an absolute nightmare. I never finished a chapter without having to rewrite it completely. I'm glad I did it now, although I daresay if I'd been told at the time how it was going to develop, I might have been chickenhearted and declined, but of course I hadn't the faintest idea. I just thought it was going to be an abstract discussion of the question, based on my knoweldge of recent royal history, and when I wrote to the people I hoped would give me interviews I still didn't know. The letters arrived just when the whole balloon went up, so I must have been regarded as absolutely crazy, writing without a word of apology and just assuming they would talk to me.

The survival of the monarchy seems to have depended, in the twentieth century at least, on an ability to combine popularity with an almost mystical regal aura. Surely that delicate balance has been upset by recent events?

Yes, but something else has taken its place. In any case, whatever the private lives of the members of the royal family, that mystical aura would gradually have faded away because it depended partly on remoteness. The royal family in the past have been distant figures, flashing past as Queen Victoria did in a carriage, the public only just catching a glimpse. Now the people have heard their voices on television, have really seen them, and know everything about them from the tabloids and other newspapers; so the aura has been dissipated. What has replaced it is a feeling that the royal family care, that they really are involved with every person in the country, whatever class they come from, whatever walk of life they occupy. They start projects, they travel about, they work a hundred times harder than any of their ancestors would have done. On top of that you have to have one dominant figure to represent the nation, and we have the Queen who couldn't be better at it.

The impression one had from your review in The Times *of Andrew Morton's biography of Princess Diana was that he had transgressed the*

Lady Longford

boundaries of good taste. As a royal biographer, are there certain things which you would choose not to reveal?

I don't want to sound prudish or priggish, but I like to think that if I had been offered the story Morton was offered, and if Princess Diana's friends had come up loaded with all these personal secrets, I would have declined. It was absolutely wrong to publish that book, and we can see now that it was the start of all the trouble. And who benefited? In the end because life goes on and God is kind, Princess Diana may be happy; I certainly hope and believe Prince Charles will. But it was a totally unnecessary and wrong passage in both their lives. I wouldn't go as far as to say nobody should have read it; you can't ask impossibilities of people if it's there in book form, but I don't think the *Sunday Times* should have serialized it. Rupert Murdoch may say he's a monarchist, but the effect of serialization was not to forward the cause of monarchy. It's been suggested that in the end the monarchy will be strengthened by all this coming out, but those are just words to me.

Where do you stand on the great public 'right to know' debate. Is the royal family public property in that sense?

We look on the royal family in two ways which might be said to be incompatible. In one way we take pride in saying they're just like us, but in another way we like to think of them as being above us, and the two don't go together. The royal family somehow have to satisfy both these requirements, and I think they do on the whole, unless some really bad things happens, like *Diana, Her True Story*. After reading that you couldn't possibly think that a model was being set for the nation, either by the Princess of Wales herself or the Prince of Wales, or by Prince Philip, the Queen, or indeed the Queen Mother. They are described as implacable, which means that they can't be placated, that they're cruel.

Do you think perhaps there's a case to be made for more careful selection of those marrying into the royal family?

That would be very difficult. In the case of Prince Andrew's bride, for example, she was very well connected on one side and they also knew her family on the other side. They didn't know anything about Koo Stark's family, but my personal view is that she would have made a much better duchess.

Do you think the nation actually benefits in any way from knowing the inside details of the royal family's life, or is it at the level of entertainment and scandal-mongering?

It is ninety per cent at that level, but some individuals may have benefited from the knowledge that life can be very difficult even for the royal family on occasion. It used to be thought that life in the royal family was a bed of roses, and it may now be seen to be rather different. But it is better to bring this awareness in the form of *Elizabeth R*, the film to celebrate the Queen's fortieth anniversary, which showed the difficulties in a perfectly natural and yet convincing way, with no aspect of scandal. Once you get into the realms of scandal it's like the old saying: bad money drives out good, and scandal drives out good news.

You must remember Edward VIII's abdication in 1936 when he made his famous 'woman I love' speech. That too must have rocked the nation, but the monarchy survived, even perhaps was strengthened by it. Are there any parallels with what is happening today, do you think?

In that instance the rent in the monarchy was mended very quickly, because we had a really wonderful king and queen to step in, and people soon realized that a king and queen with a family was far more stabilizing than anything that the Duke of Windsor could have achieved, even if everything had gone as he hoped. I suppose he never would have had any children, so it would have come back to where it did, but only after many years. In my opinion these would have been lost years, because the future king and queen wouldn't have had the experience and practice of a long reign and long lives; that's absolutely definite. The only faint parallel I can see now is that all the pieces are in place so to speak for a very successful royal family. I have an enormous admiration for Prince Charles; he's got real ideas of what he wants to do, and what he wants to contribute to the country. He's genuinely active and not at all keen on being just a centrepiece. I can't say anything about his personal life, but at least the two princes are there in place, so the situation could develop almost as well as it did after the abdication. It is very difficult to imagine after 1992 that we are suddenly going to have an *annus mirabilis*. There will be a transitional period, but I feel full of hope for the future.

Do you think there ought to be a constitutional difficulty about having a divorced monarch, or indeed a remarried monarch on the throne? Don't you think there is something very unrealistic about expecting Charles to be a bachelor king?

Absolutely. I don't think that's right at all. We know now that there are bishops who would be prepared to remarry him, and I would say that's absolutely right, and I feel sure there will be the same attitude, if not an even more affirmative one, in the future.

You were clearly very affected by the Queen's Guildhall speech. Did you identify with her as a mother?

Yes. I felt I knew that she really was as unhappy as she looked at that moment.

Your own children's marriages have not always run smoothly, but you have taken comfort from their happy second marriages. In the eyes of the Catholic Church marriage is for life. Did you feel very anguished, not just at a personal level, but on a religious level on account of your children's divorces?

No, not at the time. All I can say is that if at the beginning of my married life, when my children were being born, some prophet had told me that we would be a Catholic family and yet we would have these divorces and second marriages, I would have felt amazement, disbelief and great unhappiness. But for most people life doesn't strike with one great hammer blow; it gradually happens, and you get used to it, you accept. You know the people involved, you admire them and love them whatever has gone wrong, and so you're buoyed up; you know it isn't the end. The Queen must have felt the same about her children. I don't think it's the business of parents to blame; it is the business of parents when their children are young to teach them as rigorously as possible, and to make rules and see that they're kept, but once the children are grown up parents should not reprimand or criticize; they should give support where it is needed.

I'm going to ask you a rather sensitive question, because of the religious aspect and because I am also a Roman Catholic. The marriage of one of your children was annulled, even after the birth of six children. Did you have any intellectual difficulty with the idea of that annulment? A lot of people are very critical of annulment and think it is a fudge, or a way of clearing one's Catholic conscience. How do you view it?

I used to think that annulment should be much more common, and that it should be made much easier, and I held that view for many years. It would leave the faith as it was while allowing that there never had been a marriage in the Catholic sense. But I've rather changed my mind and I now think, in my heart of hearts, that divorce is really the true state of affairs; that there has been a marriage, that there no longer is, and therefore it's ended. I don't really believe in annulment, and I believe that divorce is the way of the future. But I know that isn't the teaching of the Catholic Church and I wouldn't dream of teaching it to anybody else.

Quite a number of people in the public eye are granted annulments . . . Caroline of Monaco, Frank Sinatra and so on. Do you think this points to there being influence at play?

I'm not sure on these very difficult questions, but I now think we should used the word divorce, not annulment. It seems to me that the truth about most broken marriages is that they weren't always broken; the argument for annulment is that they were broken from the start, only one didn't realize it. That does not seem to be the accurate description.

Are you saying that if you divorce, the Church should be able to marry you a second time in the faith?

Yes. That is what I am saying.

Your own marriage has had a wonderful symmetry – Frank converted

Lady Longford

politically into your camp, and you converted into his religious camp. Did this bestow a kind of equality in the marriage which made it endure?

We laugh about it; it's really too symmetrical for anything but a joke, but it did happen just that way. We were like two magnets for each other, and if one moved in one direction, the other followed. The teaching about marriage, two being as one, is very true in many ways. I often know what Frank's going to say, and he often knows with me, but of course that's perfectly rational and explicable in two people who have lived together for over sixty years.

You have headed a kind of literary dynasty. Your children and now your grandchildren having carried on the tradition of writing. You must feel immensely proud of that.

Yes, and very thankful too, because it's such a happy pursuit. If it has disappointments they're nearly always one's own fault; there are no resentments and regrets as in some other professions.

I detect that the task of writing your own life may have been much more daunting than writing the lives of others. Is that because you dislike being introspective, or that your curiosity about other people does not extend to yourself?

Both are true. I'm not an introspective person by nature. I'm sure I would have benefited from psychotherapy, but I couldn't endure being on a couch and talking about myself. I can only just enjoy the business of talking to you. Various people suggested I should write my memoirs and naturally I listened to them, but the obvious difficulty was that nothing had ever happened to me. I'm not dissatisfied with life, and I feel I've been very lucky, but that's doesn't make good reading. You need disaster, then to be restored, then hard work, then another dreadful fall, and so on – that's what's interesting to read about. Also when I began doing it, I suddenly felt rather unhappy in a very unexpected way. It brought home that all these happy times really were past, the children being born, and Frank and I being young. I'd never quite acknowledged that these things were over and were never going to happen again. It was rather a melancholy discovery.

Lady Longford

You once wrote, 'Frank's lack of interest in appearance and possessions gradually earned him a halo for eccentricity. This was kept polished by his own activities.' This seems quite an indulgent attitude – have you never minded his eccentricity?

No. When I first married him, his great friends, the Birkenheads, told me always to have plenty of safety pins because his clothes were all kept together that way. I soon knew exactly what they meant, but it's a very superficial thing; it isn't like somebody belonging to the great unwashed. He has beautiful manners, he was extremely well brought up, and he still stands up when a lady comes into the room. I try to stop it, but it's ingrained. He doesn't take an interest in possessions and surroundings, doesn't even look at them. When we had a burglary, he suffered for me, and was very unhappy because I lost things, but he was not unhappy for himself, for he did not notice what was gone. It is just as well – it would be terrible to have two people moaning together.

Are you ever indignant about the way your husband is portrayed in the press sometimes?

Yes, I used to be, but only about one thing: an absolutely scurrilous suggestion was made that he only visited prisoners who were well known, in order to get publicity for himself. This couldn't be more untrue. He visited prisoners for years and years before the famous ones that he is now connected with, and he visits totally unknown prisoners still.

He is well known for his campaigning on behalf of Myra Hindley, something you shared in. Did you understand the strength of public feeling against that?

Oh yes, because I felt it myself when I first heard the news. Frank understood perfectly well too, but one of the most important things about Christianity is that you've got to help people who are in trouble. There's no point in helping people who are doing well; they don't need your help. If you're lucky in your own life, in your own circumstances and in your friends and family, you're all the more bound to help the people who are not. Whether it's their fault or not doesn't make any difference; if they are in that position now it's your duty to help.

Lady Longford

He also campaigned for many years against pornography. If pornography is corrupting, why has he himself not been corrupted long ago?

I don't think he had the douche quite long enough. He only had one expedition to Copenhagen, but supposing he had gone there every week for a year, it might have had some effect, who knows? I'm very glad he didn't.

Isn't there something disagreeable and paternalistic about the idea of censorship, about some people being able to decide for others what they may or may not see or read?

Certain things cause so much damage in human relations that it is right to prevent people seeing them. Personally I would put pornography quite low on the list, but at the top I would put any kind of racialism or anything that incited teenage children to bully. There is a very difficult line to draw between freedom and censorship, but it's the duty of people in government to find that line and not go over the edge in one direction or the other. Since the 1960s we've tended to favour licence and freedom without considering how far we're affecting other people's lives. All human life is a compromise of one sort or another, and freedom should not mean the right to complete licence ever.

Like most people who have lived a long time, you have had your fair share of sadness, and more than your fair share in Catherine's tragic death at the age of twenty-three. Many people at such times are disappointed in their religion. Were you, or were you consoled by it?

It was and still is an appalling pain, and I still suffer. Religion doesn't stop you suffering, but you don't suffer in a meaningless way. What's so awful is the feeling of waste in the case of premature death. Catherine was twenty-three, just beginning life with everything before her. She was very pretty, had lots of friends and an interesting job; it was just the most appalling waste. But I felt an absolute conviction that she was all right. I know she's all right, and I feel that because of my religion. Religion also prevents you from asking the purely selfish questions: why me? why should it happen to me, when there are millions of other people it could have happened to? why should I suffer? why should God allow suffering if he's a

Lady Longford

loving God? Those are the questions you ask before you're religious; you don't go on asking them afterwards, which is a great blessing.

Catherine was the first of your children to be born a Catholic ... was that to prove to be a solace to you and your husband, or did it merely add a special poignancy to her death?

I don't think it was relevant at all. There was no room for more poignancy.

Do you feel that you're going to see each other again?

I find that very difficult to visualize. In a sense I believe we shall, but we are not going to have mortal bodies, so how are we going to recognize each other? I don't know how these things work . . . but then as I don't even understand how a simple thing like television works, I would be amazed if I understood a great mystery like the afterlife.

What do you regard as your greatest achievement?

The creation of one of the fifty million families in this country. I really do believe that. The second best I suppose is to have written some books which may be of interest, possibly even for another fifty years. Luckily if it turns out that they're all sent to the Christmas bazaar at Sir Thomas More's church, I shan't know.

SIR BERNARD LOVELL

SIR BERNARD LOVELL

Bernard Lovell was born in Gloucestershire in 1913. He was educated at Bristol University and in 1936 became Assistant Lecturer in Physics at Manchester. By 1951 he had risen to Professor of Radio Astronomy, a post he held until 1981. He was founder and director of Jodrell Bank experimental station (now the Nuffield Radio Astronomy Laboratories). He gave the Reith Lectures in 1958, taking as his subject 'The Individual and the Universe'. He is the author of several books on radio astronomy and its relevance to modern life and civilization. His works include *Science and Civilization* (1939), *Radio Astronomy* (1951), *Discovering the Universe* (1963), *The Story of Jodrell Bank* (1968) and *Voice of the Universe* (1987).

Sir Bernard Lovell

You were the son of a lay preacher – on the face of it, an unpromising start for a scientist. How do you look back on your childhood?

Very happily. Childhood remains an extremely powerful influence on one's life, and although I went through periods of great turmoil, particularly when I got to the university, I'm now extremely thankful in old age that I had such an almost fundamentalist upbringing. My father's knowledge of the Bible was greater than that of any other man I've met. When he reprimanded me it was always with biblical quotations. But he was a kindly, often indulgent disciplinarian and my memories of that time are really very happy. I had the sort of life which is now very rarely found.

From what I read of your background, there was nothing to suggest the path that you were to follow. Do you think these things depend largely on chance, or do you think they are genetically determined in some way?

That's an extremely interesting question. My immediate instinct is to say that it is all by chance, and that is almost certainly the correct answer since I can see no means by which my subsequent career was genetically determined. My life as a scientist really began at school when I was at an impressionable age. Quite fortuitously I joined a party going to the University of Bristol to hear a series of lectures by Professor A.M. Tindall on the electric spark, and that event transformed me. Before that I had not been interested in science and wanted to leave school and do something else, but after that I just had one ambition, and that was to become one of Tindall's students.

During the war you worked in the radar research team and your discoveries were crucial to the war effort. Were you aware at the time of the colossal influence you had?

I think not. I imagine you're referring to the blind bombing device which I was ordered to work on in 1942 – very much against my will, since I had to drop the project in hand which was a device against German night raiders. But by the time Churchill summoned me to Downing Street, the situation was entirely different. We had in fact just suffered a terrible disaster: the Halifax bomber I was using had crashed in the Wye Valley and had killed most of my small team, and also the people from the EMI who had been

Sir Bernard Lovell

given the contract to make it. Churchill wanted the blind bombing apparatus to be ready by October of that year, an impossible task, but the system was operational by the end of the year. As I talk about it now, it is almost as if one is disembodied; it is very difficult to believe that it was me who was involved in all of that nearly fifty years ago.

The H2S system was also capable of detecting submarines surfacing at night and as Hitler himself acknowledged this proved a major setback in the U boat assault. One imagines that you must have felt exhilarated at the part you played in history, or was it not like that?

At the time I don't think we realized how dramatic the effect was. It's only in the historical context, forty or fifty years later, that one sees what a turning point it was. We now know that without it there could have been no invasion of Europe, because the ships would not have been able to bring the American troops across the Atlantic.

Did you ever doubt the morality of what you were doing?

Not then. When the war ended all I wanted to do was to get back to university research. I remember refusing to go on a flight to look at the devastation over the Ruhr and Hamburg; I wanted to forget. But more recently I have thought, my God, the device I helped develop led to the devastation of Hamburg. When I wrote my book *The Echoes of War* [published 1991] I had to read the official history of the strategic bombing campaign, and in the forth volume of that there is a report to Hitler by the police president of Hamburg describing the state of that city after the bombing raids of 1943. It was rather chilling to think that it was the planes that carried our equipment which actually marked out those cities for bombing. But then I immediately had the consoling thought, illustrative of the dividing line between good and evil on all sides: the device that was used to destroy German cities saved us from starvation. Of course the dividing line between good and evil in most of science is a very thin one.

What was your impression of Churchill during your dealings with him?

Sir Bernard Lovell

What one thinks of him from meetings fifty years ago is possibly coloured by everything one has read about him since that time. What I remember most about that particular July 1942 visit to the Cabinet Room was the fact that nearly everybody was terrified of him, even the commanders-in-chief. He was in control, there's no doubt about that. Another interesting thing was his faith in Professor Lindemann who became Lord Charwell. Churchill regarded Lindemann as his key adviser and would refer any scientific question to him. 'What does the professor think?' he would ask. And what the professor thought was usually what Churchill thought, but what the professor thought was very often cause for dismay amongst other senior people at that time.

Was Churchill justified in referring matters to him all the time?

I think not, but on the other hand, it's an appallingly difficult question to answer today, because if Charwell had not had his way about the priority of the bombing, then our device would not have existed. Therein lay the irony, the thinness of the dividing line once more. People analysing Charwell's decisions tend to reach an isolated conclusion, and they often forget this remarkable ancillary fact.

In 1952 your dream of a radio telescope was on its way to becoming reality, but the next five years were marked by delays and mounting costs which became the subject of a House of Commons committee. Was it very difficult to keep the faith?

I never lost faith in the project itself, but it was a very difficult time. Scientists like everybody else have instincts, and my instinct told me it was going to be extremely important. If I'd been asked in the 1950s how it was going to be important, I probably couldn't have given the correct answer, and almost certainly would not have placed so much emphasis on its significance outside the purely astronomical field. So although I never lost faith, I didn't understand precisely how that faith was going to be realized.

Were you terribly frustrated at the time by all the delays?

It wasn't so much the delays, it was the attitude of the faceless people in

Sir Bernard Lovell

offices in London that was enraging. They hid behind their official positions, they never stood up to be argued with, and they did not understand the situation.

How did you withstand the pressure? Did it not detract from your scientific purpose?

I suppose it must have had an effect, but the irony of the situation was that these pressures began in 1957 when the telescope was nearly finished, and the worst attack came when other things made it inevitable that a solution be found. If the Russians hadn't launched sputnik and we had not been able to demonstrate the unique capacity of the telescope against the carrier rocket I do not know what would have happened. I was under threat of imprisonment because of false evidence which had been given by a government official to the public accounts committee, evidence which could not be contradicted. It wasn't until two years later that the committee accepted that false evidence had been given to them – that's almost unique, by the way – and when that was done, then we were clear to move forward.

The prime purpose of Jodrell Bank was to add to man's knowledge of the universe by radio astronomy, but it was its secondary function in tracking satellites which rescued it from public criticism. Were you disappointed or angry that its primary purpose was usurped in this way?

Not at all, and in any case the primary purpose was not usurped. From the time when sputnik was launched in 1957 to the landing of the man on the moon in 1969, when interest began to wane, only ten per cent of the operation time of the telescope was used in those activities. Nine-tenths of the time was still used on astronomical work, and some of the most important discoveries in its whole history were made during that period. Besides, the case that I made for the telescope in the 1950s included its use in tracking what we then called earth satellites, for scientific reasons. The only extraordinary thing was the public interest, the amazement at the launching of the sputnik.

Since the telescope was built in the face of a great deal of criticism, did you

Sir Bernard Lovell

perhaps view this as a modern manifestation of the long history of perscution endured by astronomers?

I didn't take it in that personal sense. I took it as an indication of the stupidity of much of the bureaucratic administration. The trouble I experienced was really the beginning of the tightening up on university research and research generally, as a result of which it's now become so controlled that a place like Jodrell Bank could not happen nowadays. You see, I didn't come here to do the sort of work that's being done; the new features in space were encountered more or less by accident. Nowadays if you want to use even small amounts of money to do research you have to write papers to be mulled over by committees and boards and panels, and if that had happened when I came here in the late 1940s Jodrell Bank wouldn't exist, because I would have been told that what I proposed to do was impossible. The situation is much worse now. In a place like this the young people ought to be doing research; but they're either away on committees or writing reports, or formulating requests.

It is often said that in terms of supporting research programmes, Britain is one of the least accommodating countries and that is why scientific progress is made in spite of rather than because of government support. How true is that nowadays?

Science is underfunded, but that in my view is not the only problem. It's also the way it's organized, and the fact that so many people who ought to be at their workbench doing research, are having to do other things. Scientific research of the sort that I've been engaged in throughout my career, apart from the war years, is a risk activity; yet the whole of the bureaucratic structure is designed to prevent people taking risks. Too many people are concerned with the organization of science; an immense bureaucracy has grown up because there has been a terrible lack of understanding of what research in a place like Jodrell Bank means. People get it all mixed up with technological development, but research and development are entirely different things. Research is a risk business which should be financed with relatively small amounts; instead equal amounts of money are spent trying to stop the risk being taken. Development on the other hand is another matter – it can be tied to a target. The pragmatic attitude of this country during the last few governments has been appalling. Government ministers pronounce: 'What is good for science is

Sir Bernard Lovell

what is good for the country tomorrow.' What a lot of poppycock. It was an attitude which began with the 1965 Wilson administration when I was on the Science Research Council. Secretaries of State for Education and Science used to come to our council meetings and demand to know what we were going to do to help the economy of the country. Development and technology may be like that, but not research. And one of the great evils of the structure of science today is the failure to understand this difference.

The system in this country seems designed to frustrate those who possess vision, those who pioneer and invent . . .

Yes, that's true, but it is not peculiar to this country. We've inherited all this paperwork and bureaucratic administration from the United States where it's excessive, even more so than here. In order to improve the system the government has to understand that research needs funding and organization separate from development and technology. The other problem is that so many people are involved in these assessments of proposals for research that many of them inevitably have vested interests in the money; that is not an accusation, it is just an inevitable consequence of the tremendous bureaucratic structure.

Isn't it also true that those who assess projects are sometimes not capable of assessment?

I don't want to appear to be accusing certain people, but what you say is inevitably true. As soon as you begin to have people who are not deeply involved in the particular subject, you are bound to get bad judgements. But the essence of the whole of research is that you can't plan it; if you plan it you'll kill it.

Apropos of funds being allocated by administrators rather than by scientists themselves, you said about twenty years ago, 'We may enter into another intellectual dark age.' Did that come to pass?

Yes, I believe we have been in an intellectual dark age for the last twenty years. Please don't take what I say as a political judgement; it is simply a statement. The dark age was initiated by a Labour government and has

Sir Bernard Lovell

been carried forward by both political parties. Regrettably, the government under Mrs Thatcher was pre-eminent in the demand that you put your money in what was going to be good for the economy and the country tomorrow, so things became very bad for science during that administration. I hope that we can recover. The trouble is that so many of our good people have now left the country.

Success at Jodrell Bank was eventually a much bigger and more complicated triumph than could ever have been envisaged at the outset. Did luck play a part, do you think?

I'm never quite clear what people mean when they say luck plays a part. The phrase I prefer is that one creates one's own luck, which is not meant to sound arrogant or bumptious. Of course the fact that the telescope is still engaged in work of international importance thirty-five years after it began work is to a certain extent fortuitous in the sense that it was the kind of instrument which could easily absorb the new techniques of electronics and computing. But I wouldn't use the word 'luck'.

Your belief in the possibilities of cosmic exploration by radio astronomy was something of an act of faith, was it not? Were there times when you doubted what you were doing?

Never. We built the telescope for astronomical purposes, and although the media interest was on another very important function, that after all was a sideline, albeit an important international sideline which carried us in the middle of the sandwich in the Cold War between the Soviet Union and the United States. I don't for one moment deny the importance of that sideline, but the telescope has always been at the forefront of astronomic research.

In 1962 you addressed a congressional committee in the USA and said you were open minded about the possibility of life existing on other planets. Thirty years later, is your mind entirely closed to the possibility?

Not entirely. It's a subject on which people tend to make arrogant statements. My own view is that the conditions which led to Earth being a habitable planet are extremely rare in the Universe, and rare in the sense that they're not properly understood. For example, if biological evolution occurs, does consciousness automatically develop? Nobody really understands this. All I would say is that I think the chances of the present searches for intelligent signals from outer space are more or less doomed to failure, almost on statistical grounds. But undoubtedly one must accept that there are about four billion galaxies in the field of view of modern telescopes and a galaxy contains about a hundred thousand million stars, so even if a small percentage of them have planets you end up with an extremely large number. I therefore don't think one would ever ever be able to discount the proposition that life may have emerged elsewhere, but my present feeling is that it is going to be extraordinarily difficult to obtain any proof of that. There is, however, one extremely interesting consideration: the subject known as astrochemistry has undergone tremendous developments in recent years and over one hundred molecular constituents in the great gas clouds of the Milky Way have been identified; and if the emission of amino acids were discovered, and this is by no means impossible, then it would be very hard to deny that biological evolution must have occurred elsewhere. That would throw the whole question wide open once more, and it would be very interesting to see how the theologians would deal with the possibility of a demonstrated life elsewhere.

You have been very critical of experiments which risk contaminating space before their effects have been properly studied and understood. Do you have the same rigorous approach to contamination of the earth, the sea, the atmosphere, and so on?

Indeed I do. In the case of the planet Venus we have a very grave example of what could happen. We tracked the first Soviet capsule to descend through the atmosphere of Venus, and the results were quite astonishing. The surface temperature turned out to be so hot that mercury would boil, lead would melt, and the pressure of the atmosphere was about ninety times that of the pressure on earth, and furthermore it was poisonous. As every astronomer knows Venus and Earth are almost twin brothers in the solar system; there is only a few per cent difference in their size and their mass; it is simply that Venus is ten per cent closer to the sun and therefore much hotter, and the favourable conditions which prevailed on Earth – and which are now being jeopardized by our contamination of the atmosphere

Sir Bernard Lovell

– took place at a very early stage in the history of the evolution of the planet Venus. So I think we have a grievous lesson there, though not one which calls for panic. I think the panic of a few years ago had a largely political basis.

But do you think there is ever a real risk of our planet being destroyed?

Certainly, but some of the risks are not fully appreciated. One which I scarcely ever see referred to is the danger of a celestial impact. The President of the United States has set up a commission to report on this, because it is not impossible that something could be done about it if one had suitable detection equipment to divert an approaching object. Many of the near-Earth objects which might collide and do collide with Earth get burnt up in the atmosphere, though we know the orbits of only about one per cent of them. The last great minor catastrophe was early in this century when a meteorite devastated an enormous area of Siberia. If it had fallen half an hour later, it would have destroyed the city of St Petersburg. There is also the very powerful and possibly correct theory that the extinction of the dinosaurs was due to a great celestial impact, so I think when you ask about the future danger to the terrestrial globe it is not only the man-made devastation which we have to worry about; it is also this other danger I describe which has been present for all time.

Science has become increasingly involved with power . . . military, political, economic power. Would you agree that power, apart from being enthralling and intoxicating, is often corrupting, and how well do you think scientists deal with this?

Power is nearly always corrupting. How well do scientists deal with it? Very badly I would say, because they are nearly always tools of the society in which they live and work. This, I'm afraid, is inevitable in the present structure of science.

You once said, 'The post-war belief that scientists could be instructed and science could do what it was asked for the benefit of society was absolute nonsense.' What prompted such a remark?

Sir Bernard Lovell

I don't remember the occasion when I made that remark, but I think it's perfectly true. There's evidence everywhere in the demands that science should work for the good of the state. The biggest demonstration of that fallacy occurred in 1965 during the Wilson administration when there was much talk of 'the white heat of the technological revolution'. Blacket used to say, 'science is a magic wand that will turn a poor country into a rich country', but after a few months in the new Ministry of Technology he was saying that science was not a magic wand at all, it was just one important cog in a large wheel which determines the progress of society.

Do you think that special conditions pertain in time of war so that it is morally permissible for scientists to be so instructed by governments?

I can only speak from my own experience of World War II, when as far as I was concerned, there was no alternative. As young people we had been living under the shadow of Hitler's Germany and war had become inevitable, and in the period after Munich we were just desperate to do something to change this awful state of affairs. And part of being a good citizen demands obedience to the state. Of course it's an entirely different matter if in peacetime one opts to go into a military establishment to make weapons of destruction.

Have you ever had cause to regret the use to which some scientific discovery has been put?

I don't think so. You see, my only involvement in those matters was when I was ordered in 1942 to make a destructive weapon which in the end, entirely accidentally, turned out to be the weapon of salvation of this country. You're asking questions which belong to the whole of the civilized world and certainly to society as a whole, not so much to individuals. But in times of national emergency, in times of war, it is one's duty if one is a good citizen to work for the state.

Would that equally apply to the enemy?

Of course. That is one of the dilemmas of mankind.

Sir Bernard Lovell

What is the greatest difficulty facing radio astronomy today?

Many people would immediately answer 'lack of money', but that would not be my answer. Mine is rather more fundamental. Science has developed in a technological, highly computerized way, and although the most marvellous work is being done by young people, much of it has tended to be along given lines of development. It is very difficult to prove this, but technology may have actually closed off opportunities for new discoveries. There have certainly been none to compare with those in the decade 1950–60 when everyone's mind was more open. I find it hard to believe that in the second half of the twentieth century man has been privileged to discover all that there is to be known about the universe, I just cannot believe that, and it worries me that all the breathtaking discoveries since the war have been limited to one decade.

Presumably you would agree that knowledge should always be tempered by humility towards what is yet to be discovered. How difficult in practice is it to achieve this?

Arrogance is a major problem with a lot of scientists today, arrogance in the face of new discoveries. But experience leads one to the conclusion that there is no final answer. You solve one problem, and in solving that problem you raise a whole host of new problems. When our telescope came into use in 1957–8, I was convinced that we would find the major answers to the origins and the evolution of the universe, but the discoveries we made simply deepened the problems which have to be solved. Progress brings its own complexities in a very dramatic way, and when people talk of knowing the mind of God and coming face to face with God, that is the antithesis of the humility which is necessary to progress.

One has the impression from reading your books that you are a man all but overwhelmed by the immense complexities of your own undertakings. Did you ever doubt the wisdom of embarking on such undertakings?

I was never overwhelmed by the practicalities, at least as long as I was director and they were under my control. But I was overwhelmed by the intellectual, theological and philosophical import of the task.

Sir Bernard Lovell

Your interest in man and the universe seems, curiously for a scientist, to border almost on the theological . . . why is that?

Because I think it's one of the great intellectual problems which faces the civilized world, and I feel very humble before it.

If you contemplate the origin of the universe, do you still have to part from the realm of scientific observation and knowledge into that of philosophical speculation? Or has science cracked it, do you think?

Science has not cracked it, and I think it is inherent in the fundamental laws of nature that science never will crack it. Science has apparently penetrated very close to the origin of the universe in which we live, but what kind of origin it had is quite unknown and never will be known. It is a matter of the utmost arrogance when scientists claim that they can investigate and understand from a purely material point of view how the universe came into existence; they do not understand that their conclusion is inhibited by the fundamental laws of physics.

Are you satisfied that modern telescopes penetrate to the limits of the observable universe? Is there anything beyond which is not observable?

Modern telescopes penetrate into regions of space time which take us back more than ten thousand million years. This takes us to a condition when the universe was a very hot compact of radiation. We subsequently developed into the granulated structure of galaxies and stars which we see today. Whether that means that we comprehend the universe is another matter. Cosmology has become very highly theoretical, and theoretical speculations, alas, now lie in regions of space time where I think there is no possibility of penetrating observation. You reach a stage where you have to infer to an earlier time, and some of the best brains in the world are at work on the inference to this earlier time, but as in all science if a particular solution is found, then a whole host of other problems will be revealed.

Although you deny any sort of religious fervour, religious belief clearly plays a part in your life. How important is that side of things for you?

Sir Bernard Lovell

It is very important in a particular way. I have a passion for the organ and the Church to me is associated with some of the greatest music that has ever been written. Every individual has his own reaction to the question you've just asked, and that is mine. I go to church regularly, but I must say it is the ethos and the music which always take me.

But what about real faith? Do you believe in God?

It's incredibly difficult, having been brought up by a very powerful parent, a lay preacher in the faith, to rid oneself entirely of the feeling that hell is below and heaven is above; this is all part of the very powerful synthesis that survived into the middle ages. We still use these idioms in our daily lives – we talk about the sun rising and the sun setting, whereas we know in fact that it is the earth which is rotating. Of course I cannot share the anthropomorphic image of God that my parents had; few people do nowadays, but that doesn't stop them being deeply religious. Science for me is only part of existence, and although my life would be entirely different without it, a lot of my life has been lived outside the scientific world.

In times of personal crisis, would you seek refuge in religion?

I had a personal crisis a year ago, so I can answer that question. My wife suffered a severe stroke, and although she is still alive my intellectual companion of fifty-four years was effectively removed from me. My duty has been to have her attended to and to make her as comfortable as possible. In other words my reaction to that sort of crisis has been entirely practical.

Since religious belief is by definition an act of faith, and to that extent quite irrational, it is difficult to see how that is to be reconciled to science which is only concerned with demonstrable truths.

This is part of the synthesis which is necessary. I think it can only be approached with humility from both sides of the divide. Some of the sermons I listen to make me mad, but occasionally you hear a sensible approach being taken to these questions.

Sir Bernard Lovell

Do you believe that science and religion are different paths towards the truth? Is it the same truth, or a different truth?

It must be the same truth in the end; they are different approaches to the ultimate truth.

Early astronomers were persecuted on religious grounds. Do you think the Church has made advances in proportion to those made in astronomy?

No. One despairs sometimes of the attitude in the established Church and its lack of guidance and coherence in important moral issues. When one sees this failure it makes me feel that it's all the more important that the Church should become a coherent body in its statements of beliefs and attitudes to the modern world. Again it is a question of humility, this time from the leaders of the Church and theologians.

In 1958, when you gave the Reith Lectures, you said apropos the origins of the universe: 'The optimism is tempered with a deep apprehension born of bitter experience that the decisive experiment nearly always extends one's horizons into regions of new doubts and difficulties.' Did that continue to be the pattern?

I'm glad you've quoted that since it encapsulates all that I have been trying to say about these new discoveries. I'd completely forgotten I'd said that thirty odd years ago, but how much I still agree with it now, and all that has happened since then illustrates that it is the case.

You mentioned feelings of fear and humility with which you approached the lectures. Were these born of a consciousness of the limits of your knowledge?

No. It was a consciousness of the misuse to which scientific discoveries can be put. At that time the intercontinental missile had just been used by the Soviets to launch a purely scientific satellite, but, since sputnik, space has become militarized. About ninety per cent of the rockets which have ever been developed for space activities have also been developed for military purposes. That is where I saw the fear, and that fear manifestly still exists.

Sir Bernard Lovell

What do you think has been the greatest contribution made by radio astronomy?

In the broadest terms, the extension of man's penetration into the universe. Beforehand, the 200-inch optical telescope was believed to be the greatest instrument possible since it could penetrate some two thousand million light years into space. That was the extent of our knowledge of the universe. But radio astronomy broke that barrier, and has continued to do so.

What do you think of Stephen Hawking whose books on cosmology have notched up millions of sales worldwide?

I don't think I'm going to answer that. Scientists have generally been very reserved when faced with that question.

Why is that?

Hawking's terrible physical state places great inhibition on any criticism. He has undoubtedly contributed substantially to theoretical astrophysics, but the question as to whether there is any degree of uniqueness or any lasting quality in his theories cannot yet be answered.

I believe you have very mixed feelings on being a public figure. What has been the most difficult aspect of that?

When I look back on those dozen years when I was under constant public gaze and the BBC were around all the time, I think I was extremely fortunate in having journalists of such integrity who understood that I would do my best to answer their questions, and left it at that. They didn't do what they tend to do now, to penetrate one's private life. Occasionally, if they phoned me at home, they would nearly always apologize. I would hate to have that sort of public pressure now; I think it would be an horrific experience. I very rarely come face to face with journalists today, so my judgement is based only on what I read; and what I read about in the papers fills me with alarm, and makes me feel jolly thankful that I don't have to face the public press now as I did in the 1960s.

Sir Bernard Lovell

Looking back, would you say you have had a hard life?

Yes, but a hard life of my own making. Even now, there's no reason why I should keep going to the office. Ten years ago when I retired, I could have just gone away, but it was inconceivable. It never entered my head that I could walk away and sit in the deckchair in the sun. I'd hoped I might spend more time doing other things, but even that doesn't seem to have materialized.

As a scientist, do you believe in an afterlife?

Not in the sense of an anthropomorphic state. I'm always intrigued by the problem of the cosmic ethic, but it's very difficult to talk about this because it's one of the problems one's still trying to enunciate. It does occasionally seem to me to be exceedingly difficult to deny the existence of an all embracing cosmic ethic, but I don't think anybody understands this. I certainly don't. I suppose that something of one's own ethic must survive, inevitably so, in its influence on society. I cannot believe in the simple form of afterlife that I was brought up to believe in, but that is not the point. I think there is something much deeper than that about the universe which is not understood, and that is the only way in which I can answer your question. It's tempting to say, 'I just don't know', but I don't think that's an adequate answer; there is a more positive answer than that, and I would hope one day to be able to talk about it more clearly than I can now. Cosmology is one thing, but there is something ill-defined beyond cosmology; this is a major problem between science and things which are not science. I don't think there are any real answers at the present time, but I would never give a final negative. I prefer to say I'm still thinking about it.

JOHN MORTIMER

JOHN MORTIMER QC

John Mortimer was born in 1923 and educated at Harrow and Brasenose College, Oxford. He was called to the bar in 1948 and participated in several celebrated civil cases such as the *Oz* trial. His series of novels featuring an amiable defence barrister have been adapted for television as *Rumpole of the Bailey*. His other novels include *Paradise Postponed* (1985) and *Summer's Lease* (1988). His acclaimed autobiographical play *A Voyage Round My Father* (1971) was filmed for television in 1982 and won an International Emmy award.

John Mortimer

Yours was the sort of childhood that, had you grown up into a complete neurotic or developed almost any other kind of psychosis, it would have been entirely explicable in terms of your early years. How on earth did you turn out to be so normal?

It's a question whether I am normal at all. In many ways, however, I had a very happy childhood because I had a father and mother who treated me very well and always as though I was grown up; and I was an only child which has its advantages in that you grow up very quickly. I was treated like a good friend, especially by my father. He flew into terrible rages with other people but never with me, and my mother was long suffering and loving. So although I was very lonely because my father never wanted visitors who would see he was blind and feel sorry for him, I didn't have an unhappy childhood. I went to ridiculous English schools which I didn't like, but on the other hand I was able to adjust to them and survive them because I had a very secure relationship with my parents.

Both your parents were adept at not acknowledging reality. Your father did not admit to his blindness and your mother, long after his death, continued to behave as if he had not died. This phenomenon of making light of sorrow and grief, if that's what it is, is something quintessentially English. Is it something that you have inherited, is it something you perpetuate in your own life?

You're right – it is quintessentially English. There is a wonderful story about Lord Uxbridge whose leg was shot off at the Battle of Waterloo, and when the Duke of Wellington said, 'By God, Uxbridge, you've lost your leg,' Lord Uxbridge looked down and said, 'By God, sir, so I have!' And nothing else was said on the subject. But that isn't altogether a failure to accept reality; it's more a stoical attitude to life which I think is quite admirable. Whether it's stoic courage or whether it's a refusal to face facts, I'm not quite sure, but that's how I prefer to live. I can quite easily put unpleasant facts out of my head – I don't think about death for instance.

Are you confident that you can look back now and remember your father as he really was, or has the act of extensive writing about him to some extent fictionalized him and put him beyond reach?

John Mortimer

I find it very difficult to separate fact from fiction. A writer is constantly taking life and turning it into fiction, regurgitating it, and sending it out to the world, altered or not. Certainly when I wrote the play about my father, I wrote many lines for him which he never said in his life, and now it's quite difficult for me to remember which ones were his and which were mine. He's become a sort of fictional character and not like other people's fathers who are contained entirely in themselves and their memories.

Was it partly your intention when you wrote A Voyage Round My Father *to lose your father?*

Not at all. I wanted to write a play about my father and also to celebrate the peculiarly English middle-class attitude to life of that period. That was my intention, but the effect of it has been perhaps that my father has vanished or turned into a different character from what he really was.

Woody Allen once said of Jesus that he was very well adjusted for an only child. Do you think the same could be said of you?

I don't know whether I'm very well adjusted. I've had a very easy life compared with anyone who has lived in Europe or in other parts of the world, and the period I've lived in has been very safe. Only children are fortunate really, in that they very quickly have to learn to live a grown-up life and they have terrific resources within themselves. I led a very strong imaginative life when I was a child, and was able to adjust well to most things in life.

Despite your professed loathing for public schools, you seem not to have been too unhappy at Harrow, or was that an attempt to make the best of a bad experience?

Apart from being very homesick, I had a good experience at my prep school, the Dragon School in Oxford, which was a very good school indeed. I was treated very well, and it was a progressive school for the time and even had a few girls. Instead of having to play games which I hated, I was given a bar of chocolate and sent off to the Oxford Rep Theatre, which was very agreeable. Then I went to Harrow where I was just indescribably bored. It was full of vaguely upper-class people whom I learned to dislike. I wasn't bullied or beaten – none of those dramatic things; I was just bored and being educated slightly above my station.

Is it the idea of sending a young child away at so early an age which is the basis of your objection?

Yes. It's a most extraordinary English habit, and I never quite forgave my mother. Strangely enough, I could understand my father wanting to get rid of me, and I sympathized with him, but I couldn't quite understand why my mother did. I didn't know what I'd done wrong to be dismissed to some draughty distant building. Not that I haven't had children at boarding school myself, but that was when I was young and busy and less thoughtful, less considerate perhaps. But the idea of handing over the upbringing of your child to strangers is very weird, and I think people who run English prep schools also tend to be extremely weird. My son went to Bedales, a coeducational boarding school, which I suppose is rather different. He liked it there and met the girl who is now his wife, and they've been together ever since. And I myself owe a debt to the public-school system, since it gave me an immense amount to write about it. Making fun of public-school attitudes and English upper- and middle-class attitudes, has been my stock in trade over the years, so if I hadn't been there I don't know what I would have to write about.

You have often said that you believe in middle-class virtues. Can you explain to me what these are?

They are really the virtues I saw in my mother and father, those virtues I was trying to celebrate in *A Voyage Round My Father*. To begin with, it wasn't anything to do with money, for they felt money was quite ridiculous and certainly not the most important thing. They were both liberal, my mother a sort of Shavian new woman, my father an old-fashioned Lloyd George Liberal. They were professional people, my father especially in the sense that he gave very good service to the clients he was acting for. He didn't think about doing it for money, though he liked being paid. In those days barristers often did cases for nothing, and I certainly started that way. There was a kind of tradition of middle-class professionalism, of tolerance, liberalism, all of those things, which I

John Mortimer

admire. The middle classes have been the source of most of the strength of England, and most writers have come from the middle class. With the exception of Byron and Shelley, the aristocracy hasn't produced many writers, and working-class traditions have tended to keep people in rather stereotyped conditions of mind. Political change also has come mainly from the middle classes, and all the best revolutionaries have been middle class.

Your books and plays have evoked, often savagely, the moral decline of the middle class. Do you consider yourself to be part of that decline?

The moral decline in England came really in the Thatcher years, when all of those values I admire were derided. The idea that making money was important and everything had its price and had to be sold at the best price, all of those things marked the decline, in my view. And no, I don't consider myself any part of that. I consider myself to be an old-fashioned liberal middle-class person.

There is a character in Paradise Postponed *who is in favour of the working classes running the country while at the same time doubting if these were the kind of people she would have to tea. Does that perhaps epitomize the dichotomy in your own attitude towards the working class?*

In *Paradise Postponed* I wanted to be as rude about my side as I was about the other side. I was getting at a type of mandarin left-wing person, particularly of that era of the Webbs, Virginia Woolf, Leonard Woolf and those sort of people, who managed to combine the view that the working classes should take over the world, with the feeling that they themselves, being extremely privileged Bloomsbury persons, wouldn't have them to tea. But I don't honestly think that that's my own attitude. I'm as sceptical about liberal left-wing policies as I am about everything else. The radio quarrel with Julie Burchill when she accused me of being a snob made me think very closely about whether I am one, but I honestly don't think so.

You have sometimes described yourself as a 'committed leftie'. What does that mean in fact?

A committed leftie is how I would be described by other people, but it's quite a difficult thing to explain. When I was at the Dragon School the Spanish Civil War was on, and I read – perhaps quite ill-advisedly – a lot of Auden and Spender and T.S. Eliot when I was really quite young, so those attitudes of the 1930s, the republican side of the Civil War, and so on, all of that was very immediate to me. Then when I went to Harrow which was upper class and full of rich people I became a one-boy Communist cell. There was an English public school Communist Party and I used to get messages from King Street but I stopped being interested at the time of the Hitler-Stalin pact. Then I went into something called the Crown Film Unit, making documentary films during the war, and it was there, for the first time in my life, I met the working class, the workers so to speak. I became a member of the union and I felt extremely left-wing, and then came the great Labour victory of 1945. All those events throughout my life have encouraged me to believe in essential equality and in some version of socialism. But there are all sorts of leftie things which I'm not in favour of, like eating museli or being against fox-hunting. I don't really accept the entire left ticket, but I would always vote Labour, though with increasing scepticism.

Do you think your views have changed dramatically since the early days of 1945?

No, but perhaps if that government had never existed, then it would have been difficult to remain faithful to the Labour Party. Those memories and those ideals have kept me going.

Isn't that a very English attitude in the sense that those who vote Conservative do so all their lives, and those who vote Labour continue to follow the Party line? Do you think that's a good thing?

I think it's a good thing not to vote Conservative, for whatever reason.

Your fellow barrister Geoffrey Robertson said of you: 'There is a legal part of John Mortimer's work which is deeply conservative, deeply rooted in the law.' Do you think that was the case when you practised?

It is absolutely true to say there is a part of me which is deeply conservative:

John Mortimer

I want the countryside to be kept as it is, I don't want the English landscape to change, and I want English country life to be kept as it is. I'm also very conservative about the British Constitution which I think works very well, and about the British system of justice. My whole attitude towards being a barrister is that the law is a kind of disease and you should try and cure your clients of it as quickly as possible. I always regarded the law as something which was getting in the way of a client's life, liberty and pursuit of happiness, and that my business was to extricate him from the law as mercifully as possible. When I started as a barrister the divorce law was absolutely ridiculous, in that you had to try and establish who was guilty and who was innocent, whereas there's really no such thing as guilt or innocence in marital breakdown. So what you had to do was to try and solve people's problems, and get them out of the clutches of the law. That's how I always regarded my work as a barrister.

When you say you believe in the British Constitution, does that apply to the monarchy?

My theory about the monarchy is that it's much better to have a head of state who isn't political. The mistake of America is to have the head of state who is the prime minister, so to speak, which gives an American president a quite undeserved patriotic glow because you can't really criticize the president without criticizing America. It's an excellent thing to have a head of state who does not have any political powers and for that reason I've always thought the monarchy a good idea, though I'm becoming increasingly unsure about whether it can survive, even though it has good constitutional uses. The ridiculous thing is that people expect the monarchy to mirror decent family life or moral standards, but any hereditary line is going to have people who behave extremely foolishly from time to time. We have to evolve our own moral standards and not look to the monarchy to do it for us.

You married for first time when you were twenty-six and inherited a ready-made family of four children. After the solitude of your own childhood, did the prospect of a large family attract you, as it might have terrified others?

I think it did. I was really entranced by the idea of a lot of children and since then I've never lived without children around. I have children now of all possible ages, from forty-two to eight years old. I think it did have to do with the loneliness of my childhood.

Since your wife had first to secure a divorce before you could be married, you went to considerable lengths to be cited as co-respondent. One imagines that in those days it was a rather sordid business with a great deal of stigma attaching to it . . .

It was particularly difficult for me because my father was the doyen of the divorce bar, and it was difficult for him too, although his colleagues behaved very well about it. We used to go to endless numbers of hotels and try and make people remember we'd been there. No one ever did, but in the end a private detective called Mr Smith came to the house and found our clothes in the same bedroom, and I then made a confession. Mr Smith later gave evidence in court that we were living together. The following week I was conducting my first case as a barrister and I had to call this same Mr Smith as a witness to the adultery of the people whose case I was handling. For the next thirty years I called Mr Smith to testify about once a week. We sometimes had coffee together but we'd never refer to the time when he came and inspected my bedroom. One day Mr Smith was walking across a pedestrian crossing and a police car came buzzing along and nearly ran him over, so he hit the police car on the roof in a fit of anger, whereupon the policeman arrested him. Mr Smith sued the police for false arrest. As he needed a witness to say he was a thoroughly reliable and decent chap, I went to court and said I'd known Mr Smith for thirty years and he was an absolutely truthful, honest character. He got substantial damages.

Your marriage to the first Penelope was legendary in its tempestuousness. Most people would find perpetual fighting draining and debilitating, yet you continued to work hard and write hard. Did you perhaps find a certain exhilaration or energy in the conflict?

Not really. I had £5 a week from my father, four children to feed, a very large house in Hampstead, and another house somebody gave us in the countryside. So I really had to work. I not only earned money by divorcing people, but I wrote anything – stories for women's magazines, anything. Two writers married to each other is an impossible situation, because you're using the same material and using each other's lives. It was certainly tempestous, but it gave us both a lot of material, and it wasn't without moments of happiness. When I look back on it now, however, I can't think how I survived it, not only because the marriage was at times stormy, but because I was working flat out as a barrister and a writer, and also enjoying myself quite a lot. I must have had enormous stamina. The funny thing about that time is that I would often leave the house in the morning battered after some long argument or angry scene, and then I'd go down to my chambers in the Temple and give advice to elderly company directors on exactly how they should conduct their married lives. Everybody else's life was absolutely easy to put right.

Your father was much given to angry outbursts. Did you inherit his predisposition to anger?

No. His anger made me very calm, and I have very few angry outbursts. What I have in common with my father is a well-developed sense of the ridiculous. He had a long succession of jokes about his life, which he told very well, and he would laugh until the tears ran down his face. We share a sense of the absurdity of life, coupled with rather a sentimental attitude to it also. My father would weep in the theatre, yet he would make an attempt to deal stoically with life, which is what I liked about him. I actually miss him all the time and I'm terribly overshadowed by him. When I came to live in his house I found it difficult to do anything to it, to change anything about it for a long time, and I do find myself with the feeling that I'm repeating his life.

In Clinging to the Wreckage *you describe your married life as a feverish round of longing for lucrative divorce briefs to defray 'the family's extraordinary demands for Farex, Ribena, Johnson's Baby Powder and knicker linings'. Were there compensations to offset this heavy load, or do you remember it as unmitigated wretchedness?*

Not at all as unmitigated wretchedness. The children really were a great pleasure, and it's very nice that I still seem them a lot. And there came a time when the desperation to buy the knicker linings calmed down; Penelope had a contract with the *New Yorker*, and I was beginning to make money by writing plays and doing bigger divorce cases. So it didn't go on forever.

One of the things you learned from being a divorce lawyer is that people on the whole don't rush into divorce as they do into marriage, and that – as you put it – 'any human relationship, however painful and absurd, can seem better than the uncharted desert of divorce'. Was that the sentiment which kept your own stormy marriage going for about twenty-five years?

I think it was the children really, and it certainly wasn't stormy all the time. What a lot of my clients feared was being alone; they would rather have the quarrels, or they'd even rather live with people they never spoke to, than be alone. I don't think I thought that. I didn't think I'd be alone if I was divorced, so it was really the children, and also there was a lot of affection.

Did you see Penelope Mortimer's The Pumpkin Eater *as a sort of revenge?*

I honestly didn't. I thought it was a very good book, and I don't really feel that I'm like the person in *The Pumpkin Eater*. You've got to write about what's happened to you; that's what I do too, and it's not revenge.

Your play The Wrong Side of the Park *contains thinly disguised elements of your first marriage. Did writing that make you feel better about the painful aspects of marital breakdown?*

Yes, I think it did, but again I don't think it should be seen as a deliberate personal act within a relationship. It is an example of the writer's solitary way of trying to translate his experiences into some form of art.

In much of your writing the distinction between fact and fiction is rather blurred. Are there any dangers in this, do you think?

Of course there are, and it's a very interesting subject. Nothing is the literal truth, or the whole truth; everything is somebody else's creative choice about the truth. That goes for journalism, documentaries and novels. In a sense the most truth comes from fiction. Tolstoy is the writer who comes nearest to telling the truth about life; you get much nearer the truth by reading Tolstoy than you do if you see some documentary or read a book which is meant to be a discussion of history. History is all written from somebody's point of view; it's a question of choice. Fiction is telling a story to make people want to know what is going to happen next, but it is really the writer's attempt to make some statement about life. The facts of the story need not be true, but the statement should be true, it should be a statement of the truth.

After the breakdown of your first marriage you had two promiscuous years. Were those the years you should have had before you married perhaps?

Absolutely. I became middle aged quite early on, and then I had to go back to being young again. I didn't go totally mad, but I was always on the look out. I think I'm naturally somebody who wants to live with a family and children, and I wouldn't now like to have to embark at my age on a promiscuous period. I think it would be very exhausting – all that planning and wondering and making telephone calls . . .

Your father thought that sex, like love, had been greatly overestimated by the poets. Did you have any sympathy with this view?

I disagreed with it at the time. He derived tremendous fun from pricking any preconceived ideas and making them look absurd. For example, he would always say that travel narrowed the mind, and you learned much more by staying at home. So he would dismiss any kind of large idea that sex or love was the greatest thing in the world. Yet he was very much in love with his wife, and she with him.

Are you a romantic at heart?

Yes, I would say so. I like romanticism mixed with – not exactly cynicism – but common sense, as in Stendhal, or Byron.

John Mortimer

You wrote in your autobiography: 'The basic morality on which law is founded has always seemed to me inferior to those moral values which everyone must work out for themselves.' That would seem to suggest that our legal system is very crude and unsophisticated . . .

Yes, I think that's right. The legal system is like some sort of public utility: cleaning the drains, washing the streets, stopping people knocking each other on the head, or taking each other's wallets . . . but not much else. The subtler points of life will not be decided by law. That's why, for instance, I'm against all censorship laws, because I don't think the law should tell people what they should read or what they should not read, or intrude into their private morality. Those are things they must discover for themselves. The law can do simple things, like stopping robberies, and compensating if you're run over, but when it gets into the intricate realms of morality it makes a fool of itself.

Would you agree that our adversarial system is not necessarily conducive to the truth and that success is often due to powerful rhetoric?

I'm in favour of the adversarial system. An English trial isn't an exercise to discover the truth, it's an exercise to discover whether in a criminal trial the prosecution has proved its case beyond reasonable doubt. It's absolutely right that people should not be sent to prison unless their guilt is proved beyond reasonable doubt. That doesn't mean that at the end of a criminal trial the truth has been discovered; the person might be guilty but there might not be enough evidence to satisfy a jury. That's a much better system than having the judge as a kind of Hercule Poirot trying to ferret out the truth which he may be wrong about. I have grave doubts about how much rhetoric alters the adversarial system. You can lose cases by making mistakes, but I think it's quite difficult to win unwinnable cases with rhetoric.

You used to say that when you grew up you would decide between being a writer and a barrister. Since you have left the Bar, does that mean you have finally grown up?

A good question. I didn't decide for years and years to leave the Bar, and I think I left it about ten years too late. The great advantage of old age is that you can behave quite childishly, whereas when you're young you're very anxious to appear grown up. I always was a writer who did a bit of barristering, like a girl who wants to be an actress does a bit of waitressing as a day job. But I still don't know whether I've finally grown up . . .

You claim always to have felt somewhat out of place at the Bar. Why was that?

When I started everybody was frightfully correct and conservative, and called each other by their surnames, as though they were at English prep schools, and generally behaved in a sort of English public-school manner; and there was I, rather left-wing, writing plays, going off at the end of a court to go to rehearsals and take actresses out. So I was slightly out of place, though not completely, because I had of course been a child round the Temple. When I first went to the law courts, the ushers used to call me Master John. It was rather like the young squire taking possession of the house.

You defended some famous cases, including Oz *and* Gay News. *Were you aware at the time of the significance they would have for years to come?*

No. I got into all that because I was a QC and also a writer. The first book I defended was *Last Exit to Brooklyn* and I got that off on the appeal, on the basis that the description of sex was so disgusting that it put the British population off sex for about a week. It was a frightfully moral argument which the Court of Appeal liked. The *Oz* trial just came upon me; like most things in my life, somebody asked me to do it, and I did it. It turned out to be absolutely typical of that strange flower-power generation, which seems to me much more distantly in the past than the 1930s or the 1920s. However, I'm not sure now it did change the face of England.

You grew up in an agnostic household and have never been able to bring yourself to believe in God. Have you ever felt that as a particular loss? Have you envied other people their faith?

I wasn't ever christened or confirmed, so I grew up with no religion, but I never missed it at all. And I always admired my father, because although he went blind and had awful things happen to him, he never turned to God. But I am very interested in religion; I think sometimes atheists become obsessed with religion, and I certainly love talking to bishops, or arguing with cardinals. My problem with religion, or with an omnipotent deity, is to see why he puts up with all the evil in the world and why he allowed eight million Jews to be massacred and why he lets Bosnia go on, if he is all powerful. I can't quite work it out and I can't work out whether I would like God if he existed; that's a kind of intellectual argument which I'm always trying to get the answer to, but I never succeed. There have been more horrible deeds perpetrated in the name of religion than for anything else, and it's difficult not to believe that the religions of the world have done more harm than good. As a writer, however, I am aware that Catholicism has provided a wonderful kind of starting-off point for novelists. If you're Graham Greene or Evelyn Waugh you can have a kind of framework for your life and your writing which I don't have, and which I suppose I might envy. I also do think that a totally materialistic view of life can be a kind of stunted philosophy; you do want to attach some kind of almost mystical importance to something, otherwise your life becomes rather Stalinist.

But as you get older, don't you hanker after some sort of faith?

No, I don't, honestly. And I certainly don't hanker after immortality. My father used to say that immortality of the soul would be like living in some kind of transcendental hotel with nothing to do in the evenings; and I don't really look forward to that. It is important to believe in something outside yourself, more important than yourself, but having some political beliefs and also believing in the importance of literature is enough for me.

In your autobiography you quote from Wordsworth's Tintern Abbey, *as if it gave expression to some scarcely acknowledged religious impulse. Have you yourself felt that 'sense sublime of something far more deeply interfused, whose dwelling is the light of setting suns . . .'*

Yes. What you have to find is the mystic importance of the moment of time, that moment when you're experiencing the country, or solitude, or whatever. And I suppose the nearest I can get to religion is a sort of Wordsworthian reaction to the countryside and pantheism and the

John Mortimer

importance of nature. I can understand the mystic qualities but not the intellectual qualities of religion.

You once said, 'Loyalty is a stultifying emotion.' Can you develop that idea?

I think that anything which is uncritical is stultifying. You should be able to criticize everything and so if you're devoted to somebody totally uncritically, it is stultifying. But in saying that I really meant loyalty to groups, or parties, or the old school, or whatever.

Does loyalty extend to fidelity? Is fidelity also stultifying?

No. I think it's probably liberating in a way because it removes a lot of complications from your life. It's something people have to deal with for themselves, but I think on the whole fidelity is rather freeing.

You disliked Mrs Thatcher and all that she stood for, feeling she epitomized what was worst about the 1980s. Is her legacy likely to darken the 1990s equally?

Yes. It was her legacy that destroyed basic industries in Britain; we're producing service industries and computers, but nothing basic is being made in the country any longer, and I dislike the whole morality of everything having its price and the idea that nothing was important unless it was making money. Political idealism died in the 1980s and became an object of derision. We're still living in that shadow.

You made no secret of your loathing for the SDP. Does that extend to the present Liberal Democrats?

Yes, I can't stand the Liberal Democrats. They're just there to spoil everything. We've had Conservative governments for so long because the opposition has been split, and when they could have voted against Maastricht and against the government – quite legitimately because they weren't having a referendum – they kept the government going for no reason whatsoever. I dislike them intensely.

You have often been criticized for being 'a champagne socialist' and have defended yourself by claiming your role was to infiltrate the Establishment in order to change it. Do you think you can claim success in that respect?

I just believe champagne should be freely available to all. Nye Bevan was forever drinking champagne, and that was a very good sign. I also don't think attacking the Establishment from the outside has much effect. The best form of attack is humour, to laugh at the trappings. If you get the jury laughing in court, you know you've won the case. But I don't think I've succeeded very much in changing anything. The great thing about the British Establishment is that it is totally impervious. All a writer can do is to try and promote people's understanding of each other and their sympathy with each other, and to make established institutions look ridiculous.

Beneath your own cheerfulness and bonhomie, *I suspect there is a grim pessimism, and* malaise . . .

Pessimism is a very good basis for a cheerful outlook on life. If you don't expect too much you don't get disappointed. I always used to tell my clients that they could go to prison for six years, and when they ended up by being fined £2 they were frightfully relieved. But if you'd told them they were going to be fined 10 shillings and they were fined £2, they would have been very cross. So I think it is better to expect the worst. I do have a fundamentally pessimistic attitude to life, but I hope I don't have too much *malaise*, except in the afternoons when I often get depressed.

Your preferred genre for writing is comedy. Do you think that is the best way of saying important things, or is there perhaps a danger that important issues will be seen to be trivialized?

That's a very good question. Comedy is the most important and the most difficult form of writing. Anybody can be tragic, but to be funny is really hard and requires great skill. It's a great English tradition from the

John Mortimer

comedies of Shakespeare like *Twelfth Night* and *As You Like It*, which are quite sad plays really, through to the novels of Dickens which can be tragic and comic and savage at the same time. Comedy is also the most truthful thing; if you rule out comedy you rule out half of the truth. Does it trivialize the truth? I don't think it does. Just the reverse.

You are very sensitive to criticism and unfavourable reviews. Haven't you reached a stage where you can afford to ignore adverse comments?

I've now stopped reading reviews. They are just quite irritating, and it can be bad for the confidence. Dickens never read reviews, then suddenly he read a bad review of *Little Dorrit* by mistake and got into a terrible depression. Writers are very uncertain about what they've written, and if it gets very well received, that's a wonderful relief and a surprise; if it is badly received, it's depressing.

There are many contradictions in your character which I am sure you are aware of. You are an upholder of traditional values, but a defender of liberalism; you are both wordly wise and apparently starry-eyed, and so on. Have these contradictions ever worried you? Have you ever tried to resolve them?

Oh no, I wouldn't like to resolve them. I would cease to exist if I resolved them. The contradictions are essential, and if you're writing, you have to have the tensions in your writing which are the different parts of your character.

I have the impression that the fact that you were unable to get close to your mother, even at the end of her life, was one of the hardest and saddest things for you . . .

Yes, it's one of my greatest regrets. I think because I had a very strong relationship with my father, she was rather left out. Also she came from the English tradition of – not coldness, because she was not in the least bit cold – but of not being demonstrative. Her father committed suicide while she was in South Africa and her family just sent her the local paper with a note saying, 'This story will probably interest you.' As a family they didn't talk about anything like that. And although we weren't quite so remote, it was never as close as I should have liked.

I believe you are infuriated by the thought of dying. Wouldn't you be comforted by the thought of an afterlife?

No. My father's immortality is that I remember him and that my children are like him. The only sort of immortality I believe in is when people remember you, or people's lives have been shaped by you to some extent. I don't want some sort of strange and detached existence floating about the universe.

Looking back on your life, what are you proudest of?

Of the good things I have written, *Clinging to the Wreckage, A Voyage Round My Father*, and I'm also rather proud of *Rumpole*. It's quite difficult for a writer to keep going in a lot of different generations, and I'm pleased to have done that. I'm proud of my children, and happy to have kept my parents' house in the condition it's been accumstomed to. I don't think my achievements have been really great. I hope I've been on the side of tolerance, liberalism, letting people alone, and social justice, but millions of other people have said all those things, so it's not anything I feel particularly responsible for.

You have sometimes said that to conduct an interview is much more difficult than to be interviewed . . . do you still take that view?

This has been such a good interview that it's made me think very deeply. I was never quite so well prepared as you, and it is always nerve-racking until the interviewee suddenly says something extraordinary and then you can relax in the knowledge you've got the bloody thing wrapped up. I remember interviewing Hailsham and asking him what he did when he sat on the woolsack looking bored. And he said, 'Well, what I do is whisper bollocks to the bench of bishops.' And I knew that since I had got him to say that, everything would be all right.

MARJORIE PROOPS

MARJORIE PROOPS

Marjorie Proops was born in Woking around the time of the First World War. She started work at the *Daily Mirror* in 1939 and after the war was a journalist on the *Daily Herald*. She returned to the *Mirror* in 1954 where she established her reputation as an agony aunt. In 1969 she was voted Woman Journalist of the Year. Her publications include *Pride, Prejudice and Proops* (1975) and *Dear Marje* (1976).

Marjorie Proops

Your mother's perception of you as the plain unattractive child was terribly hurtful and it affected you deeply. Did you ever manage fully to come to terms with it, and if so, at what cost?

It's not entirely true that my mother rejected me, which is what this question implies. My mother was a very practical, sensible lady, and she couldn't help but recognize the fact that I was a plain kid with buck teeth and glasses, someone who would never dance at the London Palladium. I also had a very pretty younger sister, and she realized very early on that I would have the disadvantage of not having looks and style, but she used to say to me that I was the one with brains and talent. She encouraged me to develop the few skills that I had for drawing, music and singing, while my sister was praised for her looks. My sister and I still laugh about this, and there's never ever been a hang-up for either of us. My mother cherished us both and loved us both equally.

You were teased at school because of your Jewish background. Did that make you feel ashamed of being Jewish or did it lead to the more common feeling of being part of a persecuted but superior minority?

At the beginning when I was teased in the playground and called 'Becky the Jew girl', I used to run home crying to my mother, who said, 'Isn't it lucky you've got another name? We'll just call you Marjorie from now on.' And when my name changed the teasing stopped. But I was very aware at an early age of the prevalence of anti-Semitism in London. It was the time when Mosley and his blackshirts were marching and menacing people. I was too young to analyse it but I felt the terror that every victim of anti-Semitism feels. It does bring you closer to the community – you need the protection and comfort of other Jews. Every Jew I've ever talked to is aware of that menace, always present. It is rising again now in Germany and Europe, and it could rise again here, which is one reason why the Jewish community is close. I haven't been a practising Jew since I was a teenager; years ago I abandoned any formal religious worship, and I married an atheist. Proopsie was born a Jew but did not believe in any form of religious worship; I'm still a 'don't know' when it comes to religious affiliation. I got married in a synagogue simply to please both families, and we never went again except for the odd barmitzvah or wedding, but I still identify enormously with other Jews.

Marjorie Proops

Do you think of yourself as being British first and Jewish second, or the other way around?

British first. My mother's family came to this country in the 1880s, and my father's family originally came from Holland and had been in England for about 200 years by the time I appeared on the scene. So yes, I see myself as thoroughly British and I'm very patriotic; I love this country and it upsets me when things go wrong for us as a nation.

Your upbringing was characterized by a fierce protectiveness and a certain snobbery. Do you remember questioning your parents' values at the time, or only afterwards?

Only in retrospect. When you're growing up you don't question anything. My mother was a snob, but my father wasn't. He was a very happy-go-lucky gambler, handsome and irresponsible, and my poor mother never knew whether we were going to have any housekeeping money at the end of the month or whether my father would gamble it all away. Like many gamblers he was so immensely generous and warm and giving that he'd give everything away, which was another problem for my mother. All her life she felt insecure because of this, and one of my lasting memories of her is that she used to sit in the sitting room of our flat over the pub, wringing her hands. I now realize this was a sign of her anxiety. She became agoraphobic in the latter part of her life and for many years was unable to leave the house. Yet the day my father was buried, when she was in her late sixties, she suddenly ran out of the house, down the garden path, shouting, 'Alfred! Alfred! Take me with you, I cannot live without you.'

You have very early Socialist leanings fostered by a young awareness of class division. Have your Socialist views ever been seriously tested, do you think?

For a brief spell I was unfaithful to the Labour Party, partly because of Shirley Williams to whom I was very close. When Shirley and her three confederates formed the SDP I remember she was very distressed at the time. She'd been through her divorce with Bernard Williams, and had talked to me a lot about that. She was very emotional about it because Shirley is a Catholic, and to divorce was an awful sin for her. Then when she left the Labour Party she rang me up weeping and said that it was like the divorce all over again but she felt she had to do it. She asked me to join her and I agreed, not out of any conviction at all, but really out of friendship for Shirley and because emotion in my friends affects me deeply; somebody has only to cry and I'm there with them crying too. I was one of the very earliest members of the SDP, but I very quickly pulled myself together; politics is not about being sentimental, but about conviction and what you believe is right for the people of this country. So back I went into the fold and here I am, still in the fold.

Were you an admirer of Neil Kinnock?

I liked him very much personally. He has qualities that many people don't know about, one of them being that he questions himself and accepts that he's made mistakes, something which is very difficult for a politician to do. Who knows whether he would have been a good Prime Minister; but I liked him and certainly I voted for him; I hoped he would be Prime Minister, and was deeply disappointed when he didn't succeed.

As you grew up you viewed the prospect of being an old maid as extremely frightening, a fate you would have done anything to avoid. If you were starting out now, do you think being alone would hold the same terrors as it did then?

No, but I'm a very different person now. I'm a bit wobbly on my feet because of arthritis, but mentally and emotionally I'm very strong indeed. When I was growing up, however, a young unmarried Jewish girl was unacceptable. You were a total failure if you hadn't married by the time you were about twenty-three; you were therefore conditioned, not only by your own appearance and by your family but by Jewish society as a whole, to believe that this was the way life had to be.

Did you view motherhood seriously?

Oh yes. I wanted a child very much, although I don't know now whether I wanted a child for the right reasons. When I knew that Proopsie was going to go abroad and he would probably be away for a long time, I suddenly realized that I was childless, and I very much wanted not to be. Women are bred to breed, and it's a natural instinct over which we have no control. I was very glad that I did have a child and would have liked to have had more.

You were a virgin on your wedding night and describe your introduction to sex as 'a tremendous intrusion, frightening, disagreeable ... a hideous and very painful experience'. Do you look back on that time more in sorrow than in anger?

If I'm forced by this sort of question to recall it, then I relive it all now, this minute; I see this ugly penis thrusting towards me and penetrating me, and I feel the intrusion I felt then. I knew nothing at all about sex. I didn't know what happened, so it was not only a physical shock but a tremendous psychological trauma. One of the reasons why I'm able to emphathize with so many readers who have been raped is that I know what it's like, because in effect that's what it was. I wasn't a willing partner responding to someone I loved as the culmination of a loving relationship; it wasn't like that at all.

But presumably you weren't entirely without some physical experience?

When I was a kid there were the usual attempts by boys to fumble in the playground, but mostly they attempted to fumble my sister; she was the one whose knickers they liked to get into. At that time I could draw, and I was also writing poetry and composing music, so I didn't worry about any of this sex business. Then when I got engaged to Proopsie, we'd go to the cinema and come back and sit in the saloon bar of my father's pub, but when he put his arm round me and started to touch my breasts, I'd shiver and move away; I didn't want him to do it. And Proopsie was a very courteous man, not the sort to force his attentions on me; in fact he had a very low sex drive as I realized in later years.

You have described childbirth as 'a very private personal struggle', during which time you wanted to be on your own. Do you think men should actually be excluded from something which is widely perceived as an entirely natural and creative moment, often a very special moment between couples?

Everybody has a right to choose, but I do know there are some men who would run screaming at the very prospect of being present at a birth. They can't face the blood, the mess and the screaming, and I don't think that any woman in her right mind would demand that a man should share all this with her, however much she might feel she needs him. You feel a bit like an animal, and you want to go into a corner and do it on your own. In my case it was a very long and painful labour in a little nursing home in Stafford, and I had to be on my own anyway because Proopsie was in the army, but even if he hadn't been I certainly wouldn't have wanted him there.

You go on to say that you felt there was something akin to indecency in the act of childbirth. Would you accept that this remark is at best quaint and backward looking and at worst offensive to a great many women?

Yes, it probably is, but it is a personal expression of my feelings. Other women don't have to share them.

You always wanted more children but this proved to be impossible. Do you think that more children would have lessened or increased the difficulties in the marriage?

I don't know the answer to that question, but it's true to say that both Proopsie and I loved children. We took a little Nigerian boy into our home – he's now nearly sixty and a distinguished doctor working in Portsmouth. We took him into our family when he was about eleven or so, and loved him like a son – I still do. I think if we'd had more children it wouldn't have made any difference to what happened in our marriage. It would only have made life a bit more difficult for me from a practical point of view, but I'm a very philosophical woman; if something hasn't happened, I don't waste my life regretting it.

Your experience of fostering another child was to go tragically wrong. Although your motives were beyond criticism, did you tend to blame yourself for it?

No. We simply picked him out of an orphanage like a goldfish out of a bowl, and right from the start he resented the fact that I wasn't his mother. He longed to have a mother and wanted to punish me for not being his real mother. He got on well with Proopsie but he was like a puppy around me, and then he began stealing money from my handbag. At first I shrugged and ignored it, but then the thefts increased. He ended up a professional criminal. Proopsie and I used to visit him in Wormwood Scrubs where we would sit in a room with all the other relations till our name was called. The prison governor eventually advised us not to come any more because the boy had told everyone I was his mother and was using my name for fraudulent purposes. The governor also thought I might become one of his victims. I was broken-hearted about the whole thing, and I still feel the pain of it. I haven't seen or heard of him for twenty-seven years.

Your husband's return from the war signalled the beginning of serious difficulties in the marriage. Do you think that like a lot of other women you had learned to be too independent in his absence?

Before he left I was very dependent on him and still very timid, but four years of managing, of keeping myself and my little boy in lodgings, did make me independent. He was an entirely different man when he came back, and I was an entirely different woman.

It was also the start of a father/son jealousy, which never really resolved itself. Was that a source of heartache for you?

Yes, it caused great pain. Robert was an infant in arms when his father went away but a schoolboy when he came back. Proopsie's rejection of Robert started from the moment of his return. The first weekend Proopsie was home, we went with Robert to see my mother and father in Walton-on-Thames, and during the train journey down, Robert was over-excited and wild. When I kept telling him to sit down in case he hurt himself, Major Proops said to me in his best army manner that he hoped I hadn't been bringing the boy up to be a namby-pamby mother's boy. 'Better that he should break a leg than break his spirit.' I glared at Proopsie. When it was time to leave my parents' house Robert, aged five, ran up the stairs and dived to the bottom, ending up in hospital in Walton with a broken leg. Now that was a Freudian accident if ever there was one.

In describing your husband's propensity for taking charge and expecting people to conform to his rules, you say that in some ways you were quite frightened of him. You also feared Philip, the other man in your life, to some extent. Where do you think this fear of men came from? Did it start with your father perhaps?

My father was probably the one man in my whole life of whom I had never been afraid. I've always had this curious relationship with men where I feel that they are physically and in every way superior to me. I'm always attracted to men who are much stronger and liable to be bullies, I don't know why it is. It would take a school of psychiatrists to sort that one out. It could of course be penis fear; the poor old penis is responsible for a hell of a lot. Lots of women have penis fear and there's a good deal more sexual frustration among women than people realize. I cannot tell you how many letters I get from women who have never had an orgasm, women who fake orgasm every time. I find this very interesting, and in a way comforting, because it makes me realize I'm not the only one.

You decided to send your son to boarding school at the age of eight; there will be many who remain unconvinced by your explanation that you didn't think it was right to subject your child to strictures you might impose on yourself. Are you quite sure you examined your motives rigorously?

No, I'm not sure. It is very difficult years later to face up to the fact that decisions you made might have been the wrong decisions. I'm sure that if I had my time over again I would not send Robert to boarding school at the age of eight, but at the time Proopsie was putting pressure on me to send him because he wanted him to be independent and not mother-dominated. He was also jealous of Robert's closeness to me. If I had been the woman I am now, I wouldn't have made that decision.

The public-school system is seen by many to perpetuate the worst class divisions in society. How was it possible for two self-declared Socialists to be party to these divisions?

We always believed that you shouldn't impose your own religious or political beliefs on your children; you should allow them to grow up strong enough and intelligent enough to make their own decisions. Robert now feels that it was probably a good experience for him to go to boarding school, and though he hated it at the time, he in turn sent his own son to boarding school.

But your son was so unhappy that he kept running away . . .

He did, but it was more of a game really. He had formed a kind of escape committee at school. One night he was picked up by a couple on the road. I wouldn't have sent him back again, but his father said he had to go back and learn to be a man. That was Proopsie's motivation throughout his whole life.

Your son has said that you and your husband had options vis-à-vis your marriage which you decided not to exercise, and that your stated fear of losing your son in a custody battle was not soundly based. What do you say to that?

I've always disagreed with Robert on that, and I've even taken legal advice since, quite recently in fact. At that time an erring wife was often deprived of her child, or at least stood a chance of being deprived of her child. I still believe that a divorce judge would have been sympathetic to Proopsie who would have claimed, quite rightly, that he'd been away in the war for four years, fighting for his King and Country, only to be rejected by his wife on his return. It was a risk that I never could have taken.

You say in your book that it was Proopsie's attitude of superiority that made you so determined to have a life outside the marriage. Was it really as rational, as calculated as that?

I doubt it. What happens is that in the day-to-day rough and tumble of living you do things to protect yourself, and though Proopsie and I continued to live together after the final breakdown, I then concentrated more and more on my work and on the other passionate interest in my life which was politics. It's something that happens to you gradually; you meet people, you make relationships – I don't mean sexual relationships, because I didn't have that till many years later – but you certainly develop other interests that make it possible for you to lead a fuller and more separate life.

You claim to have been revolted by your husband and quite unable to 'endure' sex – an attitude which you suggest is quite prevalent among women. Do you think large numbers of women still 'endure' sex, as you put it?

A large number of women certainly endure sexual practices which they absolutely abhor. Anal sex is what most women detest, but they will put up with what they consider to be perverted sex acts rather than have to fend for themselves. It's all very well if you've got money or a wealthy family to support you, but if you're an ordinary woman with no profession, and all you can do perhaps is go out charring, then you put up with being raped . . .

But aren't we talking about a very small minority?

No. Very few women really enjoy anal sex, but a lot of men do. They write and describe their needs to me, and they complain that their wives or girlfriends won't put up with it. I've always taken the view that nobody should have to endure sexual practices that they find abhorrent and unacceptable, but when a woman is dependent on a man for the roof over her head, the food she eats, and for the care of her kids, then she's going to put up with whatever sexual practices he demands.

Why do you think men have the urge to have anal sex with women?

It's a fairly basic animal instinct probably, but it does highlight the deep difference between male and female attitudes to sex. The majority of women need to feel that they love their partner, or they need to convince themselves that they do, whereas a man can have sex with a total stranger – he just gets his rocks off, and that's fine. But you would know much more about male sexual impulses and instincts than I do . . .

You are a veteran champion of women and the main tenets of feminism, and yet in some ways you have been dominated by men all your life. Why do you think that came about?

One of the reasons why I've always been a strong feminist is that I hope other women will be stronger than I've been. I will fight to the end for the right of women to run their own lives, to do what they want to do, to have abortions if they want to, but attitudes are personal and you can't change what you are. No matter how long I live, I will always be a woman ready to be dominated by a man.

Some people have also detected the whiff of anti-feminism in some of your articles, and there was the famous attack on lesbianism . . . was this because you found the whole feminist tract a little hard to take?

I think I went through a phase, probably in the 1970s, when I thought that the whole thing had gone over the top. It became too militant and basically unattractive, and I found it distasteful. I now have a rather gentler approach to feminism. There was a time when I marched up and down with banners and banged on the door of No. 10, but that was a phase and I have matured a little since then, the edges have softened.

In your early days as an agony aunt your approach to people's problems tended to be quite simplistic, even flippant on occasion. Was that simply inexperience or did you come to view your job much more seriously and responsibly than at the outset?

It was inexperience and nervousness. My first few columns were very tentative and I had no confidence at all. I then had some good private training from a psychiatrist, Dr Chesser, who sent me on various courses including marriage guidance counselling. The more I learned about the job the more difficult I realized it was going to be. Dr Chesser taught me that each letter represented a unique individual, a person in pain, in trouble, worried, inadequate, usually sad. That was the first and most important lesson I learned. Gradually I gained confidence and knowledge, and I began to realize that people were beginning to trust me and seek help from me. I had mixed feelings about it, because I felt it was the most tremendous responsibility; still do. That's why I get mad with people who joke about agony aunts and the work they do.

Marjorie Proops

Would you accept that a newspaper column is an imperfect way of dealing with the complexities of human problems?

Of course I would, but the vast majority of people who write to newspapers and to people like me have nowhere else to go, so we're better than nothing. A large number of people say at the end of a tortured letter: 'Now I've got it off my chest and I feel better.' If we serve no other function, we are still valuable.

You must be aware, more than most, of the terrible burden of human unhappiness. How do you cope with that?

At times I get very depressed, and I lie awake for hours at night and think that I'll have to give it up. Then I pull myself together, I listen to the radio, and there's another day tomorrow. But I can't pretend that I can just shrug it off at the end of the day.

Were you conscious of an irony in the fact that you spent a great deal of your life trying to solve other people's problems without ever being able to solve your own?

I'm still immensely aware of that irony. It is very difficult for people to solve their own problems because we make excuses for ourselves, we can't accept the fact that we're as awful as we are, that we've behaved as badly as we have. It's very hard to pass judgement on yourself.

One doesn't have any very clear impression from the book as to whether the arrangement you describe of having a sexless marriage and a long-term lover outside marriage was one which combined the best of both worlds, as it were, or whether it was deeply unsatisfactory.

It was the worst of both worlds. I did love Proopsie in a funny kind of way, especially towards the end of his life, when we became very close. He was my best friend, and I miss him now, oddly enough, more than I miss Philip. My relationship with Philip was always unsatisfactory because we'd snatch the odd hour or two whenever we could, and it was almost always ninety per cent sexual, which is not what one really wants. Philip was a man of great erudition and style, highly intelligent and interested in politics and the law; so I wanted much more of him and he wanted much more of me. He wanted me to go home to him, not to Proopsie, which I wanted too. But good sex is also important, and Philip opened up a whole new magical world. I was in effect a virgin when I met Philip, certainly I hadn't experienced orgasm, and he was able to make me appreciate sex with total lack of inhibition.

In 1986 you became mentally ill and struggled for the next three or four years to become well again. Your son remains convinced that your illness was the result of drugs which interfered with your mental processes; you and your psychiatrist thought otherwise. Looking back, who was right?

My son proved to be right, because for four years I'd been taking a drug which was first prescribed for depression and anxiety. I didn't know that I was allergic to it – there are only a small number of people who have this reaction, and I was one of them, but nobody knew it. Robert went to see the psychiatrist and had a bit of a row with him. I was taken off the drug and I was back at work within three weeks.

I have the impression that you are very reluctant to criticize your psychiatrist, Tom Kraft. Is your attitude principally a result of gratitude to him, or is it perhaps based on fear?

It's gratitude, because despite what Robert says about him, he did help me a lot. I had awful obsessions and terrible nightmares during this period of breakdown. For example, I had an obsession with death – I couldn't pass a hearse or a funeral parlour without coming out in a sweat. And Tom really did help me cope with all that.

What do you think caused it?

I have no idea. Perhaps it was a build-up over the years of all the tensions and stresses in my life, and the various guilts. I was beset by guilt, which Tom Kraft helped me face.

Marjorie Proops

You must be one of the very few people who still remember Robert Maxwell with affection. Even your sympathetic biographer says that for all your wordly wisdom you sound like a total ingénue *when you talk about Maxwell.*

Maxwell was a very affectionate man who could charm anybody, especially women. I first met him when he was a Labour MP, and when he came to the *Mirror* he was glad to see a familiar face. He invited me to have a cup of coffee with him and he asked me a lot about the paper. He suddenly asked me if I was a director of the company, and when I said no, he said, 'Well, you are now.' I told him that it wasn't legal, and that certain procedures had to be followed, but he simply said: 'If I say you're a director, you're a fucking director.' Sure enough I became a director and was advised by the company secretary, 'Never argue with him; never even try because you won't win.'

How did he behave at board meetings?

I only went to one. He was the great dictator, a bully . . . maybe that was one of the reasons I was attracted to him. He shouted at everybody else but was very gentle and affectionate towards me, treating me as a cross between a helpless two-year-old and a ninety-five-year-old. I didn't know at the time that he was a crook, a liar and a thief, that he was robbing the pensioners.

Your friend and colleague Geoffrey Goodman says that you could not distinguish between those who were genuinely fond of you and those who were trying to use you. Looking back, do you think Maxwell's affection for you was genuine, or did he view you more as a valuable asset to the newspaper.

I would think that his first consideration was my value to him commercially. We know from market research that my column is the most widely read of any part of the paper. I have no illusions about that, but I think in addition he did have a genuine affection for me, as I had for him. I still miss him.

Marjorie Proops

You had a very close, often flirtatious relationship with Maxwell. Do you accept that many people, your friends included, found that distasteful, particularly since Maxwell was behaving in such a cavalier way at the Mirror *and manifestly interfering with editorial policy?*

He had that sort of relationship with so many people, it wasn't just with me. It suits people now to be a bit selective in their recollections, and some of the comments are coming from those who were fired by Maxwell. Ex-editors, ex-executives, ex-directors, ex-journalists who still have axes to grind have seized the opportunity to have a go through me at Maxwell.

But don't you think now that like a lot of other people you were taken in by Maxwell?

Of course I was. Everybody was. And the people who now say they weren't are liars. At the same time, everybody, or almost everybody, who came into contact with him was fascinated by him in some way or another. It was palpable. I remember once when one of these ex-editors had written a book, and there was a launch party at the Groucho Club; Maxwell wasn't expected – I don't even know if he'd been asked – but suddenly in this room absolutely packed with people all shouting and drinking, he appeared, head and shoulders above everybody else, and at once there was silence; just for a second or so there was total silence, and then the noise started again. Immediately he appeared anywhere people were aware of his presence. I don't know what it was about him, but he did dominate people. He dominated the board, he dominated all the people that he robbed, and those people who pretend now that they knew what a villain he was, didn't act like it at the time, I can assure you.

You subsequently resigned from your directorship of the Mirror. *What prompted you to do that?*

Proopsie and I had taken a short break in Majorca, and while we were there, I got a phone call from the company secretary asking me to meet him at the airport to sign some documents. I left Proopsie at the swimming pool and went to the airport where this man handed me a stack of documents and asked me to sign quickly. When I asked what they were about he said there was no time to read them and I was just to sign. I told

Marjorie Proops

Proopsie when I got back and he blew his top, insisting that I resign as soon as we returned to London. Proopsie never liked or trusted Maxwell. In that respect he was very shrewd and had much more sense than I had.

You were very much the symbol of respectability at the Mirror. *Did you never think it was hypocritical to trade on that image given your own personal circumstances?*

No. Remember that my main journalistic function is to help people with their problems, and I never ever moralize. I leave people to make their own moral judgements, and I never offer advice unless I'm asked for it. My private life therefore doesn't impinge, and has no need to impinge, on my professional life, or on my relationship with my readers. They may well say that I'm a hypocritical bitch, and they're entitled to say that, but I think my experiences of pain and unhappiness, far from being a disadvantage as far as my readers are concerned, have helped me to understand them.

Wouldn't it have been more honest and perhaps beneficial to others to have come out in the open earlier? After all, with your tremendous popularity you could have done a great deal to promote an understanding of marital problems and extra-marital love.

I wouldn't have dreamed of doing that while either Proopsie or Philip was alive. They died four years ago, both of them, within a fairly short time of each other. I was widowed twice in effect, and it wasn't until after they'd died that I agreed to do the book.

Why did you tell your story? You say that it was to put the record straight for your son, but that could surely have been done more privately. What was the real reason?

I simply gave in, partly to pressure from Maxwell who wanted to cash in on my popularity as a journalist. I also decided that if I was going to do it there was no point in inventing a whiter than white character, a sort of Saint Theresa Marge who would be totally false and unreal. If it was going to be done at all, then it had to be honest. I talked to Robert at great length, and told him the whole story of my marriage to his father, as well as my relationship with Philip. I told him that if he thought it would harm him or his children, then I would forget about it. I hadn't signed any contracts at that stage. He thought I should go ahead, and when I pointed out that people might criticize me to him and the children, he said: 'If anybody criticized you to me I'd tell them to fuck off, and my children, believe it or not, know that word too.'

There have also been revelations in the press that Philip was two-timing you. Were you aware of that at the time?

I knew this lady. She was a very old friend of his, whom he had known for many years before he met me. She had been a refugee, and he was very fond of her. Philip was a very kind man and he looked after her – in fact I sometimes drove him to her flat.

But there was no physical relationship between them?

How would I know? There may have been. By the time I met him she was a very frail, very old lady, a good deal older than he was; but there may well have been, and good luck to him. I didn't expect that I was the only woman ever in his life, any more than he was the only male relationship in my life.

Did you have other lovers?

No, I didn't. I was never promiscuous . . . flirtatious, yes, but Philip was my only lover.

Your own paper called it 'a story of deceit, the story of a flawed woman living out a secret existence . . .' Did that hurt?

Not at all. The truth doesn't hurt. Everything in the book is true, and I authorized it. That piece about Philip and Miss Meitner, as I always call her, was another bit of very nasty spite and people putting the dagger in, but I feel sorrier for them than I do for myself. If they've got to dig that deep for dirt in order to try and cause me pain, they have failed, because I had twenty years of happiness with Philip, and if he had happiness before he met me, why would I begrudge him? I loved him.

A fellow journalist has said of you: 'The flame of her ambition has never for a moment flickered', the implication being that you must have known what sort of publicity would follow the revelations in your memoirs, and you could be sure it would do your career no harm. That may be a cynical view, but can you honestly say there is not some truth in it?

Absolutely no truth in it at all. Here I am, thirty-eight years on his newspaper; no journalist could be more valued than I am. Nobody could have more affection and respect from her employers than I have. When that piece appeared in *Today* about Philip and Miss Meitner, the editor of the *Daily Mirror* rang me up at twenty to nine in the morning and he said to me, '*Today* has done a very nasty piece and I wanted to warn you. I don't want you to be upset by it. It's all a load of crap, we all know that. I just want to tell you that we all love you very much indeed, that we are here to protect you and care for you, so don't let it upset you.' What more could I want? I achieved my ambition many years ago, and I've never been motivated either by money or by power.

Virginia Ironside whom you replaced on the Sunday Mirror *is reported to be very hurt that you did not tell her she was about to lose her job to you, especially since she considered you to be a special friend. What do you say to that?*

First of all, I'll tell you exactly what happened about that. The editor of the *Sunday Mirror* came to see me and asked me how I felt about doing the *Sunday* as well as the *Daily*. I told him I had enough to do, and that in any case, he had Virginia, and that I wouldn't take a friend's job. But he told me not to worry about Virginia, and that she was going to leave. I didn't ask him whether she was going to go anyway, but I got the feeling that she was. I know they were not happy with her column, and neither was the previous editor. I believe also, although I haven't been told formally, that what they want to do with the *Mirror* is to draw the *Sunday* and the *Daily* a bit closer to each other, and as I'm the only possible link, it makes sense from their point of view. I didn't actually want the bloody job, because it's going to mean twice as much work for me, but he told me it was going to happen anyway and that he would tell Virginia. I also tried to telephone her but couldn't get hold of her, and she rang me first and was very upset about it, but she said she understood it had nothing to do with me. I asked her to have lunch so that we could try and sort it out between us. The next thing was that awful piece in the *Mail* which made it clear that she does blame me; and OK everyone needs to blame somebody. You have to be a very strong person to blame yourself for losing the job.

Despite what seems to have been a fairly disastrous marriage, you say that you still miss Proopsie more than Philip even though, in your words, 'Proopsie bullied and cowed me, whereas Philip gently led and supported me, and whatever I did, whatever I am now I owe mainly to him...' Why was your husband's death harder to accept, do you think?

Because Proopsie was there all the time. When he retired I thought I was going to have a very difficult time with him, and indeed the first day of his retirement when I went out to work, he said to me, very sarcastically and very coldly, 'Do have a good day at the office, dear, won't you?' and slammed the door behind me. So I went and had a bloody miserable day, but when I got home that night he apologized. After that he was mostly kind and warm. Remember that by this time Philip had more or less disappeared from my life, because he was ill and he'd gone to live in Brighton. He had aged very quickly and he'd deteriorated both physically and mentally. It was Proopsie I went home to every night; he was the one who was always there, helpful and supportive, although he continued to bully me and boss me around until the day he died. That was the sort of man he was. When he died I missed the friendship, the companionship, I missed this man sitting in the other armchair, I even missed the bullying...

KATHLEEN RAINE

KATHLEEN RAINE

Kathleen Raine was born in 1908 and educated at Girton College, Cambridge where she became a fellow in 1956. She is a distinguished poet and Blake scholar and has won many prizes for her work including the W.H. Smith Literary Award. Her publications include *From Blake to a Vision* (1978), *Blake and the New Age* (1979) and *The Inner Journey of the Poet* (1982). She has also written three volumes of autobiography: *Farewell Happy Fields* (1973), *The Land Unknown* (1975) and *The Lion's Mouth* (1977). The last of these describes her friendship with Elias Canetti and her intense relationship with Gavin Maxwell. She is founder of the Temenos Academy and in 1993 she won the Queen's Gold Medal for Poetry.

In Farewell Happy Fields *(1973), you wrote: 'I understand now that it is to my mother that I owe the happiness of my infancy as I remember or have since imagined it.' That sounds as if it took most of your life to make that discovery . . .*

Yes, I was horrible to my mother when I was a little girl. I was very spoilt, rebellious and difficult, and now more and more I see I owe her everything.

You say that your mother belonged to the 'golden race'. What do you mean by that?

I'm thinking of Yeats' words, 'The golden race looks dim . . .' My mother lived entirely by spiritual values, in a world of beauty and poetry and imagination. She would notice the birds, or a leaf falling from a tree; she wouldn't notice anything about the money market – she would have been bored by that sort of thing. She had wonderful gifts and if she had been a poet she would have been a better poet than I; I am alloyed with the world, she was totally unalloyed.

Your father was a lay Methodist preacher . . .

Yes, every Sunday and most Wednesdays he was off preaching for the Wesleyan Methodists. He was also a very enthusiastic member of the League of Nations Union, and a great pacifist; he adopted wholeheartedly every kind of available idealism. One good thing to come out of this was that because Gilbert Murray was a tremendous pacifist, my father somehow accepted his translations of Greek drama, which I'm sure he wouldn't otherwise have done. He took my mother and me to all the productions of Gilbert Murray's plays at the Lyric, Hammersmith, which was a great joy to us both – Mother and I didn't care much about pacifism or any other good cause, but we loved the drama and the poetry.

You wrote that your father was not free of the 'sin of righteousness' but that your mother, who never thought herself good or made any effort to be so, was indeed free. You could hardly I suppose have had two more different role models . . .

That's true. It's been very difficult, but I think in the course of my life I've satisfied their different desires for me. My mother would have wished nothing more than that I should be a poet, and now I seem to be deep in education which my father would have wished. He would have believed very much in what we're doing with the Temenos Academy, which is seeking to sow the seed of a different kind of education. I won't say a new kind, because it is perhaps a very old kind: education based in truth, beauty and goodness, not in profit and the latest trendy 'ism' from some American university. The basis of the Temenos Academy is to be as universities have been in the age-old past, schools of wisdom, because wisdom is more important than information. I'm sure the sciences are well taught in universities, but when it comes to the humanities, the value and meaning of life, it is miseducation rather than education. The first time I met Prince Charles I made him laugh because he asked how I had come to the ideas I held, and I told him what Ananda Coomaraswamy had said: 'It takes four years to get a first-class university education but it takes forty to get over it.' And the Prince replied, 'I have been working on it for twenty.' What the universities are teaching now would make Socrates or any great teacher of the past turn in his grave. It is not wisdom, it has nothing to do with the basic values of humanity, or what man is and what the universe is; that is the final validation of truth and wisdom because it's written in us, it's our nature. We're a long way from that.

Even your mother, free spirit though she may have been, was not without a certain censoriousness, the Calvinism of John Knox's Scotland. Children tend to absorb their parents' attitudes and prejudices – was that something you found difficult to shake off?

I don't think so. John Knox really didn't go deep in my mother. Once when we were talking about *The Pilgrim's Progress* which my father loved, I remember her saying, 'I think that is a book that has outlived its usefulness...' To her the truth of the imagination was the most important thing. The Scots have a very schizophrenic imagination; on the one hand they accept all this gloomy stuff of John Knox, and on the other the fairy world somehow slips through all that, and in the balance the judgement of the imagination counts for more in Scotland. The ballads of Scotland don't take the side of the righteous so much as the side of the beautiful; and imagination is kinder than morality.

Kathleen Raine

From your beloved Cumbria you moved with your parents to Ilford which seemed to encapsulate for you everything which was drab and despicable about the modern world. Do you think that perhaps without Ilford you would not have been able to escape so completely into the world of dreams and poetry?

Finally, at the end of my life, having selfishly tried to escape all these things, I seem to have been led full circle round to try to help the people who are imprisoned in Hades. That is what education is for; it's not to follow one's dreams, but finally to give what one can to others who are trapped, which I now feel to be my task. I found Ilford particularly false, but there are thousands of Ilfords, neither rich nor poor, absolute victims of all their falsenesses. The very poor are up against it since they have to confront just the sheer problem of survival, the tragedies of birth and death, and of all those things. On the whole the working class help one another as they do in villages, but in what I mean by Ilford, they keep themselves to themselves; there is no nourishment of mind or heart coming through those garden gates. Ilford is the world of people who watch television and never exchange friendship or love with their neighbours, and who absorb all the false values of the media. They are prisoners, spiritual prisoners.

You describe most movingly the pain associated with your experience of young love. Is that a feeling you can still recall, is it something you still carry around with you?

It's strange you should say that, because I recently went to a production of *Romeo and Juliet* at the Barbican with the architect Jane Drew, who is, like me, a great-grandmother. I was sure that it would be no good and that we were both too old, but we were both absolutely overwhelmed by the words of Romeo and of Juliet. It wasn't a marvellous production, but both Jane and I were absolutely *bouleversées* by the beauty of that young love. Yes, one carries it in one's heart, I think, forever.

How do you remember it?

Through Romeo and Juliet's words essentially. It's not the person one was in love with or the person I was; it is just that some things have the quality of eternal beauty and truth in them, in the love as such. We all experience it, we forget the person, but we remember the love, because that is real. Though my first love died many years ago, one remembers him still. I've met his son and that was quite moving but it's not a personal thing. Love is something more than personal; it's a vision, a way of understanding the world. That purity of young love is absolute – you can't imagine that you may ever feel this for anyone else.

You describe the time when you won your scholarship to Girton College as 'the last moment after childhood when I was not at odds with the world'. Did you feel this as something you were powerless to control, or was there an element of wilful rebellion?

As soon as I got to Girton I began discarding all my father's values straightaway. I was very glad to escape from the trap and the cage of a rather Puritan form of Christianity which contained elements that to this day I can't accept, like the doctrine of the atonement. Feeling that my father had ruined my life, I became very rebellious at Cambridge. That idea was too extreme really, but at the time that's what I felt. And Cambridge was there with all its trendy, atheistic, nihilistic types, not to mention Huxley and the Bloomsbury world, and everyone was so clever, and I fell absolutely for all of it. I'm deeply ashamed now. I see now much better who my father was than I did then, and I think I would have been just as severe on my children if they'd behaved like me.

But in retrospect you came to regard Cambridge as being just as alien to your poetic vision as Ilford had been. Why was Cambridge such a disappointment?

The values people at Cambridge stood for were purely cerebral. Their apparent cleverness embraced agnosticism, atheism, nihilism, but they denied the sacred springs of life, which are the imagination and the heart. The poetry was also hard and clever, and all the poets I'd loved up until then, like Keats and Shelley, and Shakespeare and Milton, they were absolutely out. At the Temenos Academy we are now trying to re-establish the idea that the arts must grow out of a vision of the sacred. The sacred is not the same as the religious, though all the great religions have been grounded in a vision of the sacred, and most of them have lost it since to a great extent. The sacred is the nature of things, it is the reality of the cosmos, it is the depths of the human soul. When Moses saw the burning bush and heard the words, 'Put off thy shoes from off thy feet for the ground whereon thou standest is holy ground', this was an experience of the holy, but in our culture it has become more or less impossible for any well-educated person to encounter this burning thing. Certainly first love is an experience of the sacred, so is any love; this is something that is our birthright as human beings. I often think of a phrase by D.H Lawrence, that knowledge is an experience and not a formula; yet at Cambridge, and I'm sure at Oxford too, and at every other university in the United States and indeed, heaven help us, in India even, this idea is killed. Education nowadays is all right for computers, but it doesn't open the human being, it doesn't expand the consciousness, it doesn't nourish the soul or the spirit. There isn't even the Communist Party to pin our faith on as there was when I was at Cambridge. That was where the better world was going to come from, a universe of peace, freedom and equality. Now the Communist empire has fallen, and something else is desperately needed to transform the world, and I'm afraid the politicians are not going to do it for us. A friend wrote to me the other day that she loved the way I embrace all the lost causes. But I don't think the cause of truth and reality ever can be lost; somehow it springs up again.

You married Hugh Sykes Davis on what you describe as 'despicable grounds' since there was a complete absence of love or even sexual attraction. Was it an act of defiance against your father, or did you feel that you were incapable of loving again as you had loved, or were you in some way not in control of your actions at the time? Or all three?

All three. He was also unconventional, and it was a way of joining the world of the rebels and despairers. I certainly thought I would never love again. In a sense I never did. Years later, I did know a different kind of love. But sexual love had been completely killed off at the time by the axe descending on my first love. And yet, one sees *Romeo and Juliet* and one thinks, how marvellous. Shakespeare understood all that. But in Christianity there has always been a curse on sex, and it's very wrong. When finally in my later years I reached India, where the erotic is sacred, and there is the beauty and adornment of women, the sari and the jewels, and the linga for the Lord Siva at every street corner, one begins to realize that this Christian ban on the erotic is terribly misguided. In the New Age,

Kathleen Raine

whatever that means, I think they're not going to accept that any more, although one has to admit that our young get into trouble when they have premature sexual experience without love. Sex has somehow been separated from love, and people are rebelling against puritanical culture in this country but have no alternative to put in its place; so we seem to be living in the worst of all worlds at the moment. There is no culture as there is in Eastern religions, and somehow this country is in a state of negative rebellion against the good without having discovered an alternative which will humanize and consecrate something that has so long been under a ban.

You wrote of that time in The Land Unknown: *'If the sexual instinct was at that time my undoing, it was not through its strength, but through its weakness.' What exactly did you mean by that?*

Blake said that those who suppress desire do so because their desires are weak enough to be suppressed. Shelley saw that this was nonsense, and wrote most wonderfully proclaiming what Keats called 'the holiness of the heart's affections'. The erotic poem *Epipsychidion* was written to Amelia Viviani when she went into a convent, which Shelley saw as the most terrible denial and desecration of something very holy; she was sensual and sacred to Shelley's vision of sex. The erotic is only one aspect of love but it's a very important one for us human beings; without it women don't love their children any more; they hate their men, hence the catastrophic state we're in. I gave a lecture at the Nehru Centre the other week on Shelley and India, and I saw why he had placed *Prometheus Unbound* on the Indian borders of the Caucasus, even though there are no Indian borders on the Caucasus. His beloved is the feminine principle of India, the goddess. She is called Asia, and she is the excluded principle of beauty and the feminine and the erotic. I'm not a feminist, quite the contrary, because it seems to me it's not feminism we need, it's the feminine, it's the woman. All this business of women trying to get high positions as executives is all so irrelevant; it's not that we need, it's the restoration of love in its full sense.

You left Hugh Sykes Davis and eloped with Charles Madge who was in love with you and wrote you poems. Did you love him?

Not really, not truly . . . it was more an escape into poetry. We should simply have been friends; of course we are friends and to this day I think he loves me, but I'm very thankful I didn't stay with him. It was a great wrong I did him.

You suffered from feelings of guilt and shame because of your elopement. Was that because of the spirit of the age or did the feelings go deeper than that?

Oh, much deeper. I felt I was betraying everyone, including my father of course, and my mother, because these roots die hard. Looking back on my relationship with Charles, I should not have allowed him to rescue me, and I don't know why I jumped into one marriage after another. It was partly cowardice – I hadn't the courage to stand on my own feet. You are very searching in your questions . . . anyway, that is what happened, and I'm deeply sorry. It's what we have done to harm others that embitters old age, it's the pain we've caused which catches up with us.

Motherhood did not seem to alter your priorities in the usual way, it did not seem to deflect you from your poetic destiny. Has that been a source of conflict or regret in your life?

Indeed it has, bitter, bitter regret. I was not a good mother and my children and grandchildren suffer from it to this day. I don't think it is in the nature of women to follow a complusion, a vocation – I won't say a career because that's something quite different. Women should love first of all; we are the mothers of the human race, and we should love our children and bring them up. If women had had it in their nature nothing would have stopped them from writing the works of Plato or Dante or Shakespeare or Beethoven; women have been in the world as long as men, but this is not what women are. These things are sex-linked, they are characteristics like beards, and they belong to men. Who has ever seen any work by a feminist except another work about feminism? I know myself I'm as good as any woman poet who's written in the English language, but I know my place. I'm not Yeats, I'm not Eliot, I'm not Shakespeare; it's a very minor gift I have, and women and men are different. In doing what I have done as a writer, I suffer from a sense of guilt and betrayal of a much more profound nature than that of merely betraying my parents and my children; it's a betrayal of woman. I have not fulfilled the true tasks of woman, either as a daughter, a spouse or a mother, and that is the price of being Kathleen Raine. I didn't see it like that, and I was not writing from ambition to get my poems on the BBC or anything like that; it was a deep compulsion, and partly it was implanted in me by my parents. Anyway, that's how it's worked out. I think the feminists know quite well that I don't like them, and they don't like me either.

When you left Charles Madge it was for an 'unrequited, unrequitable' passion. Yet you experienced with your lover, as you say all lovers do, 'that almost unendurable intensity of passion'. Why was it then unrequited, unrequitable?

For one thing he was in the war and taken prisoner. Thank God, thank God. It was all to do with my imagination. He came from Scotland and somehow touched a spring of memory in me of my mother's country, and of all the poetry and the beauty of that lost world. This had nothing to do with the practicalities of human relationships, and when he came back I realized that the whole thing was just a dream, but anyway, I'd taken the precaution of becoming a Catholic which did save me from it.

Your experience of marriage led you to believe that it was irreconcilable with poetic vision. Was this a sad discovery for you?

Yes, indeed. One wants to have one's cake and eat it. Perfect, requited love is only possible in poetry; it's irreconcilable with marriage. Everything is at the price of something else. But poetry was the driving force of my life, and now I don't really even care whether I was right or wrong; when you consider the vastness of the cosmos and the mystery, it's just another part in the epic, isn't it? We're all part of something much bigger than ourselves, and we don't know what the whole is. People who can say, 'God thinks this and thinks that' are very naïve. One does not know. The modern world looks always for a fix, or an explanation. Science hasn't proved it yet, they think, but next year it will. But we live in a profound insoluble mystery, and the things that emerge from it are unsurpassable. It's amazing what is and has been and will be; it is an inexhaustible marvel of being.

Apropos poetic vision, you write: 'All poets seek to remember and recreate what we all know at heart to be not a mere fleeting illusion but the norm we never cease to seek and create (however often it may be destroyed), because in that state alone lies felicity . . .' Do you feel now that you have arrived at this felicitous state, as it were, or does the search go on?

Of course it goes on. Sometimes one has a glimpse, and in writing a poem it's a kind of prayer or meditation; one raises one's consciousness as high as one can, hoping that some beam of light will come. While we are in this world we cannot experience a vision of paradise, for paradise is by definition what we have lost, but it is also by definition what we are, because our nature is such that we seek something. My William Blake used the word sleep, which in fact he got from Plotinus. Neither of them talked of sin and repentance, but of sleep and awakening. It's a matter of opening of consciousness and, poor human beings that we are, we have a sense that there's more to it than we've understood and we cannot but seek that which we feel to be our own. That is, I suppose, the religious impulse in its deepest sense, but easy answers and doctrines and creeds have nothing to do with it. It seems to me more and more that the older I grow the less I know.

You go on to say, 'To be exiled from the Garden of Eden is our greatest sorrow, and some forget, or try to forget, because to remember is too painful, to recreate too difficult.' Have you sometimes found it too painful to remember?

Yes, there were many years when I didn't write any poems, because it was too painful. But then I gathered myself together again, because it's the only thing that matters.

But why did you find it too painful? What had happened?

One's life had become a mess and one felt so alienated from it, and to be recalled by that music reminds one of the mess one has got into. Judging by the number of painkillers and sleeping pills that are distributed, many people can't face it and instead deaden themselves. We can just about go through the day with the help of some routine, but it can be just too painful to remember, especially when we feel we've lost it through our own fault; that's perhaps the one thing of all, that it hasn't so much been done to us as done by us.

Kathleen Raine

Do you think poetic love is irreconcilable with physical love?

I'm afraid this is so, at least in my experience, and who has ever heard of a poet for whom this was not so? Edwin and Willa Muir loved one another, and he was a wonderful poet, but I don't think poets on the whole have a record of happy marriages. One doesn't know with certainty, but I don't think they do. Poetry is the land of the soul, it is the soul's native country, but in this world you have to live according to the conditions of this world, and there are moments surely when two people who have loved one another deeply have briefly felt that this is forever; they have touched the borders of paradise . . . but then life moves on. Sometimes it remains as a tranquil happy relationship, but think of Yeats, think of Eliot, think of Milton, of Shelley, of Keats . . . it doesn't usually work.

But would you say that poetry and realism are alien to one another?

To me poetry is the reality, the soul's world is the reality, and if we lost the vision of that world we would very soon degenerate into apes; poetry is what makes us human, it is the human kingdom. We've seen what it's like when people lose the paradisal vision in some form or another; they revert to the sort of awful behaviour we see on television and in the press every day. If man loses the vision of perfection which is written in our very nature, that is what makes us mad. The Darwinians always talk about man as if he were another species, but we are another kingdom – the human kingdom. We're the working out of the spiritual destiny, and without the musicians, the painters and poets, the architects, the sculptors, without their vision we couldn't progress; it is what brings us to our humanity. Those of us who are caught in this vision know it to be the most real, the most important thing, but we're only poor imperfect human beings and we slip back. Most of us who are captured by this vision do not have easy lives, but we don't question where out duty lies; it is our dedication, we have to do it. I sometimes wonder, ought I to have given myself more completely to poetry, been less of a coward about it, and at other times I think the whole thing was a mistake anyway.

As I understand it, your poetry has been inspired by visions of a land you have glimpsed but never really known. Have you lived in the hope of knowing it?

In a sense, yes. In moments of vision one is there, in the hope of really knowing it. I'm not much concerned with the salvation of my soul or with what happens to me now. I used to feel deep repentance and mourning for all those things, but now that my personal life is really behind me, it doesn't matter any more. If one has caught one gleam of that country and transmitted it, perhaps it is all worthwhile.

Would you say that the measure of a poem's success is its ability to enable others to glimpse what you have seen yourself?

Yes, but others see it because it's in them. It's like the old image used in the seventeenth century; strike the string of one lute and on another lute the string resonates. It resonates in people because it is in them; it isn't because it's in me.

You say that it's only in moments when we transcend ourselves that we can know anything of value. Is this ability to transcend ourselves given to all of us, or is it the prerogative of poets?

It's given to all of us and it's not the prerogative of anybody. That's why we're human, that is our human destiny and task. People do it in different ways, and the most important way of all is in human relations. That is the final test, and the great sages – I don't care for saints who are horrible people on the whole – but the really holy people, though they don't write poetry, have it in their lives; their very presence in the world communicates this feeling.

When you received the W.H. Smith Award for The Lost Country, *you said that the standard of English poetry was so abysmal that you doubted whether an award should be made to any poet at all. Have you revised your opinion since then?*

I've redoubled it. It was bad enough then, but there were still a few poets alive. Heavens, if you saw my postbag for *Temenos*, you would see the rubbish that people write while calling it poetry. And the rubbish that gets published and put on the radio! None of this has anything to do with poetry. There are not half a dozen poets in this country, nor in any other country, so far as I can see. One or two in France perhaps, but not many. Given the values of this country, the total nihilistic, empty values of Western civilization, how can it produce poetry? Even the New Age people have rebelled so much against knowledge that they haven't produced any poetry either. There's perhaps more poetry in their lives but on the whole they go and grow vegetables and live a greener and better life. Besides, the English language has been so vandalized that words have lost their meaning; people are no longer taught the language, they don't know what words mean, and it's quite appalling. The situation is ten times worse now than when I expressed that view. When the Poet Laureate wrote to me and asked if I would accept the Queen's medal for poetry, I wrote back saying that it was a poor show if I was the best poet to be found. I accepted it anyway, for I would not wish at this moment to dishonour the Queen's award in any way because, poor lady, she's having a bad time too.

You obviously think that the arts are not in a healthy state at the moment. What is the reason for that, do you think?

I have at least tried to keep faith with the world that poetry comes from, but the soul of the age is very sick. That's why we get Francis Bacon. The arts themselves are projecting the sickness of the soul of the age; they're not healing it. Perhaps, in a sense, projecting it is healing it, I don't know, but generally they are reflecting a terrible spiritual ill or else they are dried up. I feel France is particularly arid at the moment. There's very little greatness in the world, it seems to have gone. Even biographies tend to denigrate and to dishonour rather than to see what is noble and honourable in a man or woman. I reviewed one about my old friend Herbert Read not long ago. I didn't find in it the man I knew who did so much for us and for so many people. He was so generous, and he was a seeker after truth, but this book was simply in the kindest possible way minimizing him. It appears you have to minimize or you won't sell the book. If you can prove that someone was a homosexual, then you're fine, you get a public; you have to find something that demeans or dishonours, such as incest or promiscuity ... well, promiscuity is respectable now ... but all the noble virtues, the truly human virtues, are discredited.

You were bitter that you did not get the Oxford chair of poetry in 1968.

Kathleen Raine

Was this because you regarded yourself as the best candidate, or was it because you lost out to Roy Fuller?

Roy Fuller? He's no poet. Of course I was the best candidate, but I'm glad I didn't get it; it would have taken a lot of time, and I had better things to do in my life. When did the Oxford chair of poetry go to a real poet? I suppose Seamus Heaney is – he's written a few good poems – but I don't really give him very much thought, nor Ted Hughes who, although very gifted, portrayed man in books like *Crow* and *Woodwo* in a way that I felt was not a true and valid image of man. But of course there is never an Eliot or a Yeats to give it to.

You said in 1972 that you thought that your scholasticism was being 'censored out of existence'. What did you mean by that?

They didn't like my unearthing all these buried roots. My scholarship was on Blake. I didn't understand a word of his longer poems so I decided to find out, and I began a process of reading the books he'd read, a study which opened out a whole body of what I've called excluded knowledge. In the humanist revolution of the end of the eighteenth century, the tradition of neo-Platonism was just not in, and all this new scientific stuff led to an entirely different point of view about the universe. My work on Blake uncovered the sources of his awareness of the whole excluded tradition of this knowledge. Christianity was totally without anything to contribute by that time in this country. The Hebrew tradition, the Islamic tradition, the Platonic tradition, the Vedic tradition – these are the great mainstreams of human wisdom and it can't be otherwise. To try to make a complete description of the cosmos in material terms may produce extremely interesting discoveries, and indeed has, but modern physics itself has come to the frontiers of the explicable in those terms. We have to return to the mainstreams of wisdom, and Blake has been a sort of sacred book for the New Age people. I don't think they understand very much of him, but they get something. They feel that this man understood something, and indeed he did. I did a great deal of work on him and made very sure that I let no knots remain tied because I knew it would be attacked. There were two lines of attack: one was to ignore me, and the other was to say, 'Oh well, she's a poet,' in other words, 'She's a fool.' But I'm not ashamed of it and I wouldn't go back on it, although I think I would write some of it a little more clearly now.

Kathleen Raine

You have always rather shunned literary circles. Do you think you would be bored by them?

Very bored, although I've known some wonderful poets and writers. I knew Edwin Muir very well, and David Gascoigne was a lifelong friend, but on the whole they're a boring lot. Literary circles are more concerned with getting their works published than with literature and that is why I refused this ridiculous honour because when I looked at the list of people who had received it, they were really writers of entertainment for readers of the Sunday papers; it's not anything to do with what poets will die for, as Keats did, as Shelley did, with what I have suffered for, as David Gascoigne suffered. Poets are not in the service of literary reputations, of getting their books published, and that sort of Booker Prize mentality, no, no, that's not what it's about at all.

Have you refused literary honours?

I never refused any honours until I refused the Companion of Literature. Until then I was never offered an honour to refuse. But I have the love and friendship of Prince Charles, what Saint Jean Perce called, *l'amitie du Prince*, and that he writes to me 'with love' means far more to me than any honour would; and he probably won't even be king, poor man.

You have never had any time for materialism, preferring spiritual riches to the material kind. Is it not some kind of torture for you to live in London surrounded by signs of material wealth?

Yes. It's dreadful. I look in at the windows in Portland Square and can see nothing in the house that makes one feel, ah, I'd love to be in that room, what a wonderful room! David Jones' room had all sorts of things: a photograph of the little dog that the Russians sent up in the first sputnik, a spoon that had belonged to his mother, a general muddle of pencils and boxes, and a lovely chalice that he put flowers in. It was a room that scintillated with life. Edwin and Willa's room was an untidy muddle, and the cats walked in and out, but theirs was the sort of creative room I like. When my house was burgled the only things they took were my cameo brooch, a very small chain of pearls and my carriage clock – they didn't see anything else they wanted. They didn't know the value of my pictures. I've kept *Temenos* going by selling paintings which various friends either sold or gave to me when they weren't famous. I'm sure they would understand and appreciate that it was right to sell them and let them go in order to bring up *Temenos*. The only thing I've got left is a David Jones' inscription.

You describe yourself as anti-Socialist in the sense that you believe in the rule of the wise, not the mob. Are wisdom and Socialism mutually exclusive? Is there no such thing as the wisdom of the mob?

Not of the mob. The mob unfortunately is led; it doesn't think for itself. Rupert Murdoch and the gutter press control the mob. Ghandi-ji had a vision of a Socialism that came from below upwards, where the wisdom would be vested in the village communities, where Socialism would not be imposed from above, as was the case in Russia, or indeed as it was imposed by Nehru. If it were possible, and I think it would have been possible but no longer is in India, this would have been a wonderful kind of Socialism, because there is wisdom in people, but not in mobs. And if the mob is swayed by the media, that is a betrayal of the deep innate wisdom there is in ordinary people. How that's going to be overcome, I do not know. Someone recently said to me that what Prince Charles should do is speak to the common man, as the king always did; the king used to take the side of the people against the barons – we see that in Shakespeare. But how can you reach beyond the *Daily Mirror* and all the other tabloids which serve out poison every morning? My father was the son of a coalminer, and he went to Durham University, took an M.Litt. and became a very scholarly and well-educated man, but when he was educated there was no such thing as bad education; you either had it or you didn't. There were cheap books in the Everyman and World's Classics series, all sorts of literature of certain excellence published in cheap editions so that the poor could buy it as well as the rich. The idea of bad education and miseducation has been the horrible invention of people who thought there was money in it, and now we have not an uneducated public – would to God we had – but we have a miseducated public, and that is a very terrible thing. I don't see how we're going to recover from it, except that of course there are reactions and who knows . . . For the moment we have every kind of exploitation, not the innocence there used to be in country places like the Western Highlands. One knows people exist in remote parts of the world who still have a kind of dignity and innocence, but that's all being obliterated.

Kathleen Raine

In the cottages when I first went to the Hebrides, people used to tell stories and sing songs; now you have the same kitchen and the same dog under the table, but now you have the television set. Even if you go to the remotest village in India, what do you get? . . . *Dallas* and all that rubbish pouring in. I don't see how that tide can be turned.

You were converted to Roman Catholicism in 1941. Was that a sort of road-to-Damascus conversion, or was it a long and winding path to discovery?

Neither of these. It was just I thought I must do something about my life which was in such a mess. Half my friends were Catholics and I think instinctively I wanted to make it impossible to marry the man I was so very much in love with. When he came back from the war, I wanted to say, 'I can't marry you because I'm a Catholic.' And it was also a sort of argument with myself, an assertion that religion was a good thing, the idea that I was born into Christendom, therefore I ought to be able to use the Christian religion, and not go hunting after Buddhism or Sufism or some other religion to which I was not born. I argued myself into it, but it didn't take at all, because it didn't engage my heart.

You now dismiss your conversion as an aberration. Did this feeling come about because of uneasy relations with the Church?

Yes. I just wasn't like them at all, I felt I'd got into the wrong party. Oh, some were lovely people . . . Father Pius, for example, an Irish Carmelite, was a wonderful man . . . and my dear friends later in life, Hubert Howard and Lelia, they were deeply involved in the Church. But they were born into the culture. For me it was when I breathed the air of India that I felt home at last.

Would you say you were Wordsworthian in your religious outlook? Have you felt 'the presence which disturbs with elevated thoughts'?

Absolutely, absolutely. My father wrote his M.Litt. on Wordsworth, I was brought up on Wordsworth, I feel all of that very deeply. Or rather I did, for that was nature; since then I think I have progressed towards the human kingdom and understood that it is in mind and not in nature. Blake said the divine presence is in us. Christians are so set on original sin that it clouds the deeper vision which is that there is a spark of the divine in every human being, every creature. In India this is stoically taken for granted.

Do you believe, along with Jung, that at least part of our psyche is not subject to the laws of space and time, and that this part might survive after we die?

I don't believe anything. I simply don't know. I was talking to an Indian friend not long ago about the Sanskrit poem *Bhagavad-Gita* in which the Lord Krishna says: 'Don't mind about killing these people, they'll all live again.' I asked my friend if this was to be taken in the sense that individually they'll live again, or simply that the spirit always renews itself. And he told me that of course they would live again, for it was the only thing which made sense of life. And I can see that. When you think of young lives ended, and soldiers killed in a war when they've hardly lived, those lives are so inconclusive... It would be nice to think that one could have another go with the knowledge that one's perhaps gathered, that one could try again and do a little better. But it may not mean that; it may mean simply that the universal spirit continually renews itself. I have no idea. And I don't think it matters.

You have always insisted that the arts have a higher purpose than entertainment. How would you elucidate this higher purpose?

To kindle light in the darkness, as Jung described the sole purpose of human existence. The arts must serve as a mediation, the channel by which a vision of – call it what one will – is given substance. Shakespeare said: 'The poet's eye, in a fine frenzy rolling,/Doth glance from heaven to earth, from earth to heaven;/And, as imagination bodies forth/The forms of things unknown, the poet's pen/Turns them to shapes, and gives to airy nothing/A local habitation and a name.' The arts give form and sometimes form so wonderful, especially when one thinks of Beethoven or Schubert or the other great composers. Music always seems to me the greatest miracle of all because it contains meaning without the intervention of words; it is almost pure meaning, it creates the thing it is about. It lifts one, takes one to paradise, it is an enchantment.

If you postulate a higher purpose, isn't there a danger that the arts will be put beyond the reach of ordinary people whose lives might otherwise be enriched by them?

Of course not. Beauty is very simple. Difficult art usually has something badly wrong with it. Anyone can understand beauty, though not perhaps at once. In Scotland, for example, poetry is for everybody, it's not for a cultured élite. I think you still have in Ireland the traces of unity of culture, although when Yeats wrote his introductions to Rabindranath Tagore, he said, 'I envy him because he has what I have always longed for, a culture in which rich and poor participate equally.'

Iris Murdoch is regarded by many as a supremely good and serious writer, combining the bite of the philosopher with the vision of the mystic, and so it comes as rather a shock when you dismiss her as 'a mere journalist'. Doesn't this suggest a kind of intellectual élitism?

No. *She* is the élitist, she follows all the trendy things. For God's sake, how much does she read the real philosophers? How much does she read the Bible, the Ghita, the Sufis? What she calls philosophy is a sort of rock-pool phenomenon in Oxford, people like Isaiah Berlin and I don't know who; one has never heard of them outside Oxford. She absolutely embodies all the sort of phoney values of our culture. I'm sorry, but I cannot accept that Irish Murdoch is an important thinker. She has no sense of wisdom.

When you were sixty-four you thought you only had a year or two to live because you had heard a voice telling you so, and you believed it to be true. Have you grown to mistrust the voice which speaks to you?

It hasn't said anything recently. I take each day as it comes and wake up with some surprise, thinking here I still am, so I'd better get up and get on with it and not waste time. And when one is old time is one thing that becomes very precious.

Kathleen Raine

About ten years ago you embarked on a crusade to restore the arts to what you consider to be their proper place in society. How did it come about that this place was lost, do you think?

The secular values which have gradually overtaken the West have virtually destroyed the civilization which once seemed so highly successful. In the industrial revolution, we produced such wonderful things and we had an empire, and we thought we were absolutely top of the world, and now we see that it's come full circle and is self-destructive in the end. It's destroying the very humanity which it should nourish. Man's intellectual vainglory has resulted in a loss of the divine vision. I don't want to dismiss science, and there are plenty of brilliant scientists now, particularly in physics, but they are only describing certain phenomena within the realm of nature. Although the exploration, the mapping of the natural world by the scientists is not a thing to be scorned at all, I do think that the attempt to explain the world in materialist terms results in the loss of knowledge of the mental world, which has been the source of human wisdom in all other human civilizations. It has been the world of the human mind and the cosmos that the thinkers have explored; it's been the mystery of human consciousness that has exercised the minds of the wise. Nature had to be explored too, but as a part within the whole, and the world that has built itself up on a supposition that the material universe is the whole of reality is fatally flawed.

I understand Prince Charles regards you as something of a soul mate. Some people may feel a certain ambivalence about that designation. Do you?

When I saw him, I thought, that poor young man, anything I can do for him I will do because he is very lonely. He himself has a vision; he uses words like sacred and hope and vision and he believes in these things, and I think he's determined to stick it out in the awful situation to which he's been born – most unenviable, you must admit. He's trying to do something, and if I can help I will. I really came to know him through Laurens van der Post who has always supported the prince. A soul mate? Well, I'm an old woman and he's a young man, and I just feel . . . what shall I say . . . protective.

Kathleen Raine

You described the time after the war as 'sad shelterless years'. What did you mean by that, and from what were you seeking shelter?

I had no man in my life, I was alone, trying to struggle to make ends meet and quite incapable of bringing myself to do an ordinary job. What madness to think one can live by writing poetry and doing scholarship! I wasn't even at a university doing scholarship, because I was in rebellion against that too, so I was on my own trying to bring up two children. It was all very difficult.

When you met Gavin Maxwell in the 1950s, did you feel that at last you had found someone to share your vision of life?

What we shared was a vision of nature, where we were born, the country we loved. It wasn't the vision I'm speaking of now, it wasn't the human vision we shared.

Despite his homosexuality, you fell in love with him. Did you really believe that you could transcend the physical and have a truly Platonic love?

Yes, I truly did, and how wrong I was. But I truly did believe that.

Did you in your heart disapprove of his homosexuality?

Oh yes. In my heart of hearts.

You describe how you spent a night together only once, and that although there was no sexual encounter, you felt bound to him as if in marriage. You write: 'Every night of my life since then I have spent alone.' Was this something you resolved upon or was it the way things turned out?

Oh, it was the way things turned out. Curiously enough, only today someone sent me a letter I'd written to Gavin, in which I had said, 'I don't think a sexual relationship was at all what it was about ... I felt that you were more than a brother, something closer than that.' He didn't particularly attract me sexually, it was somehow deeper than that. I don't know why one loves certain people. Maybe the fact that he was homosexual made it possible for me to love him, because it left one free; in a normal relationship with a man, the man wants to be close and possess one, but with this distance it was ... oh ... what a mystery it all is! But it didn't work out, because to a woman a homosexual man is an angelic figure with no sex; but in fact the homosexual man has his own dark sexual world, which I refused to see, or in so far as I did see it I disapproved of it in my heart.

Eventually in your despair you uttered your curse over the rowan tree: 'Let Gavin suffer as I am suffering.' It was a curse that was to take terrible effect. Was there ever any doubt in your mind that you were responsible for the tragedies in Gavin's life?

Perhaps I was ... I don't know ... but then, one human being cannot take responsibility for another's destiny. I was the stronger character, I felt that he was a little brother, not a big brother, and that was a terrible thing to do to one's brother. But I didn't mean it as a curse. I wanted him to suffer but I didn't mean it to harm him. I meant ... oh for heaven's sake, can't you see?

You couldn't accept forgiveness for what you had done?

No. It seems to me forgiveness can't undo what one has done. Remorse, yes, but how can one forgive? What is done is done.

You still carry that burden to this day?

Probably. But that's not the worst thing I've done. I carry worse burdens than that ... my parents and my children. Yes, I have gathered some terrible burdens of guilt, but I have to do what I have to do in spite of them, and never mind the guilt.

I have the impression from your book that the discovery that Gavin had after all not loved you was the hardest thing of all to bear. Am I right?

Kathleen Raine

Yes. It just didn't seem credible. Yes, that was absolutely shattering. But I wonder if it was true; deep down I still don't believe it, because not loving is a negation and at heart all human beings love. Love is the deepest thing in any relationship really; it is the holy spirit that runs through our whole race, and therefore there is only finally love.

Gavin was later to accuse you of destroying all those who had been close to you, your parents, your children, your husband, and himself, all the people you had loved. It was a judgement which you did not question. How was it possible to bear such a burden and come to terms with it?

It wasn't. It wasn't possible.

When Gavin died, you laid on his grave a bunch of rowan berries from the tree. Was that an act of atonement? Or of love? Or grief?

I suppose it was grief.

Edward Muir said that no one knows the whole fable, only parts of it. Do you feel you know more than most?

Given my own part in the epic, I feel I've played it out, and I wouldn't say I understand it, for it's been a very strange one, but it has been increasingly significant. Curiously enough, it's only since what one might call the end of my own story that life has begun to make sense. I'm completely fearless, because when one has nothing to gain or lose, one can be truthful and one can be fearless. Also it can be very enjoyable to sit back and watch the lovely comedy. It really is a marvellous soap opera. A lot of people love me... I can't think why... not my children, but that's understandable. I have played some part in the epic, it may not be a major part, but it's quite a significant one, and I don't just mean Prince Charles. The High Commissioner for India, for example, said recently that I am also loved in his country because I have done more than most people in making a bridge between Indian and English culture.

Jung wrote near the end of his life: 'A creative person has little power over his own life. He is not free. He is captive and driven by his daimon.' Has that been your own experience?

Yes. I'm afraid so. But now I feel free both from daimons and from my own life and everything else. In a curious way I know what to do. I don't think it's to do with old age, because some people never grow up. It's more to do with having lived out one's life, and having been shattered in a thousand splinters. Suffering teaches us a great deal about life, but I am bound to say, and this is the bitterest wisdom of all, so do one's own shortcomings. You wouldn't learn much by doing everything right, and keeping all the rules and never putting a foot wrong. I was so driven by my own daimon that I failed to give my love to those to whom it should have been given . . . parents, children, husbands . . . everybody . . . I simply ruthlessly swept through life looking neither to right nor left; I just did what I felt had to be done, and it was usually disastrous.

Do you ever reflect on death?

I find it very hard to concentrate on death. In theory of course I'm perfectly aware that the length of my days cannot be very great now, but one is so used to being here and waking up in the morning that's it's very difficult to fix one's mind on death. And I don't want to fool myself with all kinds of theories about death because belief is neither here nor there, it's only what we know that counts, and I do not know.

How would you like people to remember you?

I'd much rather they didn't, much rather. But if they do, I should like Blake's words to be said of me, that in time of trouble I kept the divine vision.

DAME CICELY SAUNDERS

DAME CICELY SAUNDERS

Cicely Saunders was born in 1918 and educated at Roedean and St Anne's College, Oxford where she read politics, philosophy and economics. During the war she trained at St Thomas's Hospital taking her BA in 1945 and MA in 1958. After working as a medical social worker she took her MB and after junior hospital appointments at St Thomas's and the Royal Waterloo Hospital, she moved to St Mary's to take up a clinical research fellowship. She is the English founder of the modern hospice movement and was medical director of St Christopher's Hospice in London from when it opened in 1967 until the mid-1980s. She has received many awards for her pioneering work including the Templeton Prize (1981) and the BMA gold medal (1987). Her publications include *The Management of Terminal Disease* (1978), *The Living Idea* (1981) and *Living with Dying* (1983). She was awarded the OBE in 1967.

Dame Cicely Saunders

You have tended to describe your childhood as unhappy. Was the unhappiness a feeling which consciously registered at the time or was it something you became aware of in retrospect, as it were?

I certainly knew that I was unhappy at school, and that was fairly early. I was then sent to boarding school at the age of ten, and I knew that I was not happy there. My unhappiness at home was very much a feeling that at the beginning of the holidays everything I did was right and at the end of the holidays everything I did was wrong, and I didn't quite know why. On the other hand my parents both tried in their very different ways to help but found it difficult to do so, and part of the problem was that they weren't getting on with each other.

Your father was very ambitious for you. Was that a mixed blessing?

No. I'm very glad he was, because if you have a discontent with the way things are you can either retreat or go on to attack life, and his influence had the second effect. I was determined to do something with life, though I didn't know what, and although I didn't like the difficulties at the time, I'm very glad it all happened the way it did because nothing has been wasted. An understanding of what if felt like to be unpopular and rejected was very important in the work I did later.

You didn't like Roedean. Do you think that if things had been happier at home you might have been less miserable at school?

I might have found it easier to make friends. At home I was made to feel I was difficult, and that did not help me make relationships easily which is what counts at school. But I came through and I finished up head of the house.

Do you think Roedean and Oxford prepared you well for the life that lay ahead?

My housemistress at Roedean, who went on to run a girls' borstal, and my very special tutor at Oxford, Miss Butler, with her tremendous social consciousness and her delightful humour, were both a very great influence

263

on me. Anybody who met those two had touched absolute pure gold, and to have known them was enormously important and beneficial. The other thing about Oxford is that it made me work and sharpened my ability to think.

Your parents' marriage was not a success. Opinions are very divided on the question of whether parents ought to stay together for the sake of the children. Given your own experience, where do you stand on that issue?

I think parents should stay together but they should be more honest about what they are finding difficult and not try to hide it. To think of involving the children would often help. Children find divorce so harmful because they feel that somehow it is their fault, and to experience failure at a young age is a very difficult thing in life. When my parents actually separated I was torn between the two. I was very much on my father's side since I found my mother extremely difficult but I also felt a degree of responsibility for her. It was all extremely difficult, but it's a very long time ago now and the wounds have healed.

What was it that triggered your conversion to Christianity . . . was it a reaction against an atheistic upbringing perhaps?

I had been searching for a real Christian meaning for several years and had been reading Archbishop Temple, Dorothy Sayers, C.S. Lewis, so I had come quite a way with the head. It was only when my parents finally separated, however, and I felt to a degree responsible for it, that I really reached the end of what I thought I could cope with. The trigger was essentially a sense of need. I also met some people who were much more straightforward about becoming Christians than any I'd met before, and although that is a version of Christianity that I have left behind, at the time it was simple and accompanied by a degree of mystical experience. I felt an absolute assurance that I had been turned around and told that all the work had been done and I only had to accept; and that instead of having the wind in my face I had it behind my back.

Your earliest participation in the Church was evangelical – prayer meetings, Bible study and so on. How do you look back on that period?

Does it seem now to have been a rather immature approach to religion, or a substitute for something missing in your life perhaps?

No, it was a good start. That way of taking a fairly cut-and-dried approach to religion is perhaps not very adult, but it suited me at the time since in many ways I probably wasn't mature. I'm very glad I started that way, because to know the Bible well and to have it as a resource for the rest of your life is worth an enormous amount. I owe the people who helped me at that point a very great deal, but I had to move from the feeling that this was the *only* way into seeing a much broader perspective. That took quite a long time, but it happened from quite a solid foundation.

You founded St Christopher's in 1967 – only twenty-five years ago – and yet the hospice movement is now almost universally accepted. Do you think it was an idea waiting to happen?

Yes. I don't think there are too many original ideas in the world, but what happens perhaps is that you respond to a need. I had done a lot of travelling, an enormous amount of reading, I had listened to a great many patients and what emerged was the need for pain control, for the whole breadth of pain – in body, mind, spirit and family – the need for home care, the need for solid research, for education. All these came in different ways, and it was like putting them into the kaleidoscope, giving it a shake, and watching the new pattern take shape in the form of modern research and the whole hospice idea. In general ideas find people, rather than people finding ideas; you just have to have your antennae up.

It's only comparatively recently that we have focused our attention to any degree on the process of dying, the care of the patient and members of the family. Before the hospice movement people were simply expected to cope and on the whole one assumes that they did . . . or didn't they?

There was a great deal of isolation, suffering and distress. One effect of medical advances was that there was a concentration on cure, and symptoms were seen only as signposts along the road to a diagnosis which then might make cure possible. To deal simply with the signposts was considered to be very second-class medicine, but we now recognize that the need for control of symptoms, while the search for a basic cure proceeds, is very important. We have to concentrate on the old principles of care and caring, not in the sense of 'tender loving care', but in the sense of efficient, competent, but still concerned and loving care. It is not merely nursing; it involves a whole team – doctors, social workers, chaplains, therapists, all working together to enable patients to live as fully as they can until they die. We're not just about peaceful dying; we're about living until you die, completing your life, relating with your family, family living on afterwards. Living as well as dying.

It was your experience with a dying patient after the war – the first man you loved – that made you determined to start St Christopher's. Did you interpret this as God moving in mysterious ways?

I did at the time, yes, and I still do. It was very much a feeling that this was what was meant, but not in a way that I could sit back and let it happen, but by working as hard as possible.

Falling in love with a dying man must be very traumatic, because you know from the start that death will interrupt the normal process of consummation . . .

I don't think we're very free about falling in love. I agree with Christopher Fry who says at the end of his play *The Dark is Light Enough*, 'we're elected into love'. It is something which happens, and the fascinating thing is that you still feel in a sense that it is one of the freest acts. (This is a very interesting comment on the idea of free will and the love of God, but that's another matter.) I loved him, David he was called. It was very short, very simple, and I remember him with great fondness. He completely altered the course of my life, which was a wonderful thing to happen from one man alone. He gave us the whole hospice movement, and the phrase, 'I'll be a window in your home'. His was a commitment to openness, a commitment to everything we could bring together from the mind with the friendship of the heart. When he very quietly and privately returned to the faith of his forefathers – he was Jewish – without ever seeing a rabbi, he left me with the assurance that he'd found his own way, and that everybody in my care would in turn find theirs. In spite of the fact that at that point I was a fairly evangelical Christian, I came to understand that patients must think in their own way as deeply as they can, and it matters not if it is different from my way. All that comes from David.

But to fall in love with a man who is dying is almost like a fusion of hope and despair . . .

No . . . it didn't feel like that at the time. There wasn't really an alternative; it just happened. It was much the same when I fell in love with the second Polish man years later. It was the most intense and liberating experience. I was profoundly sad afterwards, but I wouldn't have missed it.

After the death of the second man you loved there followed a period of what you describe as 'pathological grieving'. How did you eventually come to terms with that?

By an absolute assurance of his happiness – because I do believe in a life beyond this one – and my own gratefulness for what I had learned. And of course I met my third Pole in due course, and although we had to wait a very long time before we could marry, he is now nearly ninety-two and we've been enormously happy together.

But tell me, why do you always fall in love with Poles?

I haven't the faintest idea. I have really no answer other than to say that is what happened.

You have said you believe in an afterlife. Does that mean you expect to meet those you have loved after you die?

I hope so.

You expect to meet all three men?

That would not present a problem for me.

Dame Cicely Saunders

Do you now feel immune from the grieving process, or have you simply learned to manage it better?

I'm quite frightened of how I will miss my husband. He is pretty frail and I have a certain amount of anxiety as to whether he will get through this winter. I know I shall miss him and grieve for him terribly. But I am a more fulfilled person now because of being with him, and therefore I have a better chance of handling it. I have also learned to express grief and accept help, so although I don't anticipate that it will be anything other than devastating, I shall survive.

The phrase 'helping people to die', suffers from a dangerous ambiguity. Hospice work involves control of pain by administering drugs, easing the path to inevitable death without actually promoting it. Isn't the dividing line sometimes very thin?

It depends on how you start your definition. Instead of helping people to die, I prefer to say helping people to live until they die. We concentrate on the quality of life left to them, and that may be weeks or months; we're not here just for the last few days. There are many patients who come here and are discharged again; people tend to think there's only one way out of a hospice, but it's not true. People go out for weekends, they go out for holidays, they sometimes go out for good. The sooner you are in touch with a hospice, the more quality of life you will have, and with some people the whole trend changes and they have longer than they ever believed possible. We once had a girl of seventeen who was transferred to us from another hospital, and she lived eleven years, and although that is a rare occurrence, people living months longer than expected is not at all unusual. Living better, even for a short time, may make an enormous difference to the way they feel about themselves; it also helps their families find the strength they hardly realized they had, and the ability to carry on afterwards.

Nowadays ethical dilemmas present themselves on an ever-increasing scale. How best are these resolved – by government committees, by the Church, by philosophers . . .?

They are certainly not best resolved by having a private member's bill through Parliament because that tends to produce a very emotive debate and the major issues are simply not addressed. The commission would have to include the Church, philosophers, the medical and legal professions, but the selection of people for the commission has to be given the most careful consideration, because it is easy to rig the results by selecting certain people. What is required is a debate of rather better quality than we usually have in the media where easy answers are aired, such as the suggestion that patients should be able to ask a doctor to end their lives if they feel their suffering is intolerable, without any consideration of the pressures on the rest of the community. This is a very unsatisfactory way of tackling these complex issues, but that's what tends to happen at the moment. In the recent case of the doctor who gave a lethal injection to his patient there was no evidence that he had consulted experts in the field of terminal pain. You don't have to kill the patient to kill the pain, even in those circumstances, and I think there could have been another way out. It has made the public very afraid, and fear does not produce good laws. For example, whatever we may think about abortion, there is no doubt that when David Steele brought in his bill he did not intend there to be abortion on demand, but that is what has happened. I am not anti-abortion in the way that a lot of pro-life people are – I think it is unfortunate but understandable. But what we don't have is an adequate support system for the children who come forward for abortion. Similarly, we have to provide proper help and support for those who are dying. If we simply pass a law saying it is all right for physicians to assist suicide, to promote the right to a quick way out, it would have the same effect as the abortion bill. And there's no way of pulling back once the floodgates are opened.

In one of your books you set out your views on euthanasia, quoting the Church's position: 'In order to permit euthanasia it would be necessary to show that a change would remove greater evils than it would cause.' How can you be certain that these 'greater evils' would follow?

In a sense, I can't be certain, but neither can Ludovic Kennedy be certain that they won't follow. There is some evidence in the Netherlands, a country which is tremendously pro-euthanasia, that elderly people feel a degree of pressure, and although the doctors reported to the *Lancet* giving the impression that everything was well in the Netherlands, they also pointed out that the guidelines are often not applied, and that patients are reported as having died a natural death when they haven't. There was also a study showing that a great many elderly people were very concerned about what was going to happen to them.

But the fact that something is open to abuse has never been a sufficient reason for banning it altogether – drinking alcohol, sex, etc. Why shouldn't we grant a terminally-ill patient his wish to die sooner rather than later?

It would pull the rug from under a whole lot of vulnerable people, and as was said in the House of Lords when Baroness Wootton's bill was discussed, the right to die could all too soon become a duty to die. I don't believe ours is a society in which that would not happen. People don't awfully like the old, they don't like looking after dependants, they don't like thinking that somebody is in pain, they find it unpleasant and disagreeable. To cut it all short seems like the answer, but I take Churchill's view: people who have simple answers to complicated problems are usually wrong.

Is it ever a greater evil not to allow a person his wish to die?

You have to be very careful and tease out what that person is saying. If he is saying, let me die, he is usually actually saying don't do every last treatment to prolong my life, and if you reassure him that you will not do that, that you will help him with his individual needs, that you will not abandon him, he will usually stop saying, let me die. When people say that it is usually as a result of unrelieved pain and poor communication, both of which we can do something about. There are very few who actually say, kill me, and mean it. It is mostly people who are perfectly fit and healthy who say they would not want to be kept alive with Alzheimer's Disease, or to be in a state of dependence on others. But if you have good friends, if people are good neighbours, if you have competent care, dependence can have good qualities. I remember a long time ago a young man with progressive paralysis looking at another patient, and saying that if his illness ever deteriorated to the same extent, he would want to take his own life. But when he did get to that stage he felt quite differently about it, and I remember him saying to me, 'I can't see round the next bend but I know it will be all right.' The situation can seem very different once you're in it.

This is not to deny that we have lonely people, people with unrelieved pain and inappropriate treatment, unsatisfactory nursing homes and shortage of money, but if people go on wanting to die, it is society's failure.

Have you a clearly developed view of what happens to us after death?

No, I don't think anybody could have. It remains a mystery. But I have seen many people whose spirits have become stronger as their bodies have become weaker, people who at the very end of their lives meet you at a depth which is quite difficult and frightening for those of us who are well to reach. I believe that the essential inner spirit of man survives. Why should the mind and spirit leave no trace? Even in life we have glimpses of mystery. For example, I happen to love singing in the midst of a good choir, it's the most wonderful feeling; it matters what you do and yet you are unimportant. Some things are beyond ordinary understanding but none the less real.

St Christopher's is a religious foundation but religious faith is not compulsory for those who work or are treated there. How in practice do patients respond to St Christopher's?

They find it a good place, a welcoming place, a place without pressure. There are very simple prayers morning and evening in the ward but you don't have to listen. There is chapel, but you certainly don't have to go. Many of our staff don't have that sort of commitment because what we are concerned with is the whole spiritual side of life which is much wider than the strictly religious. We are very conscious of the contribution of people of many faiths or none. Those who come to us are often searching for answers. What has my life meant? Those who are able to say, as someone said not long ago, 'I feel as if I'm a person again', are reaching the stage in which they will perhaps be able to come to terms with their situation. If they can do that, if they can find some sort of meaning in life and it makes it easier for them to lay that life down, then we would be very happy for them. But that is said in spiritual rather than religious terms. If people choose never to say anything, that's their freedom. We do a great deal of listening, but we don't do any converting as such.

Dame Cicely Saunders

How do you steer a path between the certainty of faith and the flexibility of tolerance?

By concern for people which rings through both the Old and the New Testaments, and which I believe is found in all religions. There is certainly a great deal to learn from other faiths. What convinces and enables me is not necessarily the same as convinces and enables somebody else, and that's a position I am comfortable with. I am not comfortable with people who think there's only one way.

You once said you were certain about what you consider to be 'a good death'. Can you enlarge on that?

I don't remember saying I was very certain, and if I did I was probably wrong. It has to be the death that is good for that person. There isn't just one, there is one for every individual.

Is it part of your experience that those with faith meet a more peaceful end than those without?

It depends what sort of faith they have. If it is a faith that God will not let bad things happen, that doesn't last very long. But if it is a faith which includes the possibility of bad things happening with the notion that God will see you through, then that can be a great support. It's also very much a question of people's personalities and of what's happened to them in life. You cannot make it a cut-and-dried matter. Anybody who makes dogmatic statements about those with faith dying well are on dangerous ground. It's an area where it is as well not to be dogmatic, but there are certainly people who make something completely creative out of dying, and in my experience those have usually been people who have had a mature tested faith throughout their lives.

Part of the hospice philosophy is to tell the truth to patients about their illness. What happens to those who are quite unwilling or unable to face the truth?

We don't tell people who don't ask. The hospice philosophy is not that people must know, but that we must answer whatever questions are put to us. Most people do know inside themselves but they may not necessarily want to share it, so we have to wait.

Britain is becoming increasingly secular. Isn't there a problem that the sort of ethos within which the hospice movement is contained is simply not available to a large number of people?

There are several secular hospices, there are lots of secular people working in hospices. We're not all religious by any manner of means; what we share is a concern for people. Many of us do have a religious motivation in our concern, but we are not here as a religious enclave into which people have to fit. This is an image which tends to be put upon us rather than the other way round. In my experience there are a great many people in this country who have a large unformed faith – we are not quite such an irreligious society as is commonly supposed. Those who work for us do not necessarily have to have a vocation as is sometimes thought; what they do have is a concern for others and a longing to help people do well at the end of their lives. A great many of our staff are here for only a couple of years before moving on, but they will take a lot of what they have learned about people into other fields, and that is very important.

Have you ever come across hospice workers who are not as kind to patients as you would like them to be?

Once or twice staff have been short with patients, and we have had to understand that they are under a lot of stress, and have given them counselling or extra time off, but generally people who are likely to be unkind don't come into hospice work. This is sadly not always true in some nursing homes – old people can be terribly maddening, and almost ask to be bullied, and there are people who just don't resist the temptation. Hospices, like the people who work in them, are not perfect, and sadly we have pilfering here in just the same way as in every hospital in the country, but on the whole the ethos is of kindness and concern and those qualities do gather in the right group of people. Everybody is taken on a trial basis for three months and you can usually sort out those who are unsuitable at that stage, but they are very few.

Dame Cicely Saunders

Some years ago you wrote in one of your books: 'We have reached a place in hospice work where there are a lot of inbred beliefs that have become sacred cows. The most constructive thing I could do to improve hospice work would be to conduct a sacred cow shoot.' What lay behind that remark, and did you ever conduct your shoot?

That goes back to a conference in the Royal Society of Medicine when people were talking in a rather unrealistic way about hospice work. I'm afraid I was speaking as something of a sacred cow myself at that time, but what I had in mind were the rather idealized notions such as everybody must have faith, everybody must have a good death, everybody must be peaceful and smiling all the time, nobody must show anger, and all the staff must be perfect and never lose their tempers. It was also the idea that such and such a drug was always the perfect answer. Did I ever conduct my shoot? Well, a great deal has happened in St Christopher's over the years, and we continue to ask questions, which is as it should be. I would much prefer that we should be referred to not as a centre of excellence but a centre of enquiry.

You are reported to have said in anger on one occasion, 'I'm not a cult figure.' What prompted the remark and what occasioned the anger?

Americans have a tendency to make cult figures out of people like me which is why I feel very fortunate that I didn't work in America. The remark was occasioned by somebody in America coming up to me and asking, almost literally, 'Can I touch you?' So I said, 'I bite.'

Your biographer describes your relationships with the first two men you loved as 'unconsummated, unfulfilled, unresolved' and yet you have not been inclined to offer your thoughts on these obviously profound relationships. Is that because you dare not, or does it come from an urge to be private?

An urge to be private. The relationships belong to them as well as to me.

You finally married in your fifties. Did marriage alter the order of priorities in your life?

Yes. My husband's priority was to his art, and mine was to St Christopher's, and it took us a certain amount of time to sort out our priorities to each other. At first when he was fit enough he had and he needed his independence, and I had a degree of freedom, even to travel to America once or twice, but once he became less well and had to give up his London studio he became my top priority. My work as medical director at St Christopher's was handed over to Dr West and I assumed more the role of elder statesman. My husband is still committed to his art, and I am still committed to St Christopher's, but he takes priority. I have many invitations to go and give talks but I refuse because I won't leave him. He's now very frail and dependent on me.

Does he still paint?

Yes, he is still doing portraits. His eyes and his hands are still as good as ever, and his portraits are some of the best he's ever done.

You often said that you felt a great need to be married. Why was that, do you think?

I think most people do. I don't think there's anything peculiar about that.

Did you ever want children?

Not so much as to be married. The work took over that need, but the need for companionship and, well, love, was much stronger than the need to have a family. I've been completely fulfilled in the work that I've done, and I'm very glad I waited to be married to Marian. He's worth everything.

Many people commented that you became a much happier person after marriage. Were you conscious of a sadness before that time?

I was conscious of a loneliness, yes.

Dame Cicely Saunders

Those who maintain that we do not fall in love by accident, might suggest that in your life love and death are inextricably linked – or is that too Freudian an analysis?

A bit, yes. Maybe it was with the first two, but after all Marian is now nearly ninety-two and it's living together, not dying together, that's been important. The fact that I did fall in love with people who were dying gave an emphasis to how important people are at this time in their lives, and although I would never have consciously chosen it, I think it gave an impetus which wouldn't otherwise have been there.

Do you view your own death with equanimity?

If I thought I was going to die before my husband I would be in a great state, because he is so dependent on me. Dying with unfulfilled responsibilities – something I have witnessed many times among many patients – is a very difficult thing to do. Dying when your responsibilities are fulfilled is easier, just as a full life is easier to leave than an empty one – feeling that you have made no impact on the world and that nobody is going to miss you is terrible. As far as my own death is concerned, I don't know if I have complete confidence in myself, but I certainly have confidence in the people around me and I do hold on to a certainty that God is there, and that I wouldn't ever be alone since He who Himself died shares the dying of all his children.

Because of the area in which you work, there is a temptation to see you as a latter-day Florence Nightingale figure, but in order to achieve what you have achieved you must have had to be very tough, perhaps even hard-headed?

You certainly have to be very determined and single-minded, and that can mean being tough with some of the people along the way. Patients matter more than anything and if you expect other people to work as hard as you do they may find that a bit much.

You have been described as a very forthright character. Some who have worked with you have even described you as autocratic and imperious. Do you think there is any truth in that?

I think there might have been in the past, but not now. A pioneer is apt to be that way, but there comes a time when you have to hand over. But in fact I was always able to delegate. For example, the sister and the doctor who developed our home care were given a completely free hand. That was in 1969, so even in my more dogmatic times I could still delegate, but I've certainly mellowed since then. After all, as things become established and more secure, you don't have to fight so hard.

How has the hospice movement faced up to the challenge of patients dying from Aids?

When we started there was a tendency for the Department of Health to look at the situation in very simplistic terms: Aids patients die, hospices look after dying patients, therefore hospices will look after Aids patients. We had to remind them that our cancer patients weren't going to disappear, and that we did not necessarily have the expertise to deal with Aids patients. Special centres were then set up – the London Lighthouse, the Mildmay Mission – and we learned from them. Once we established that there was something we could offer, we made ourselves available as did other hospices. At the same time I don't think you can expect hospices to take on everything. It was only because we focused on patients with cancer and motor neuron disease that we were able to do soundly based research and make an impact in the field of medicine. If we hadn't done that, if we'd said instead that we would take in everybody who was dying, we would never have been taken seriously, we would never have been able to speak from a position of strength.

In 1987 you said, 'We are worried that we will have to displace cancer patients if we take Aids sufferers . . . units such as St Christopher's were pledged to offer places only to cancer patients.'

We were pledged to give mainly to cancer patients with a limited number of longer-stay patients, but there is an escalating demand on our home care and our beds, very much greater than it was five years ago, and we haven't worked ourselves out of a job yet. We simply don't have the resources to take on a new job, but we are now working more and more in the community where a lot of people with Aids will want to be, and so we may become more involved. Don't forget that a great deal of the money given to us to build and to carry on the hospice movement is given in memory of patients who have died of cancer, so we do have a commitment, though not an exclusive commitment.

Weren't you worried that such a statement might be misinterpreted?

No, because you don't expect everybody to do everything. You don't expect an orthopaedic centre suddenly to take in patients with Aids, or a renal dialysis centre to take in patients with broken limbs in a time of frost. People have their own commitments, and that is a perfectly reasonable state of affairs.

I think I'm right in saying that the hospice movement was criticized by the Royal College of Nursing which claimed that hospices were refusing to treat Aids patients for fear of losing private donations.

That was an article in *The Times* based on a report from one member of the Royal College of Nursing. I don't think we need take that particularly seriously. That was in isolation.

How do those who work constantly with the terminally ill cope with the immense burden of death?

By working together as a team and by being aware of their achievements. It is draining, but it is not depressing. When you see patients and their families come in with pain and conflict all over their faces, and then within two or three weeks you see a resolution, that is a very rewarding experience. To be able to take away pain and to help a family find their own strengths, and to know you have made a difference, all that is deeply satisfying. And of course many of our people have a Christian belief that death is not the end, and that not only do we not have to worry about patients after they die, but they've set out on a good journey.

Few people can have been so involved with death and dying as you. Has it taken its toll, do you think?

You would perhaps have to ask other people. It may have taken a toll, but it has also opened up exciting possibilities. It has made me move from a traditional, perhaps rather limited, faith into an exploration of meaning. I feel I am learning all the time.

Don't you think it a cruel paradox that so much should be invested in the death of one person when death occurs across the globe often on a massive scale because of starvation, war and so on?

Concentration on a limited number of people has over and over again been shown to tease out general principles which can then be applied across the board. You can be overwhelmed by death on a global scale, but when you are committed to a small area, you can then examine how it can be made relevant on a wider scale. The hospice movement spans sixty countries, including places like Swaziland where there is major trouble but where the attitude of caring for people who are dying in the community still obtains. That would not have been possible if the pioneers of hospices in this country had not laid very sure foundations; and to do that you have to concentrate.

The hospice movement promotes 'death with dignity'. Can you sum up for me what you understand by that phrase? Do you think it means the same to all people?

I wouldn't agree that that's our major commitment. The hospice movement is committed to living until you die. Death with dignity means different things to different people; it has come to mean direct euthanasia to some people, switching off machines to others, or simply good palliative care. It is therefore a fairly unhelpful term. I would much prefer to say 'dying with a sense of personal worth'. That's what hospice is about.

You have often described death as an 'outrage', and indeed you must have seen its terrible effects countless times. Do you ever have difficulty in reconciling a particularly harrowing or poignant death with the idea of a benevolent and merciful God?

When I describe death as an outrage I am thinking in particular of the way in which we spend all our lives learning to love, and death is about parting from those we love; that is the really outrageous thing about it. But I also think a loving and merciful God gave away an enormous amount of what one might see as omnipotent power in making a free world, and therefore a flexible and dangerous world in which men and women can use their freedom wrongly. I certainly don't think that God picks out people for this and that disaster; but I am certain that he always shares it. God is within his creation in a way which means that he suffers where we suffer, and that is a burden beyond anything we can possibly imagine.

But do you think without faith you would have been able to do the job as well as you have done it?

I know there are some people who do an excellent job in this field without faith. I personally couldn't.

Does death still seem awesome and mysterious to you? Does it hold any terrors?

If you don't feel a measure of awe and fear, then I think you're not looking very clearly. But you have to go out into the darkness and put your hand into the hand of God. That is a very anthropomorphic way of talking about God, but I still think it's a helpful phrase.

A life devoted to death is by any standards an unusual life and one which is likely to remain mysterious and paradoxical to most observers. Is it something you understand fully yourself?

It all seemed very clear at the time. I asked what I should do. I believed I was told what I should do, and I got on and did it. It was as simple as that.

If you were to turn the clock back, would you have done things differently?

You can always look back and think of mistakes . . . you can wish you had been kinder, or more understanding, or learned something more quickly.

But I'm very grateful to have been able to do the things I have done. And I wouldn't want to start all over again, I must confess. I feel much too tired.

Is there anything left that you feel you have to do?

I want to tidy up all the archives. But first I want to see my husband safely away, not in the sense of wishing him away, but wanting him to go peacefully and happily. My prayer is for him to be able to die quietly at home with me.

You have obviously been very happy with your husband. Do you love him as much now as when you first met him?

Oh, infinitely more. This is one of the very exciting things in life: you feel that it's as good as it can be, and then come the next few days and it's better still. It's been a wonderful mature growing together. He has an enormous regard for me and thinks I'm splendid. With his pupils he was always a little inclined to regard all his geese as swans. And so with me. I am his swan, and that's a very nice thing to be, especially when I spent a large part of my early life thinking I was rather an ugly duckling.

LADY SOAMES

LADY SOAMES

Mary Soames, youngest daughter of Sir Winston Churchill, was born in 1922 and spent most of her childhood at Chartwell where she was educated privately. From 1939–41 she served with the Red Cross and WVS and later in the ATS with mixed anti-aircraft batteries. She also travelled with her father on several war-time journeys. In 1947 she married Christopher Soames and campaigned with him through six elections between 1950 and 1966 when he was Conservative MP for Bedford. In 1968 she accompanied him to Paris where he was ambassador for four years and in 1979 to Rhodesia where he was the last British governor. Her publications include *The Profligate Duke* (1987) and *Winston Churchill: His Life as Painter* (1990). Her biography of her mother *Clementine Churchill* (1982) won the Wolfson Prize for History and the *Yorkshire Post* Prize for Best First Work.

Lady Soames

When writing about your childhood you say that although elements of anxiety, sorrow and disappointment began to appear as the years went by, in your own recollection it is the happiness which predominates. Is that in effect a tribute to your parents who helped shield you from the darker side of life?

I wrote those lines after describing life at Chartwell and the wonderful Christmases we had there. As life went on and I became a teenager I began to know that life wasn't a garden of Eden, and it was disquieting to me because of my idyllic childhood at Chartwell. The first time I saw my mother cry was one of the most traumatic moments of my young life. I had very rarely seen grown-ups cry and to see this beautiful woman whom I loved and admired, and also rather feared, weeping and completely disintegrated with grief was a terrible shock to me. I saw my parents a lot because we children were never kept away in the nursery wing, and also I was very much the Benjamin, so I strayed around all over the house and never felt I was excluded from my parents' life when they were at Chartwell. I went to day school; I was never sent away to boarding school, and those parts of my life that my mother didn't take personal part in she organized with perfection. I also had the most wonderful duenna figure in my life, a first cousin of my mother's who came when I was a baby to look after me and stayed right through until I went away to the war; and so when my parents were absent I still had a wonderfully secure life. I adored Chartwell, believing then that it was a very large house and a beautiful house; of course now I see that it isn't a very large house and it certainly isn't a beautiful one, but I do look back at my childhood as bathed in golden sunshine.

As the youngest child you were perhaps the one to benefit most from the stability that Chartwell offered. How important do you think that was in later life?

I suppose I did have a rather different upbringing from my elder brother and sisters. I could try to count all the houses, the nannies and governesses and nurses they lived through, but that would be counter-productive. Does a very stable, almost cabbage-like existence, like a plant in the garden, with one set of influences make a great difference to a child? I suppose it does. There was Diana, Randolph, Sarah and then there was Marigold who died the year before I was born, so I was brought up almost like an only child. Sarah was already seven when I was born, Diana was thirteen, Randolph was eleven . . . they were goldlike Olympian figures. Sarah was really the one with whom I had close connections; I loved the others, but really didn't know them at all. They inhabited a different landscape from me.

You describe your relationship with your mother at that time as respectful and admiring, rather than close. Was that a retrospective analysis or something you were aware of at the time?

I grew into being aware of it and can almost date it: when I was thirteen my mother realized that Cousin Moppet had a great influence on my whole outlook on life and she saw that I was growing much closer to Cousin Moppet than to her. It was then that she started taking me away to ski in the holidays and I began to be more than just respectful and admiring. I came to love her in a much more real way I suppose, and it wasn't without some painful interludes, because I was a tiresome teenager. My mother was a complex character, and could also be difficult, but I came to love her when I got to know her better.

Although your mother was devoted and conscientious there was never any doubt that Winston came first. You seem not to have had any sense of grievance about this. Did you come to mind it later?

Not at all. We all felt that our parents had other very important things to do. I never felt neglected emotionally or in any other way by them. It was in my mother's nature to be dedicated, and it was true also of my father, luckily for him and perhaps for the world as well. However, much later, when I knew my husband Christopher was going into politics, I took a vow in my heart that I would try to give my children a greater priority than perhaps we had with my mother. But I think it very important in this context to remember that when my mother was bringing up her children it wasn't a mark of bad mothering to have nurses and governesses; it was part of the way of life in that stratum of society. I certainly never regarded her as a bad mother. She had some less than happy relationships within the family but I think that happens very often. If you have a number of children you're probably not equally close to all of them.

Lady Soames

Were you the closest to your mother?

I came to be because of my position in the family as the youngest. When the war broke out for instance, Randolph was away in the army, my sister Diana was married and had her children. Sarah was married to Vic Oliver and then went into the air force. I did go into the army eventually, but by the time I was sixteen or seventeen the others had flown the nest. My mother more and more confided in me and we became much closer, but it was an accident of timing.

Was your mother difficult in her relationships with people generally?

She was a very complex and emotionally charged character, but she wasn't difficult all the time. She had enormously high standards which she imposed with varying degrees of success on her children, but she was also very hard on herself. She adored my father, was completely absorbed in his life, and involved in his politics, and she felt it all with every fibre of her being. But she was undoubtedly a highly strung animal.

But did she clash with your father because of that?

Yes. Perhaps history would have been different if my father had married a docile yes-woman; he might have had an easier time at home. But my mother had the will and the capacity to stand up to my father, to confront him, and to argue with him, and the fact that she had that capacity is more important than whether she was always right. I don't think she was always right, but she took a passionate interest in his political life, and there's no doubt about it that sometimes her judgements about his friends were truer than his. I've always thought my father married an equal in temperament and in spirit.

Would you say that she influenced his political life as well as his private life?

She was a Liberal at heart and she never really changed, but she did have an influence on him though it's quite hard to say exactly to what extent. He didn't necessarily take her advice, but it was very important to him as a politician that she could enter into the arguments and the choices.

Did your father have time to show you affection when you were young?

Both my parents were enormously affectionate, visibly so, and he was a great hugger, my father, and loved having us around. The stiff upper lip of the British upper class had really no part in our family life; it was something I read about in books. I may have been deeply shocked the first time I saw my mother cry, because that was as a result of a great drama in the family, but I often saw my father weep and it never struck me as odd that a man should express emotion. My mother could be cold when she wished to express disapproval or to distance herself from a person, but to walk into a room where they both were was to be enfolded and embraced. We were a very noisy and extrovert family; when we were happy we laughed and hugged each other, and when we were sad we cried, and when we were angry we stamped our feet – there was never any doubt about how we were all feeling.

What kind of thing made your father cry?

He was moved by events and tragedies, by people behaving nobly, by poetry . . . I've seen him recite Shakespeare with his eyes brimming with tears. He wept easily and he wasn't ashamed of it.

I know you hate being asked what it was like to be the daughter of Winston Churchill, so I will ask something rather different. Were you aware of being set apart from your peers by virtue of your father's importance, and if so, was that something you found difficult to cope with?

It came upon me gradually. Of course, as a small child I took my parents completely for granted. It never struck me as odd, for instance, that my father wrote books, made speeches, built walls, painted pictures, but the realization of his importance and fame grew upon me. I may not have had a very profound understanding of events, but I realized that significant things were afoot. I used to listen to my parents talking, and with great events impinging on our domestic life, I came to realize that my father was an important figure who played a leading role in all this. We were all brought up with a great sense of public service. I would have thought it contemptible in me to have wished my parents to be at my school sports day; what did it matter if they saw me coming fourth in the egg-and-spoon race? When the war broke out and Papa took office, my feelings for him as his child became confused and mingled with the feelings I had as an ardent young Englishwoman. 1940 was special for us all, and my father was the hero of the hour to whom we all clung. Me too.

For much of the 1930s your father had been in the political wilderness. Then in May 1940 when power slipped away from Chamberlain, Churchill began his 'walk with destiny' for which he considered all his earlier life to have been a preparation. How great a part do you think destiny played in all this?

Destiny played a great part, because when he was a young soldier-of-fortune and seeking 'reputation in the cannon's mouth', he could have lost his life on about five or six different occasions. Although my father longed to be in office in the 1930s, my mother often said to me that it was a real blessing that he never held office then, because he couldn't single-handedly have turned the tide of appeasement and slow rearmament; he would have been involved in government in a time that came to be regarded, perhaps rather unjustly, as the dark decade when we were purblind. As it was he was able to start with a clean slate.

You served for five years with the ATS. The contrast between the life you had known and life in the army must have been stark. Did you find it an ordeal, or did the conditions of war make everything acceptable.

I was thrilled to go into the army and rather gloried in the discomforts. I really did want to do my bit and I felt I was part of this great enterprise going on. So I loved it and was a tremendously enthusiastic soldier, rather too much so probably.

But did you feel that because of your father you were looked upon in a different light?

Yes. I had difficult moments. It was always agony going to a new unit because I knew I wouldn't be treated in quite the same way as the others. I always felt I had to overcompensate, scrub rather more floors than anyone else.

Churchill offered his countrymen 'blood, toil, tears and sweat', and they responded with indomitable spirit. Do you think the strength of their response surprised him, perhaps humbled him even?

Yes. The response of the British people was something which moved him deeply. He was very conscious of all the devotion and valour and dedication, and he valued them enormously. It was a pact really, between the British people and him.

Churchill was held in near veneration during his lifetime. In more recent times the history books have not been especially kind. How do you respond to criticism of your father's wartime period?

I try not to mind too much about judgements on public events. I dislike mean judgements and those based on being wise after the event. But of course my father must stand the test of history. He didn't do everything right or make all the right judgements, but we did manage to win, despite all the mistakes, so I can only imagine the enemy made even more. One must keep these things in perspective, but of course I find it difficult to detach myself entirely, and when it's a question of personal criticism, I sometimes know his critics are actually wrong.

To be a very successful politician, particularly in time of war, you have to take decisions which might be interpreted later on, or even at the time, as ruthless, where sometimes the innocent have to pay a great price. Do you think your father ever took decisions which were perhaps good for Britain but were rather questionable on moral grounds?

My father would have done almost anything to win the war, and war is a rough business. I daresay he had to do some very rough things, but he wasn't a man who took these sort of decisions lightly. All those things weighed with him, but they didn't unman him.

Lady Soames

You refer in your book to what you call 'slaps at Winston's departed greatness'. What did you have in mind?

I don't remember in what context I made that particular remark, but I suppose I was thinking of how much I minded that, in quieter times, people took slaps at my father. But I've been brought up in quite a rough political school, so one accepts that that must be so. No true historian of the war is guilty of unjust or ill-informed criticism, but people who write meretricious histories are being tremendously wise after the event. They assume that we knew that we were going to win. But when you lived through it at the side of people like my father who were so deeply involved in it, the uncertainties were enormous. I feel that people very often don't understand how much the war was lived step by step and day by day.

Did your father ever despair?

A lot has been made of the depressive side of his character by psychiatrists who were never in the same room with him. Of course he himself talks of his 'black dog', and he did have times of great depression, but marriage to my mother very largely kennelled the black dog. Of course if you have a black dog it lurks somewhere in your nature and you never quite banish it; but I never saw him disarmed by depression. I'm not talking about the depression of his much later years, because surely that is a sad feature of old age which afflicts a great many people who have led a very active life.

Was he dictatorial?

No. He had a greater measure of power than any leader in democratic times in our country, but you must remember that every Tuesday when he was in this country and the House was sitting, he answered questions in the House of Commons. He always regarded himself as a servant of Parliament, and I don't think there is a recorded instance of his having gone against the decisions of the joint Chiefs of Staff. Of course he would argue his corner but it's not true to say he always got his way; he didn't, and sometimes it made him very cross. Sometimes he even acknowledged they were right. Several times during the war he pressed something to a vote of confidence which people found rather tiresome because of course he would always get the vote of confidence, but he wished to demonstrate to the world that this was a war waged by a democratic country, and that he was empowered by the democratic vote, even at the height of the war.

Your introduction to Christopher Soames was reportedly love at first sight . . . was he your first love?

No. I can't remember who was the very first. I was quite susceptible when I was young and I'd been in love with several people by the time I met Christopher. I was very attracted to men and fell head over heels many times. I was very high spirited and had a lovely time in a way, but when I came back from the war I found it quite difficult adjusting to my own class, funnily enough.

Were you flirtatious?

Yes; but having been brought up strictly, I was quite prim. I was also horrendously innocent. I can only say the gods look after their own and I had a guardian angel. I don't think I was very sensible.

Tell me how you first fell in love with Christopher Soames.

It wasn't love at first sight on my side, I have to say, but we met for the very first time in the British Embassy in Paris where, years and years later, he was to be ambassador . . . and that was rather romantic. My father and I were in Belgium and he was going to fly straight back to England, but the US Secretary of State was going to be in Paris and my father wanted to see him. We both flew to Paris for twenty-four hours, and in those twenty-four hours I met Christopher Soames. I think he fell in love straightaway, and I did quite quickly after that, but the first time, I really thought he had other fish to fry.

Did you have other fish to fry?

No, I was rather unhappy when I came out of the army. I'd had an interesting, exciting war – as the equivalent of a captain. I'd served in mixed anti-aircraft batteries and, in as much as it was possible then for women in England, I'd been in action against the enemy. In some ways one felt sparkling and confident and yet in other ways not. I hadn't been in my own world for five years. The men in London whom I saw when I first came out of the army were either beardless boys who seemed to me like schoolchildren, or they were young married men very occupied with beautiful young wives; and most of my friends were either dead or still in the army or abroad. I found it quite difficult to reestablish life at home and I wasn't very happy. I don't think I woke up in the morning saying I was miserable, but looking back, it wasn't a happy time in my life and I couldn't think what I wanted to do. I didn't have a vocation, certainly not a profession, and the only way I could have earned my living would have been as a lift operator or a scrubber of floors, so I was in rather a strange position. My father, although out of office immediately after the war, was enormously famous, and I was made much of and had a lovely time wherever I went with him; but my own actual personal life wasn't very satisfactory. Then, within a year of being demobilized, suddenly wonderful Christopher Soames appeared on the horizon and, like my parents, we married and lived happily ever afterwards.

In your book about your mother, you describe a certain inhibition in Clementine which made for a barrier between her and her children, a certain formality and lack of spontaneity. Was that something you tried consciously to reverse in your relationship with your own children?

Yes. My relationship with my children was quite different. For one thing it was more knockabout and workaday. It's true, I had a nanny, a wonderful nanny, who looked after them all, but Christopher and I lived in the country and life was different. I think that all of us in that age group had a freer and cosier relationship with our children than our parents had had with us.

As PPS to your father, Christopher Soames was a key figure, particularly when your father suffered a stroke and was scarcely functioning. How was it possible to keep this from the public and keep things running smoothly?

That's really an extraordinary episode, and the more I look back on it, the more extraordinary I think it is. Again fate steps in. My father sustained the stroke in the evening at a dinner party at Downing Street; the next morning he presided at a Cabinet meeting. Harold Macmillan and Rab Butler and several others were absolutely amazed afterwards when they learned of the extent of the stroke. They all said that Winston was rather silent and looked pale but none of them at the time noticed anything seriously amiss. By the morning Lord Moran had diagnosed a stroke and my father headed for Chartwell having walked to the car from No 10. When he got to Chartwell which was an hour's drive away, he couldn't get out of the car, and had to be carried inside. So it was only then that the worst effects of the stroke became obvious, and at Chartwell he was kept absolutely incommunicado. That weekend Lord Moran told Christopher that he thought my father was going to die. Christopher didn't tell me that, but I knew he was very ill. He was there for six weeks and somehow – it couldn't happen now – Christopher and John Colville between them kept the machine turning over. Julian Amery is very naughty about it: he always says that Christopher was Prime Minister, but it isn't true that Christopher ever said or ever felt that he was.

Did your husband ever resent the fact that his own natural political prowess was sometimes obscured as a result of his kinship with Churchill?

Not at all. Christopher loved my father, he loved him as he didn't love his own father with whom he had an unhappy relationship. From the first they took to each other and were great friends. Christopher had become interested in politics when he was assistant military attaché at Paris during the Peace Conference, but he knew he owed an enormous amount to my father. I never heard him express anything other than that he was grateful for the start that his relationship with my father gave him. He was actually my father's parliamentary private secretary before being officially appointed. Christopher was also able to do a great service for my father in that second period of office, first as leader of the opposition and then as Prime Minister in 1951. My father by that time was rather old and so very emiment that people were quite frightened of approaching him, and it was through Christopher that quite a number of young MPs on both sides of the House used to gain access to him.

Did the fact that Christopher was very close to your father cement your marriage more?

It was a wonderful thing. In the first ten years of our married life we lived in the farmhouse at Chartwell, and so we saw my parents constantly. It was a very close relationship, and gradually my mother became fond of Christopher. She didn't like him at first, though she was pretty good about it. But I remember one day years later, certainly after Papa's death, when Christopher, Mama and I were all sitting round at table, having a lovely cosy talk, and Christopher said to her, 'You didn't like me, did you, when I first married Mary?', and I remember it so well, she put out her hand and covered his and said, 'No darling, but I've made up for it since.'

Although his native talents were not in doubt, it was 1960 before your husband finally got out of his father-in-law's shadow. Was that a relief to all concerned?

I don't remember that feeling. It seemed progressive. He had quite a difficult time getting a seat, despite being my father's son-in-law. He was inexperienced politically and constituencies were quite wary of him to begin with. Somebody once implied that Christopher wouldn't have been anything in politics if it hadn't been for my father. It's true that he might not have had the start my father gave him, and a wonderful start it was, but if Christopher had been no good he would have just fizzled out. In fact, he held Bedford for sixteen years and increased his majority each time.

You have sometimes referred to the golden years of Paris. What is it that makes you recall that period with such fondness?

For one thing we were both strangers to diplomatic life, so it was a joint enterprise. We also had a wonderful welcome awaiting us because the French nation was in love with my father. We already had friends there and we took the school-age children with us and the others came in their holidays. Of course it had its ups and downs – the Soames affair (when the Foreign Office blabbed top-secret information) very nearly capsized the boat before we'd been there long, but Christopher survived it although his position was precarious for a while. In our time there, things were happening that were really interesting and exciting: the General died in 1970 . . . in itself the passing of an era; Pompidou became President; Ted Heath became Prime Minister; the summit took place in Paris where it was agreed that the French would remove their veto. It was intoxicatingly exciting politically, and all the time the life of the embassy was going on. I love France, and how could anyone not love living in Paris?

What did you think of de Gaulle?

I admired him enormously; to me he represented, as he did to my father whatever their differences and quarrels, resurgent France, the soul of France. I was also much alarmed by him, but he was very civil and kind to me. The only time I really had a conversation with him was at luncheon in the Elysée, when I sat next to him shaking with nerves. He was not an easily approachable person and we had an extraordinary conversation. He asked me, 'Que faites-vous à Paris, madame?' and so I panicked and I said, 'Je promène mes chiens, Monsieur le Président.' Instead of putting me down for giving an absolutely asinine answer to his question, he became very interested. He wanted to know what dogs I had and where I walked them, and then suggested I take them to the Ile de Cygnes which is a little island in the middle of the Seine. He drew it for me on the menu, and thereafter I always used to walk my dogs on the Ile de Cygnes with grateful thoughts of the General.

Did you warm to him?

I never had much time to, but I think one could have done. He was very fond of my mother, ever since the time when she flew at him for making a very anti-British remark. My father had missed it because he was at the other end of the table, and anyhow Papa's French wasn't very good, but when the General insulted the British fleet, Mama retaliated in perfect French. The next day there arrived the most enormous arrangement of flowers, and thereafter he respected and liked her very much. For years after my father died he sent my mother a personal letter on the anniversary of his death.

Many people now acknowledge that without your husband's work and popularity in France, Britain might never have joined the Community. Do you think he would have been saddened by the current wrangles?

Yes. I'm glad he's thought to have made a difference; I certainly think he did. Our vision of Europe was formed during the early crusading days, and although you can never speak for people who are dead, I expect he would be saddened by the present misconception of what Europe is meant to be.

You must have had mixed feelings about your husband's appointment to the governorship of Rhodesia. Did you ever consider not accompanying him?

Oh no. In fact, I made it a condition that if he accepted it, I should go with him. I wasn't going to be left behind. I didn't know what I was going into, but I certainly wasn't going to let him go alone.

Many people believe that there could not have been elections without bloodshed in Rhodesia had you not been such a brilliant husband and wife team. You must feel proud of that achievement.

I feel very proud of Christopher's part.

But you played an important part.

No, I was just there. The fact that there wasn't a complete shambles and breakdown was very largely thanks to Christopher and the brilliant team from the Foreign Office and the Commonwealth Monitoring Force. It was also enormously important that he was able to forge a relationship with Robert Mugabe. In the beginning their meetings were completely confrontational, and yet they became friends. I always thought it was a wonderful recognition of this when Robert and Sally Mugabe flew from Zimbabwe for Christopher's funeral in our village church.

In 1980 you and your husband were both honoured in Mrs Thatcher's list, such a joint honour being without precedent. Was that an especially proud moment?

Yes, I was staggered; it was very moving, very exciting for us. That was an extraordinary time, those winter months in Africa.

Lady Soames

The following year Christopher Soames was dropped from Mrs Thatcher's Cabinet, having been widely blamed for the disruptive strikes in the public services and for yielding to the unions. Do you think that was fair, or was he made a scapegoat?

The civil service strike was probably the breaking point, because he had advised Mrs Thatcher that certain terms should be met, and she ignored his advice. Then she dismissed him from the Cabinet, which she had every right to do, but without giving that as an exact reason. Two months later the strike was settled on exactly the same terms. I think he was made a scapegoat, but truthfully I never think of it. After all they were very dissimilar in outlook – he was one of the wets – and they weren't easy colleagues.

It is five years since your husband died . . . has time 'healed you of a grievous wound'?

I've been very lucky. I have my children and I've been very busy. The acute pain diminishes, luckily, but the sense of loss is there forever; how can it not be, if one's been very happy with somebody? It's something that's gone for good.

When you were appointed in 1989 to chair the board of the National Theatre it was rumoured that you were Mrs Thatcher's revenge. What was the truth behind the appointment?

It was the most rum appointment that there ever was. I was simply staggered to be offered the job. But I've just been reappointed for another three years so I feel that perhaps I have lived down my reputation for being Mrs Thatcher's revenge. They thought I was being sent by a Tory government to sort out pinkos on the left bank, though naturally they were too polite to voice that opinion to me, but I have to say there was never at the time of my appointment any suggestion that that would be my role, and if there had been I wouldn't have taken the job. I don't know why I was appointed. Richard Luce said he just thought it would be a good idea, and nobody was more astonished than I was. It's simply thrilling for me to have entered a marvellous new world, to work with talented, gifted people, and I've learned such a lot.

Lady Soames

Out of all the Churchill children, you alone managed to keep your marriage intact. To what do you attribute that?

Luck. And I married a very nice man. I find your question so terribly difficult – I was dreading being asked that. Why does one marriage succeed and another fail? I really don't know. I think we were both terribly lucky in finding each other, and we both tried very hard. A lot of commitment went into our marriage, but in the end it was just blessed good fortune.

Your elder brother and sisters had a far less settled early life than you. Do you think they paid for that with their marriages perhaps?

Who can tell? I really can't go into all that, because the answer is, I just really don't know. I don't think they had a bad childhood; they were very close to my parents when they were small, and it was only later that rifts and difficulties appeared, but even so, the door was never shut; it remained always open.

Your parents were obviously saddened by the marital problems of their children – 'they grieved over the shipwrecks', as you put it in the book. Did they hold themselves in part responsible, do you think?

I don't know. I never heard them say so. I often knew them to be sad about it and try in so far as they were able to be a unifying force. In any case it isn't always the result of difficulties in childhood. Two of my own children's marriages have failed, and yet they were children brought up in a united family, having the same home, the same childhood influences. It's very hard to identify the root causes. The expectations that people have of marriage can be unreal and the climate we live in is not conducive to keeping a rocky show going. Sometimes people don't try hard enough, or long enough. My parents had quite a number of disagreements and rows, and they lived through very difficult times. They weren't always well-off in a material sense, but they loved each other very much, and they also had a great commitment to the marriage, and I think that's important above and beyond the commitment to yourself.

You suggest your mother was more comprehending than your father of the difficulties which beset unhappy relationships. You describe her as gentle and fair minded. Did you try to emulate her example when your own daughters' marriages foundered?

I hope I did. But no two generations meet the same problems in the same way, and no two problems are identical.

You don't have much sympathy with the view – most current in American feminist circles – that your mother was eclipsed by your father, still less I suspect with the view that you were to some extent eclipsed by your husband . . . but isn't there a degree of truth in it, all the same?

I don't feel it in the least about myself. My life was tremendously widened and enriched by sharing in Christopher's. The idea that a life is necessarily wasted because it is to a large extent devoted to promoting a husband's career is something I don't understand. I'm always amazed when people say to me that my mother's life was eclipsed. It would never have occurred to her that she had been deprived, though of course it was a different generation. I certainly never felt eclipsed; I felt enhanced.

You write of your parents' relationship. 'She was scabbard to his sword, and she kept it shining.' Do you think that sort of commitment still has a modern application, or is it hopelessly outmoded?

I think it's a little sad that husband and wife enterprises aren't any longer thought to be particularly admirable. I'm in rather a muddle about this because I do want women to have careers, yet at the same time I recognize that it is quite difficult for women to have careers and to run families. I sometimes think that women have found liberation but haven't quite found out how to manage it.

You have said many times: 'I have lived with clever, gifted people all my life', which rather ignores your own special gifts. Is this what is known as British modesty, or is there some deep-seated need to make light of your talents?

I have always enjoyed the company of clever, gifted people, and of course perhaps something rubs off on one. I don't at all feel unfulfilled, or that I ought to have had a bigger role at all. I think I have been very fortunate in what has come my way. I never meant to write a book, for example, but once I started I rather warmed to the task. Although I've lived all my life with political people, I'm not in myself a political animal. There was never a point in my life when for more than five minutes I considered the idea of going into politics on my own.

I imagine you found it a very emotional experience to write your mother's biography – that is certainly something which comes through in the writing.

I said in my preface that it was quite impossible for me to write completely dispassionately or in an unpartisan way, but I tried to be fair, to stand back from it as much as I could. Inevitably, however, in writing about your own family, you do lose objectivity, but you also have knowledge that other people don't have and a sensitivity that outsiders couldn't have.

I suppose you discovered many things about your mother that you were barely conscious of during your childhood and young adulthood. Did you also discover things about yourself?

More about my mother. I tried to efface myself as much as possible. When I started to write I hadn't really understood about her very difficult early life about which she told me a great deal when she knew I was serious about the book. I also discovered that Mama lacked the capacity for happiness. By that I am referring to something beyond the circumstances in her life because I would never suggest that she and my father were not happy together. In fact I find it very difficult to understand the hurtful things that have been written recently, that it wasn't a happy marriage, for example, and that my mother was enormously difficult. She could be difficult, but it isn't only easy people who are lovable. She was someone who felt things very deeply and she was a rather lonely person.

Did you discover things that disappointed you?

No. I found things that explained certain other things which I hadn't understood before. If I ever revise the book I'll write some parts a little differently, particularly those concerning the period in childhood when you don't think about your parents as having lives of their own; it's later that you see it.

In the love and devotion between your parents which spanned over half a century, there seem to have been only two ripples ... one when your father wrote to Clementine saying that she absolutely had no need to be jealous, we know not of whom; the other when your mother at the age of fifty fell in love with Terence Philip. I had the impression that you tried to play down the possible significance of this attachment saying these five months had 'the unreality of a dream'. Did you perhaps feel some conflict at that point between your role as daughter and biographer?

By that time I was old enough to want to understand, and I wrote what I believe to be the truth about that relationship. I truly believe it had the air of unreality about it; it was a holiday romance, and she came back to base. She certainly didn't seek it, and he for his part was, I believe, quite lukewarm. How much do you tell your children about a relationship you have had with a man who isn't your father? I asked her, 'Mama, were you ever in love with him?' and she said, 'Well, I was rather in love with him, for a time, and he wanted me to be.' But it wasn't a commitment, it wasn't planned and plotted, by which I mean she didn't go on the cruise to meet Terence Philip. But when she came back she brought a little dove with her; it lived for two or three years with us and when it died it was buried under the sundial in the garden at Chartwell, and round the base my mother had engraved the words: 'It does not do to wander too far from sober men, but there's an island yonder. I think of it again.'

Is infidelity always damaging in marriage, do you think, or can some marriages rise above it, even benefit from it?

I'm sure some marriages can rise above it, and I'm very sorry whenever I see that lack of fidelity has caused a marriage to crash to the ground. Fidelity seems to me to be a very important ingredient in marriage; it's part of the commitment, but equally I think it's in certain people not to be able to be faithful, and one must hope then that they are married to partners who can sustain that. For my own part I would have hoped not to know about it; and if I had, I would have hoped to keep it in proportion.

On the issue of Edward VIII and Mrs Simpson, your father – unwisely as it turned out – publicly supported the idea of Mrs Simpson as queen consort. Your mother was shrewder, and predicted the political fall-out. Was your father simply being naïve, do you think, or did the marriage appeal to his romantic side?

He primarily felt devotion and loyalty to Edward VIII, and felt that he was being cornered. I'm sure he deplored his wanting to marry a divorced woman, but he so much wanted to keep the king on the throne that he did search for possible ways round the difficulty. I even remember hearing morganatic marriage talked about, which has no part in our constitution at all. Because of his loyalty to the king he didn't appreciate how much public opinion was against this situation, and of course the dominions all came in strongly against it. My father underestimated that, but my mother never did. I remember they had awful disagreements over this, and my mother was very bitter because she felt that my father's views in opposition about standing up to Germany were just beginning to be accepted by a lot of people, and suddenly this issue made it seem as if he were deliberately setting out to spike the Prime Minister's guns, which wasn't true at all. It was a really good example of my mother being shrewder than my father, but my father's loyalty was deeply engaged, as was his sense of romance. But there was a very moving coda to the story. My parents were at the coronation of King George VI and Queen Elizabeth, and as Queen Elizabeth, now the Queen Mother, was being crowned in her own separate ceremony, my father turned to my mother and said, 'You were quite right, Clemmie, the other one would never have done.' The beauty of the service had brought home to him what being the consort of the sovereign really means.

How did he view the exile of the Windsors?

He always remained on very friendly terms with them, although he had quite a difficult time during the war with the Duke of Windsor who kept making unsuitable demands; trivial requests would arrive at a moment when my father was grappling with the aftermath of Dunkirk or something, and it was by no means easy to deal with them; but he always remained his friend.

As we all know, Churchill took an instant loathing to the eightieth-birthday portrait of him by Graham Sutherland, feeling that he had been betrayed by the artist. Do you feel any sense of betrayal that you were not told of the painting's destruction till after your father's death?

That was an instance when I saw a side of my mother that did quite astonish me. She used to tell me a lot, and she simply didn't mention this. Of course I regret that she destroyed it, but I don't believe all the claptrap that she didn't have the right to. It's all a very unhappy story. Christopher and I and Mama were on our way to Jamaica for a holiday to help my mother recover from my father's death. We were on board either the *Queen Mary* or the *Queen Elizabeth*, in the drawing room, and I can remember to this day how I nearly slid off the chair when Mama suddenly cleared her throat and said, 'Oh, by the way, I think probably I ought to tell you and Christopher that I had that dreadful portrait of your father destroyed.'

You must have felt a sense of discomfort at the very least when you were forced to lie about the fate of the Sutherland portrait while your mother was alive. You say it was the correct decision – what exactly lay behind the decision not to reveal the truth till your mother's death?

We all took the view that Mama didn't realize the hornets' nest it would stir up. She was a most courageous woman, but she was quite old then, and we thought that she didn't appreciate the awful reaction it would cause in the artistic world. Christopher and I tried to tell her how strongly people would feel about it, and we begged her not to say anything. She never mentioned it again. I like to think I'm a truthful person basically, but I did for twelve years lie through my teeth when asked about it. People were always trying to get hold of it to stretch the canvas, or clean its face, or put it on exhibition or something. It was awful. But I would do the same again.

You write very movingly of your sister Diana's suicide, saying that your parents were spared the extremes of shock and grief, due to what you call 'the dulling of sensibilities' which accompanies old age. You were not spared the extremes, I imagine. How did you come to terms with it yourself?

Suicide is such a cruel thing, because it leaves a terrible legacy that people have to live with, of questioning, of self doubt. And I agonized for her children. It was a very sad time, and one of the worst things I've ever had to do in my life was to tell my mother and my father about it. My mother was ill in hospital and she was rather sedated at the time. I remember walking all the way back from the Westminster Hospital to Hyde Park Gate, trying to think how I could tell my father. I also had to tell Sarah who was in Spain. She adored Diana and was very close to her. I remember having to shriek down a bad telephone, but there you are. Diana was a marvellous person and it was a great tragedy, but worst for her children, awful for her children. I hadn't always been close to Diana, but I was growing closer; I had always been, even as a middle-aged woman, her much younger sister, and I am afraid in her eyes I was rather 'teacher's pet' – funnily enough these attitudes sometimes last into adulthood. But we were just really beginning to overcome that, and then this awful thing. She had a very unhappy life, yet my father wrote such beautiful things about her when she was born. She was such a wanted child, and much loved by both my parents, a golden child right into her teens.

Your brother Randolph died a sad and bitter man. You write most poignantly: 'As always in sorrow Clementine had little to say.' What do you imagine her thoughts to have been.

Only when I was writing my mother's life did it hit home that she had buried all but two of her five children. It's a bitter thing for a mother. She didn't have a happy relationship with Randolph, and though she always tried to be helpful and loyal, the misunderstandings were profound. And then when somebody dies, you have to wait for eternity to put them right. My mother wasn't a self-pitying woman, but she felt it all very deeply and would love to have had a marvellous relationship with both Randolph and Diana. I hate talking about these family relations, and I certainly don't do so in any spirit of judgement. But my mother was a thinking woman, not an insensitive one, and I'm sure she felt very deep regret and grief.

Lady Soames

You must sometimes have had the feeling, particularly when your father died, that he somehow belonged as much to the British people as to your own family. Did that help ease the loss, or did it sharpen it poignancy?

When my father died it was a great loss, but also for him it was such a release. Life had become a burden, and it would have been a selfish person who would have wanted him to linger after all he had done in life. It was time, it was time. It's quite a different sort of sadness from that which you feel when somebody hasn't run their course. He was ill for a fortnight, and after ten days it was known publicly that he was ill, and from that moment onwards you really felt that the whole world was there at his bedside. I can only say it was the most extraordinary feeling. The funeral I shall remember always.

You have sometimes joked that you feel like the last of the Mohicans. Am I right in thinking a certain sorrow infuses the jocularity?

Yes. One's alone in the little shelf of one's generation. I miss Sarah particularly; she was the closest to me, and when she died, it was awful. We were great friends, and she was always my heroine. She had unhappy times in her life but she was a marvellous person, and we were very close in the months before her death. I miss her very much. But anybody who lives beyond seventy or so is in the foothills of old age, and you can't arrive there without suffering anything. I think I've been so fortunate because I was loved by my parents, I was loved by my husband, and I am loved by my children. My father once wrote: 'You must accept life with all its contrasts, the good and the bad, the dark and the bright.' For me the death of my husband was and is a terrible loss, but I had happiness in great measure and I consider myself enormously blessed in that life has brought enrichment beyond anything I could have hoped for or deserved or expected.

SIR LAURENS VAN DER POST

SIR LAURENS VAN DER POST

Laurens van der Post was born in Africa in 1906. During the thirties he farmed in England before joining up. He fought behind enemy lines in Abyssinia, the Western Desert and the Far East where he was taken prisoner by the Japanese while comanding a small guerrilla unit. His experiences as a POW were recounted in his book *The Seed and the Sower* (1963), later made into the film *Merry Christmas, Mr Lawrence*. After the war he returned to active service in Java where he was Lord Mountbatten's representative. Since 1949 he has worked for the British government on a variety of missions in little-known parts of Africa. He also made an expedition to the Kalahari Desert in search of the Bushmen in order to try and save them from extinction. He is the author of many books which include *The Lost World of the Kalahari* (1958), *Journey into Russia* (1964), *Jung and the Story of Our Time* (1976), *Yet Being Someone Other* (1982) and *A Walk with a White Bushman* (1986). Laurens van der Post was knighted in 1981.

Sir Laurens van der Post

As a child you were steeped in the legends and myths of the African people which have become so much part of your make-up. Do you believe that without that very strong childhood influence you could have become the man you are today?

It's very difficult to say what one would have been if something else had happened. The fact is that it was a very important part of my upbringing, and I feel very much enriched by it. It was one of the great formative experiences in my life, and one which hasn't been diminished in importance by age.

Do you think the childhood experience was crucial – it was not something which could have been learned or acquired later?

One's whole life is a process of fulfilling the person you're born, a process of being educated and growing older without losing the child that you were in the beginning, so that one can end up as a kind of child-man, man-child. It's one of the saddest phenomena of our time that very few people seem to remain young in old age.

You were thirteenth out of fifteen children . . . how far did your being just one of a large family shape your character for later life?

I'm not aware consciously of what being a member of such a large family meant to me, except that we were extraordinarily happy, and that we had diversity. Some of my older brothers may have found it more of a strain, but I personally did not. My father died when I was young, so that I was more aware of my mother's influence. We were not a family of conformers, but a family of diversities, and all our diversities were respected and encouraged by my mother. I've often talked to my sisters and brothers about the great debt we owe our mother, because of her capacity not to have favourites. When I look back I can't recall a single occasion on which my mother favoured one child against another . . . yet, when she was dying, I discovered that she did have a favourite. It was one of my brothers who had died some time before. In a sense he might have been thought to be the least satisfactory of the children, almost what the others might have called a failure, yet when my mother was dying, although we had always thought that she would like to be buried with my father, she said to me, 'I want to be buried with my son, because I can't bear the thought of him being out there on his own.'

Africa, the place of your birth, has come to have as much symbolic significance as actual . . . am I right in this assumption?

The earth where one is born always has a symbolic significance, but Africa especially, because of its immense charge of natural life. It is the continent which contains the greatest variety and abundance of animal and plant life in the world; it is also the home of the Bushmen, the oldest living people to whom we have access. I always felt in Africa that I was very near to the original blueprint of the country, and that brings one nearer to mythology. Life comes to us consciously first as a myth; then the myth becomes a legend, and the legend becomes history. Africa in that sense has an extra root in the spiritual organization patterns of the mind which we call mythology. In Africa the myth was the earth and the earth was the myth to a degree that you don't encounter anywhere else.

You have described the story of black Africa as a horror story. Do you ever feel a sense of guilt by association, for being part of the story?

The horror story I was referring to took place before we came on the scene, when Africa was constantly being raided by the outside world for slaves. It was a great source of slave labour both for Asia and the Mediterranean world. As Europeans we were accused of being the greatest exploiters of the slave trade, but actually we came at the end of the story. We were briefly involved in the trade, but we also played a leading role in putting an end to it. One of the unfortunate results of slavery is that by the time we came to Africa the black cultures had never been able to prove what they could have done if they had not been so grossly subjected to the horrors of the slave trade. There was also disease, life was very uncertain, and people didn't live long. The further south you go, the further removed you are from the point of impact with the slave-owning civilizations, and the more integrated are the black cultures. That's why I always have such great hopes for the part of Africa where I was born; in southern Africa the people were least affected by what I call this horror story, and they produced considerable black civilizations of their own.

Sir Laurens van der Post

You have often said that the 1930s in England were the unhappiest years of your life, presumably because they were lived in the shadow of war breaking out. But it was also the time when your children must have been young. Was it not a time of joy and hope for the future through them?

Not really. At the time we lived on a farm in the West Country. My son was about five when his sister was born, and when he was six or seven, I was terribly unhappy about what was happening in Europe. I felt ashamed at the way Europe had allowed the Nazi horror to grow when its evil was so obvious to me. I had been to Japan and the Far East and I had watched the Japanese invasion of Manchuria. I love the Japanese, but I watched with horror how they walked out of the League of Nations, how Mussolini went into Abyssinia and nothing was done. I thought the war was going to come in '38, so at the end of '37 I sent my wife and children out to Africa to be looked after by my family there. But of course I was a year out. I never really enjoyed my young family because my daughter, still happily alive, was just a little giggling girl when she went out to Africa and I didn't see her again until ten years later. So I didn't have that kind of happiness you are asking me about.

Your autobiographical writing sometimes strikes the reader as fragmented and seemingly selective. For example, I could not find any account of the children you had by your first marriage, nor indeed much reference to the marriage itself.

You didn't find it because I've never written an autobiography as such. I've written about those parts of my life which seemed to me to be of objective interest to others. My own personal relationships are not there, and were never meant to be. I never wanted to indulge in writing about my sorrows; the importance of our lives is not in the outer eventualities, but in the inner eventfulnesses, and that is what I have written about.

Do you prefer to forget about those things you have omitted to tell?

Oh no, they're very precious to me. But if I were going to write properly about my life, I would have to live it a second time, and what a waste that would be. I've done it once, I don't want to do it again in books. This would be to commit the sin of looking back over one's shoulder, and all mythologies warn us against that. To do that is to be turned to stone like Lot's wife, or, like Orpheus, to lose your Eurydice. Most autobiographies are a way of looking back, making the present a past, instead of trying to make the past a present.

What were your feelings when you came to join up?

I was very glad that the sense of compromise had suddenly gone from life, although what struck me immediately was the difference between this war in 1939 and the 1914 war which I remembered as a young boy and which was the last of the romantic wars. Indeed my older brothers were afraid the war in Europe would be over before they could take part in it. But in 1939 we all went off rather sadly; there was no feeling of romance about it. The impact on the spirit of man was not in the war itself, as in the 1914–18 war, but in the demonstration of the depths to which the human race could sink if it neglected the challenges as it did in the '20s and the '30s of this century. I had been to Germany and seen the Walpurgisnacht rally in Nuremburg, and it was a horrible sight. I was reminded recently of the Walpurgisnacht march during the demonstration by the Labour Party in Sheffield just before the last election which they thought they would win. Did you see the flags flying? Did you see the holy light in their eyes? It was terrifying to watch the leaders on the platform, wearing exalted expressions as if they'd seen the eternal light. On such occasions we have to ask ourselves what will happen to the human spirit if we don't stand up and fight. You must meet the challenges of life in their right dimension, and in 1939 it was clearly a dimension which could only be suppressed by force.

You must have felt fundamentally changed by your wartime experiences. Was this what led to your divorce in 1948 – was it impossible to return to the married life you had known?

No, I don't think it was due to that at all. My first wife is still alive and she is a great friend of ours, and although she lives in South Africa we see her regularly when she comes over here. She's a wonderful person and we all love and admire her very much, but there was something that wasn't quite right. For instance, I loved living in the country, while she liked living in towns; I'd already realized that I couldn't write in Africa, but she loved

Africa and didn't want to be away from it ever. I can't blame it on the war, but what the war did, particularly for those who were imprisoned, was to help enormously in the process of getting to know oneself. My father always used to say that the most important inscription over the temple at Delphi was 'Man, know thyself.' War is a dark healer which works when all other methods of healing the human spirit have failed. One gets a heightened perspective on values; nothing but humanity counts again. In a sense war was a tremendous experience, and also confirmation of the intuition that I had from childhood; it showed me again what I had seen when I was in the Far East, that empires would never again be able to be empires in the old way, simply because of what the Japanese had done when they won the war against the Russians. They shattered for the whole world the assumption that white races were superior. It confirmed my feeling that, great as one's country is, one belongs to all of life wherever it is. When the war came to an end, I went straight from prison to take over in Indonesia. Of all the prisoners, I alone stayed behind, because I found myself involved in the great revolution in the minds of the indigenous inhabitants of Indonesia. I felt I understood it and I had to stay. When the Japanese surrendered I was weak to the point of death, but I went straight back to active service because of this insight, this new feeling of certainty that there was a job to do and I must do it, otherwise I would never live my life properly. My war went on nearly ten years before I came home, so obviously when I got back to my family, the little girl was twelve and a half, and my son had done his first year at university and was charging around on a motor bike. Divorce at that moment seemed right.

I imagine that led to feelings of profound regret and sadness.

Yes, it did . . . it was very sad. But it was also right. That helped.

Did you find it difficult to fall in love again?

I don't quite know what that question means. One's always in love with life, and if one lives one's life properly, love is so much part of it that however it arises, one recognizes it and welcomes it.

Religious feeling, according to you, comes from the fusion of what you call

Sir Laurens van der Post

our Little Memory – what we acquire in our lifetime – and our Great Memory, the memory of all life that has ever been. How does this differ from what one might call a sense of history, that is to say something one can have without the religious dimension?

Religion is a sense of where one came from and where one's going to, so it is the ultimate inexpressible intangible of history. In one of his lovely Quartets, Little Gidding, T.S. Eliot who was a great friend of mine wrote: 'A people without history is not redeemed from time, because history is a pattern of timeless moments, so while the light fails on a winter's afternoon, history is now and England.' History is now, but one's sense of religion is timeless.

You said in your book, A Walk with a White Bushman: *'If there is no God there is no point in being responsible – it's just chaos and eternal night.' Are you saying that without God there would be no moral order?*

The Old Testament says that God is that which cannot be named, and that is the best negative definition of God there has ever been. But something in us knows that when we speak of God, we speak about the ultimate sense of law and order and harmony which there is in nature. Even the primitive people I knew in the Kalahari, when they talk about the sun, they talk about it making a ringing sound. Goethe's *Faust* begins: 'Die Sonne tönt nach alter Weise – The sun resounds in ancient manner.' There is a sense of music, of order which comes from somewhere in creation, and one knows from experience that if you lose that sense of integrity in that form of awareness, your life has no meaning. People go to pieces, and the consequences are awful.

Would you allow that throughout history many acts of barbarism and persecution have been perpetrated in the name of religion, and continue to be perpetrated?

Yes, but that doesn't mean that they were religiously perpetrated. They have been perpetrated in terms of the dogma that people have made of religion. If you study the animal world, the animals don't murder; they kill for food but that's part of their law and order. When a lion stalks its prey, the other animals scatter, but the moment they know the lion has killed, they stop running away and go on grazing all night around the lions eating one of their fellows, because they know they won't be killed. The lion will be contained in the natural order; he doesn't kill for fun, only for survival. If you ask why wars break out, I would answer that a real war, something which is consciously fought, takes place to prevent a greater killing. But the terrible slaughter of millions of Jews, which I can't ever get out of my head, or the massacre at Nanking by the Japanese, that was madness, and certainly not nature. That was man; it was not God.

On the question of forgiveness, you experienced torture and starvation at the hands of the Japanese, and yet were still able to forgive. Do you think the ability to forgive is related to innate virtue, something noble in the soul, or is it more a self-protective measure in that vengeance and bitterness are corrosive and ultimately self-destructive?

Forgiveness in the great sense of the word is a natural thing, part of the natural order. Otherwise life wouldn't go on; it would be locked in an eternal feud of killing and destruction. If you have lived honestly and truly through the challenge that's been presented to you, and it's over, then the question doesn't arise. You don't have to forgive in a conscious way; you just don't hate any more. There was a man with whom I spent a great deal of my time in prison, a medical officer called Dunlop who stood up many times to a particularly cruel Japanese. This Japanese singled out an officer for terribly vicious treatment. He tortured him, beat him and at times nearly killed him, and once he said to Dunlop, 'Why bother giving medical treatment to that useless man – I might as well kill him.' But Dunlop stood in front of the apparently dying prisoner, and said, 'You'll have to kill me first.' And just by his bearing he prevented many further cruelties. When the war suddenly came to an end, it was decided that the people suspected of being Japanese war criminals should be tried as such, and they were duly lined up. Dunlop was asked to walk down the line and pick out the guilty men. The cruel Japanese stood in the line and was obviously bracing himself to be hanged. But Dunlop looked him straight in the eye steadily, for a minute or more, and then turned his back on him and walked away. This is the kind of extraordinary thing I'm talking about, but it's something people aren't interested in nowadays.

Sir Laurens van der Post

There is a great deal of historical evidence that those who have experienced evil are very often contaminated by it. On a national scale the persecuted often turn into persecutors, and those who have been abused and maltreated as children, later grow up to inflict abuse on others. You have certainly been acquainted with evil, but are seemingly untainted by it. I am interested in how this has come about . . .

So am I, and I don't pretend to know the answer. The contamination you describe happens very often when people have been exposed to evil before they have developed the natural immunity possessed by a child. When you're in a state of helplessness and you have not experienced the love and the care of parents which is natural to life, and which animals show to their young, then this does happen. It starts through having had to live from childhood with a lack of love. T.S. Eliot told me that after the Korean War, the Americans appointed a high-level committee to investigate what made some human beings braver than others. They wanted to know why some people when they were subjected to brainwashing gave way to it and others not; what was this quality in people that made them, whatever happened, resist the evil to which they were being subjected. In every case they found that the most shining examples were people who had had a happy childhood, who had grown up surrounded by love. There's so much evil around that unless there is some provision in the pattern of life to fortify us against that form of negation, there wouldn't be life on earth, it would have gone. In the final analysis there has to be something which is greater than evil.

Your appeal to preserve the Kalahari Desert for the Bushmen seems on the face of it to contain a contradiction. On the one hand it runs the risk of becoming a huge tourist attraction which would defeat the purpose, and yet if it is left completely alone then no one will benefit from the lessons to be learned. Isn't this a rather naïve approach?

Perhaps all my approaches are naïve because they do tend to be defeated. I originally thought that in a world plagued by hunger, the Kalahari, which supports such a wonderful plant and animal life, could make a contribution, that it could be put to some use. But then I discovered that you can't put it to any use without destroying it. It would have been wonderful to preserve the Kalahari as it could have been preserved in those days, and in time we would have learned what to do with it and the

Bushmen. All we have done in the meantime is to destroy the desert and the Bushmen. Tourists are destroying the world; they are part of a very nasty phenomenon. To travel, to see and to learn is wonderful, but when you make an 'ism' out of anything you're on the way to doing something wrong. We are now fighting the greatest physical battle, also ultimately a moral and a spiritual battle, that man has ever fought. We are going to destroy the planet if we don't change our ways, and we can't change our ways unless there is a profound spiritual transformation in the human being. A Roman Catholic monk in America has written of 'the comfortable disease of progress that's killing us', and he's right. We are in great peril.

This primitive and natural stage which you describe so lovingly and movingly in your books is also riven with problems and difficulties such as illness and blindness which could easily be cured by Western medicine. In fact, it is difficult to escape the conclusion from reading The Lost World of the Kalahari *that these people's lives are short and often painful. How do you reconcile these two views?*

There's no conflict in my mind at all about that. I don't want people to become Bushmen themselves – that's not the answer. I don't think they've achieved a perfect state of life any more than we have. But as I see it, they are rich in a way in which we are poor. What is the point if we cure the blind, or the sick, if in the process we give them all the spiritual ills we suffer from? You may give them hospitals, but you take away the meaning of their lives. I'd much rather stay and take my chance with life as they do, like a salmon in the sea, because life itself has been kinder to them than we have ever been. Our way of life at the moment is a way of death to them. It's just the same problem with the rain-forest Indians. We take away what is light and eternity to them by cutting down their forests, by making it impossible for them to live there. It's a horror story. You have to understand that we're not better than they are; we're only more powerful. I advised the British government not to open up the Kalahari Desert, but to keep it the way it was, or to send some officers to live with the Bushmen for twenty or thirty years and then see what they advised. But they took no notice. Every bit of that desert is staked out for destruction, whether it be for phosphate mining, opening it up for cattle, doing this or that. And once you've got rid of the desert, which according to an expert geologist took two thousand million years to create, you can never have it back. It will be gone forever.

Sir Laurens van der Post

You have a great deal of influence on Prince Charles, who regards you as his mentor, his guru. Would you say that the knowledge he has gained from you is something which is likely to distance him from the nation, or bring him closer to it?

I don't know, but please don't let us talk about Prince Charles. I never talk about him, not even in the most glowing terms.

But he admires you, and it would be interesting for people to know . . .

That's all invention. People have called me his guru, but it's a very special subject and I feel in honour bound not to talk about it. I am often asked, particularly when he's so much under attack, to speak up as a friend, but I always refuse. I'm sorry. You have to be understanding and let me off that question.

Presumably you can talk about Lady Thatcher whom you have also influenced?

No, I'm not going to talk about her either. That is another subject I never speak about. I did once give my views in *A Walk with a White Bushman* but that was twelve or thirteen years ago and I have completely pulled out of that kind of field now.

I was only going to ask what it is about her that you so much admire.

I've told you I'd rather not talk about her. I say this to you because I say this to everybody.

Perhaps you can comment on what you say in A Walk with a White Bushman? *For instance, you describe her handling of the Falklands crisis as 'a brilliant enterprise of war', and the accusations of jingoism you describe as 'radical and liberal slush'. Do you accept that that sort of language might be offensive to a great many thinking people who very much hoped that war could have been avoided?*

Sir Laurens van der Post

I can't understand how any reasonable person could have described it as a jingoistic exercise. It simply doesn't make any sense to me. The Second World War started because the Japanese walked into a little part of China, and nobody did anything, so they walked into a bigger part . . . Can't people see it was against all concept of a civilized moral order to invade the Falklands like that, when our backs were turned? And by a Fascist government in the Argentine? To be accused of defending it out of mere jingoism seems to me nonsense. It is slush, and I don't mind saying it again, it is slush. You must know what Galtieri and his people are like, you must have seen those thousands of mothers demonstrating every night for their lost children. Are we simply to allow a government like that to invade our territory and take it away by force? Is it jingoism to throw a burglar out of your house? I could not see any moral justification or any grounds for people saying it was jingoism. When I think of how quietly and with what little fuss this incredible military operation took place, and with what courage! The point is very simple: here was naked unprovoked aggression; unprovoked, because the Falklands were no danger to the Argentine, and had been in British possession for nearly two hundred years. We were wholly justified in defending the Falklands. And people call that jingoism! Let people be offended by my calling it radical and liberal slush – if they can be offended, there may be some hope for them. It's a bad rotten way of thinking.

Some people thought that Lady Thatcher favoured war above all other options . . .

All she was doing was throwing burglars out of her house. Is that a celebration of war? When are we ever going to learn the lesson? Stamp on the thing when it's small. If we'd overlooked that, God knows what would have happened in the world. I don't really want to go into the Falklands issue, but what Lady Thatcher did was the brave, responsible act of a responsible government. It became a basis and precedent to show that that kind of action is still possible in a modern world.

You've described Socialism as 'a rotting corpse whose smell in our midst has tainted the political atmosphere for far too long'. This statement is based on the fact that Socialists 'release expectations they can never fulfil, and that is immoral'. I wonder if we can be confident about the difference

Sir Laurens van der Post

between expectation *and* hope *in this context? You approve of offering people hope, yet hope may also never be realized. Why is this not immoral also?*

Socialism betrays hope. It was a fulfilment at one time of a longing rather than a hope, a longing for a better world order, but it's proved itself to be such a shambles already, so clearly not a valid means of procuring for the human species what it professed to procure, that I felt justified in making those remarks. Socialism makes shallow collective values the ultimate test of human behaviour. It has done an enormous amount of harm all over the world. Not a single culture in the world infected by Socialism has come to any good at all. Give me an example of a Socialist country that's done well; there isn't a single one. As a temporary tactical challenge of existing values it was very good in its time, but as an ongoing pronouncement of the ultimate good for the human race, it's been proved inadequate. That's why I called it those names.

In A Walk with a White Bushman, *you say that Socialism was only really valid in a nineteenth-century context when the working classes had no vote. Presumably, however, you would agree that the granting of the vote has not eradicated social injustice or deprivation, and that there is still a significant underclass in Britain and elsewhere. Isn't the idea of Socialism still valid today?*

No, I don't think that follows. There will always be injustice as long as there are human beings on earth, and even when we don't mean harm the consequences of what we do can be unfair and unjust. Socialism is not the answer to the prevalence of injustice, or indeed anything else. It was all right as a stage for clearing the mind and the structures of life for better things, but it has created new forms and perhaps even worse forms of injustice. You ask if I can deny that there is still an underclass in Great Britain. I do deny it, at least in the sense that you mean it, in the Socialist sense. People have never been more free in the history of this country to be out of what you call class, to be themselves. I don't deny that there are poor people in the country, but it's not the result of a system; it's a result of what people are in themselves. There's never been a society before in Great Britain where people, whatever their disadvantages of birth, are so free to be themselves, and not to be subjected to the sufferings of a class. The sufferings in England at the moment have nothing to do with class, because people soar out of the class system with the greatest of ease if they want to.

But is there not a difference between what we might call Socialist ideals and the unacceptable face of Socialism as deployed in the former Soviet Union . . .?

No, because Socialism always tries to solve human problems by creating systems. That's the difference between Capitalism and Socialism; Capitalism is not a system, and people are mistaken if they think so. It expresses itself in certain patterns from time to time but it's much more pragmatic than Socialism which starts with the concept of a system: life has to conform to the ideal system. But you can't do that. It is utterly impossible and dangerous for any human being to think he can devise an ideal social system and inflict it upon other human beings. The great error started with something which was meant to be very good, like Tom Paine's *The Rights of Man*. The great fallacy of *The Rights of Man* is that it ignores the fact that rights have to be earned, and that you have no right which is not accompanied by an equal and opposite responsibility. One of the basic implications of Socialism is that the so-called working man is inherently good and the person who employs him is inherently bad. There's always a villain in Socialism, and an absence of self-criticism; Socialism never sees into the totality of the human scene, and its values are always collective values. It's almost as if it regards the individual as a form of egotism; it doesn't realize that an individual can be most truly and utterly and wholly himself without damaging the equal right of his neighbour to be the same. This is expressed much better in what is called a Capitalist climate. Terrible things happen in that climate too but it's not a climate of ideology; it's part of the process of trial and error in life.

You also say in the same book that no ideas have come out of the Labour Party since the manifesto of 1848. Isn't that a bit harsh and dismissive? What about the establishment of everyone's right to education?

The right of people to be educated was recognized before Socialism. Some of the greatest pioneers of universal education weren't Socialists; they were industrialists, and some of the most idealistic schemes of education were launched by individuals . . .

Sir Laurens van der Post

But the Socialists put it into practice . . .

Not at all. The Socialists only came to power for the first time after the last world war. All the immense pioneering work in that area was done by the Liberal Party without a socialist ethic.

What about the National Health Service?

It is a good idea that every human being who needs health care should be provided for, but the Health Service as it was created is a disaster; it's wasteful, extravagant and uncreative. It's obviously done some good, but medicine wasn't at all bad before the war. You mustn't ignore the enormous role that the private capitalist world played in pioneering medicine. You must also remember that any smooth-running private organization turned bad as soon as it was nationalized; there's not a single area where this isn't true, even the Post Office. Look at the railways – we had a wonderful railway system before the war. And look at the coal mines. I can't see why the Health Service should be held to the credit of Socialism particularly; it's not just a socialist concept. These wonderful hospitals we used to have in London are run entirely by charity. Charity is thought to be a dirty word, but it isn't. To receive help out of the love of your fellow human beings is not degrading.

I know you admired Bevin. Wasn't he a worthy exponent of Socialism?

I don't think that Socialism made Bevin. There were remarkable, wonderful people who were Socialists, I don't say there were not; but they were so in spite of Socialism.

You have surprised many people by being very critical of Nelson Mandela, saying that when he emerged from prison he was 'more myth than man', and still speaking 'the moth-eaten clichés of the spirit'. Most people will regard that as a harsh criticism of someone they see as essentially dignified, unsubdued by imprisonment . . . not unlike yourself in many ways.

Did you see what I said about Nelson Mandela?

Sir Laurens van der Post

I heard, and I'm quoting.

Well, you heard wrong. I said that Nelson Mandela, when he came out of prison, had become more of a myth in the minds of people than a man, which I think is true. When he emerged from captivity it was an immense opportunity for him to speak. I had been in prison myself, and I knew it was a terrible thing to do to a human being. But I think that prison is one of the finest schools for the making of the human spirit that ever can be. I myself only did a crash course, so to speak, but he went to unversity, having been in prison for twenty-seven years. You can imagine my disappointment when I heard him talk that Sunday, when he spouted all those moth-eaten clichés, thanking the Communists and so on. I had to ask myself, has he actually been in prison? And I thought of the great examples of people who have come out of prison the right way, people like Solzhenitsyn who showed from the words he used that he had learned lessons in that prison school. What I bitterly regret is that Nelson Mandela didn't come out as Martin Luther King came out saying that he had a dream for Africa, instead of giving us a lot of moth-eaten political platitudes. I was bitterly disappointed. Nelson Mandela is a miserable figure who speaks with a double tongue. You should hear the Dalai Lama on the subject of Nelson Mandela, how after Tiananmen Square he cuddled up with the Chinese government when he was there. He's a very brave man, but he's a very great disappointment to me personally. He had twenty-seven years to think about life, and yet he still belongs to a party which hasn't renounced power and war.

Are you hopeful about South Africa's future?

In the long run, yes. It's got a long way to go, and it's on a dangerous road, but the road is not so dangerous as not taking the road would have been. No doubt they'll make mistakes, but the quality of the human beings, black and white and coloured in South Africa, is potentially so great that I think they can win through. History and life work much more slowly than do human beings. This is another part of the Socialist slush that I talked about. Socialists think they can pass laws for the betterment of mankind, and men will then be better. They don't realize that evolution of life and the human spirit is not a rational thing; it is a process of growth which you can't learn at universities. You can only bring the improvements in life that you brought in your own nature and it's a long and hard job. Nelson

Sir Laurens van der Post

Mandela still has power over people, and he has a right to it after twenty-seven years in prison, but he didn't rise to the responsibility laid on him by his imprisonment, which Solzhenitsyn and the other great dreamers of life, such as Martin Luther King, discharged so nobly. That's the disappointment.

You were very close to Jung, whom you describe as a profoundly religious person. Do you think you were on the same journey in life, only perhaps on a different route?

I don't really know how to answer that. Religion is the most important dimension in life, and in a sense I was on the same road as Jung, but I don't pretend to have been of the same calibre. He was of enormous importance for religion without organized religion realizing it. It's one of the tragedies in the world. If you listen to certain archbishops nowadays, religion is a sort of socialist ethic, not religion at all; when I hear them talk, I can never recognize the religious content of what they say, but in Jung religion is given a contemporary language, it renews itself. And it's a promotion of the whole fundamental world of the dream which the universe is destined to fulfil. Dream is a profound language of nature, particularly of nature to come. It's where we get the blueprints of life, that whole area which Shakespeare and the great artists knew. Shakespeare talked about the prophetic soul of man dreaming of things to come. In that sense, yes, I felt that I was in a similar dimension to Jung.

On the subject of religion, you say in A Walk with a White Bushman *that until you had understood and absorbed the mythology of Africa, Christianity did not come alive for you. Do you regard Christianity as another branch of mythology?*

No. I don't think of mythology as having branches. I think of mythology being evidence of a divine pattern in the human species, instinctively and wherever it finds itself. Religion is a profound instinctive pattern which has very often been cheated. It has suffered a great deal from what socialism suffered from, from being turned into rigid dogmas, rigid concepts and ideas, which were not large enough or flexible enough to express the true essence of religion. The mythology of Africa is an instinctive mythology, and it opened me up to religion from which I was excluded by my education, and particularly the form of Calvinism to which I was exposed.

Do you think the main tenets of Christianity – the Virgin Birth, the Crucifixion, the Resurrection and the Life Everlasting have a symbolic rather than an actual significance, metaphorical rather than literal?

They have an immense symbolic significance, but to me no actuality is complete without the symbolic. The symbol is an expression of the most profound actuality of the human spirit; it's not, as you imply, not real. They all deal with reality in the only way in which it can be dealt with at that stage of human awareness. I wouldn't like to consider them dogmatically. One of the great dangers that press upon modern life is precisely the absence of symbolic reality. Immense impoverishment of the human spirit is going on all around us because people don't realize how incomplete life is unless it is symbolic. Religion is not religion if it isn't symbolic.

How can different religious traditions be reconciled if it is part of their essence to exclude one another?

They're not really religions if they exclude one another. Conscious religion is expressed by human beings, and everything we do is approximate. Our observances of religion is whole and ultimate and perfect perhaps, but the expression of which we are capable is always approximate, and it is in being aware of what is provisional and approximate in our apprehension of religion, that we find very often how much other religions can contribute. Here is the tremendous importance of the symbol again, because although people may use different symbols, they are all ultimately the same. Stone Age mythology was an early expression of Greek mythology, and the link is not only highly discernible but frightfully important. It's our interpretations of the religious experience of mankind which vary, but the experience is the same everywhere.

But most religious faiths claim that their teachings alone are true, and that they are true for everyone. It follows that other faiths are mistaken. How does one deal with this problem?

This is the problem of human beings valuing their ideas too highly, and has nothing to do with religion. This interpretation of religion is not a religious interpretation. When I'm asked this sort of question I have to say, my dear chap, you're not talking about religion, you're talking about a church, and a church is provisional and approximate, and thank God, often very wrong.

Do you think you have discovered what is true for you in a religious sense?

I have a feeling sometimes that I might be on the way to discovering it, but I do know that there is a long way to go. All human beings in all societies have a feeling of impoverishment if they're not on the way. The Stone Age people I knew in the Kalahari had two dances, one for the little hunger, for food and for survival, and the other dance for the great hunger, the hunger for religion. This hunger is real and if we don't get the food for it, we decline and diminish.

But do you think that what is true for you is necessarily true for everyone?

Oh no, not for a minute. This is as far as I can testify: I live in the hope that my concept of the truth is right, but I do know that if I'm wrong it's in a way that probably I'm not aware of. How do you distinguish between truth and error in life? The struggle goes on all the time, and that's why consciousness must be increased, not diminished.

You have said that there is a kind of 'foreverness' incorporated in everyone. What basis do you have for saying that, and what exactly do you mean by it?

I can't express it more clearly than that. The little Bushman in the desert said to me, 'There is a dream dreaming us . . .' It's what T.S. Eliot called this timeless element in every human being. All of us have something in the human soul which is beyond time; it's even recognized by scientists now. The psychic nature of the human being is to behave as if it will go on forever. It is the soul of man.

Sir Laurens van der Post

Perhaps because we live in a sick, cynical age, there are those who regard you as less of a sage and more of a charlatan, a romancer rather than a mystic. Are you wounded by such criticism?

I don't know anybody who's ever called me a charlatan, certainly nobody who knows me would ever call me that. And of course I would be hurt if people thought I was. And why a romancer? A romancer in what way? Be specific, in what way have I been romancing? I can't deal with a vague statement – you must give me an explicit example.

Well, a number of people have suggested your books are hopelessly romanticized and divorced from reality. Your Venture to the Interior, *for example, is presented as a herculean journey but according to your critics it amounts to no more than a day's walk up and down a hill. Do you perhaps mix fantasy and truth sometimes?*

I did go up those mountains, and nobody can say I didn't. This is quite absurd . . . these are idiots talking. The peak of Mlanje is 12,000 feet above sea level – is that a hill? Those people who say it is a hill are liars. It's three times the height of any mountain in Great Britain. Who are these idiots, where do they say these things? I can't cope with this.

Your life experience has been so singular, so unusual as to suggest the hand of destiny at work. Is your perception of yourself that of someone singled out for a special mission?

I've never had a perception of myself. I've never lived my life by a plan, or with an ambition. I'm somebody following the flight of the bird, I just do what life suggests and I do it as well as I can. I have actually done certain things quite well in life. For example, I won a prize for the best run small farm in Gloucestershire at a three-county show. Or is that being a charlatan and a romancer? And my record in the war – is that also romancing? I shouldn't even have to respond to these remarks; they're obviously made by singularly stupid people.

You have written that death is as natural and creative a part of life as birth. Can you develop that idea?

This is how it appears to me, and it seems to me to be mythologically right too. The whole of life is a metamorphosis: growth, decay, decline, fall, rebirth. Death is a natural part of the process of growth and rebirth.

Now, in old age, do you feel a particular serenity?

I'm prevented from feeling serene because at the age of eighty-six I still have so much to do. I've just finished a book, but I have about thirteen others I want to write, so I have an increased sense of hurry, a feeling that my ration is running out and I must get on with it. It's not that I feel unserene, but I'm not at all of a philosophic turn of mind. I just try to live, that's my main preoccupation. And my sense of wonder about life never leaves me.

How would you like to be remembered?

One does certainly want to be remembered. My experience of being in prison and thinking we might all be killed, and the idea that people wouldn't know how we died, or even remember us, was a profound horror. I would like to be remembered as someone who tried to perform some service for what I think is the overall value in life, and that is what is expressed by Eros, and by St Paul as charity. Without Eros no human being has any hope whatsoever of having this immense capacity of spirit to learn to distinguish between truth and error. It's only with charity that one somehow has the sense of where the frontier is between the two. If I can be remembered as somebody who felt that particular emotion all his life very profoundly, and perhaps rendered some service to it, well, I shall rejoice...

LORD WYATT

LORD WYATT

Woodrow Wyatt was born in 1918 and educated at Eastbourne College and Worcester College, Oxford. He rose to the rank of major during the war and was Mentioned in Despatches from Normandy. He became a Labour MP in 1945 and was made a life peer in 1987. From 1965-73 he was a weekly columnist on the *Daily Mirror* and for the next ten years he wrote for the *Sunday Mirror*. Since 1983 he has been a columnist on *The Times* and the *News of the World*. He is the author of several books including *The Peril in our Midst* (1956), *What's Left of the Labour Party?* (1977) and his autobiography, *Confessions of an Optimist* (1985).

Lord Wyatt

Your autobiography reveals that your father was a much more important figure in your life than your mother, and yet it was a relationship characterized by fear and misunderstanding. Were you accepting of him at the time? Did the disappointment and agonizing come later?

There were times when I liked my father; he could be very kind in many ways. For example, he used sometimes to take me to Horsham to watch my cousin playing cricket with Warwickshire against Sussex, and I used rather to enjoy that. He died when I was thirteen, and I remember him as a rather alarming figure, perhaps because he was headmaster of the private school he owned, and he always made it quite clear that I would get no favours. He liked my brother a great deal more than he liked me, perhaps because my brother was a much nicer person, but in any case he made it quite clear that he thought I wasn't much good. I remember when we used to swim in Cornwall and the enormous breakers came rolling in from the Atlantic, he would think I was too frightened to go in. Possibly I was, but I was more frightened of the ghastly cold. I found him a very forbidding person in that way, but I suppose looking back on it now I would take a different view, and perhaps it was my lack of character that made me resent him. If I met him now I don't quite know what I should say.

When after the war Osbert Sitwell asked you if you'd killed your father yet, a reference to your tortured relations with him, the implication was that you definitely had not. Half a century later, is your father finally dead?

I think he is, yes. Osbert Sitwell had the same kind of dislike of his father as I had of mine, and that was how the conversation arose. He told me that it was very important to kill one's father, and I thought I had, partly because I'd turned out differently and I'd read a lot of books and my father hadn't. He read mainly detective stories, like Agatha Christie, and he didn't really have what you would call a liberal mind. At that age I would have preferred somebody who had wider ideas, and he was rather narrow, although the family always used to pretend how clever he was. But after four years at Oxford he only succeeded in getting a pass degree, about the same as Kinnock at Cardiff University.

Can you recall your feelings at the time of his actual death?

Lord Wyatt

I was quite pleased actually. I remember going to the cinema that afternoon, the day of his funeral, and I didn't feel any great sorrow. I kept thinking I ought to be very upset, but I didn't really feel that. We were all so frightened of him in a way.

You were never able to form a deep bond with your mother, something which I imagine may have given you a terrible sense of loss all your life. Am I right?

I don't have a sense of loss about it, because if you haven't had something you haven't lost it. She was a very good woman, my mother, but we never really understood each other at all, and she never once praised me for anything I'd ever done. But maybe there was nothing I did worth praising.

Criticism of your father led to your mother disinheriting you. What were your immediate feelings when this happened?

She was rather gaga at the time, and it arose, curiously enough, because she was very pro-Conservative, as my father was. I had written something about my father in the *Evening Standard* in which I said he reminded me very much of Mr Attlee, he had the same good qualities of uprightness and honesty; and she was horrified to have her late husband compared with this dreadful Socialist, although I had intended it rather as a compliment.

You said your parents' marriage was made in heaven and that your mother worshipped your father. Is that a necessary constituent for a successful marriage in your view?

It was reciprocal. For him she could do no wrong, and vice versa. Their temperaments clearly suited each other and she admired him for qualities he perhaps didn't have – for example, she thought he was a very learned and clever man. He admired her because she had a strong character, and when there were ups and downs at the school, she always supported him and saw him through.

Was she a very intelligent woman?

No. I think she only once read a book, and had no interest in abstract matters, or literature or art.

Your initial dislike for your school, Eastbourne, seems to have been prompted by a certain snobbishness, the fact that Eastbourne was a poor imitation of the grander public schools. Wasn't it unusual to have been so aware of the nuances of class division at that age?

Yes. I've always been a snob, and no doubt still am, because on the whole I prefer the best if one can get it, or at least to be associated with the best. I didn't feel Eastbourne was a very good school, in fact it was bloody awful, but I do give a prize every year for an essay on the subject: 'The conditions which you think would be most likely to give you a happy life.' I do this in honour of a very nice man, about the only civilized teacher in my time, called Bell, who died very young. When I went into his Classical Sixth he told us we could either work or we could just sit and dream. I chose to do the latter. Mr Bell was a very agreeable man, and had all the values of the great Greek scholars presenting the notions of happiness. I find it very interesting reading the entries from Eastbourne each year. I usually give the winners tea in the Lords, and we have a talk. They say that in many ways the school is just as bad as it was when I was there, only it's probably a bit livelier.

In your autobiography you describe how a Tory MP, Tony Bullock, left Eastbourne out of his Who's Who *entry, and you commented that you had never gone as far as that. I couldn't help noticing that you omitted two marriages from your own* Who's Who *entry . . .*

Ah . . . well, but they're all recorded in *Debrett*, several pages as a matter of fact. I left them out of *Who's Who* because they're excess baggage.

You were very pleased to leave Eastbourne and Esher behind and were much more comfortable with your social status at Oxford. Wasn't this a shaky foundation for a declared Socialist?

First of all I wasn't a declared Socialist. I joined the Labour Club which was semi-Communist, I joined the Liberals, and I joined the Conservative

Lord Wyatt

Club, so I was just sampling, wondering what politics was made of. I also helped to get Philip Toynbee, who was then a Communist, elected as President of the Union.

You wanted to rise above Esher when you grew up, you were disdainful of 'the appalling people', as you describe them, and were desperate not to have to return and live among them. Did it not occur to you that by choosing Socialism, you would be representing these same appalling people – or did you think you could make them less appalling?

I'd better explain that I joined the Labour Party because I went into the army when I was very young before the war began. When I was eighteen in the winter of 1936, I went to Munich and was pretty horrified about what was already being done to the Jews, and this made a strong impression on me. I will never believe that the Germans did not know what was happening, because if I could find out when I was eighteen, then they must have known. When I was just twenty-one I joined up, and I became an officer fairly quickly, the most unlikely officer you could imagine. One of the great things about the British army is the attention junior officers must pay to the people they have in their command, and I had a platoon of about thirty people much the same age as myself, and I talked to them a great deal. I heard a great many stories of boys who were obviously much cleverer than I who had had to leave school when they were fourteen because their parents simply had to send them out to work; of mothers who'd died because they couldn't afford medical attention, and other really distressing tales. I had also spent a few weeks with Mass Observation and enjoyed talking to the people who in a sense no longer exist, the working class. So my main motivation in wanting to represent these people was a dislike of injustice. It all seemed to be desperately unfair, and the Tories had done nothing whatsoever about it.

Was part of the attraction of Socialism the fact that your father had detested it?

Admittedly that made me feel there must be something in it, but it wasn't the moving force. I joined the Labour Party because I thought the world should be a better place and the Tories had failed to make it so. Social justice, I thought, was long overdue.

Lord Wyatt

As the possibility of war approached, you married for the first time; you say it was a marriage based on love and passion, but was there perhaps also an element of fatalism about it, a feeling that you might not survive the war to marry afterwards?

I think that was so. I felt that I was born just before the end of the last war, and was now due to be killed in this one. But deep down I never really thought I would be killed; even the people who didn't survive never thought they were going to be killed. It was just a question of luck.

Your account of those early days in the army gives some idea of how ill-prepared we were to face up to Hitler's advance. Did you sometimes doubt that we would win the war?

Never. I was always absolutely certain we would win.

Why?

Because for various reasons Britain can never be beaten in a war. It is an ingenious country when it has its back to the wall; we'd always rustle up allies from somewhere or other, and the British don't contemplate defeat. I was in the war from the very beginning, and I never met one soldier of any rank who thought we were going to lose the war. Even when France had surrendered, when Hitler was trying to get across the Channel, and the Battle of Britain was raging over our heads, I never met anyone who thought we were going to lose it; and that was when we were alone with nobody helping us, not the Americans, not the Russians, nobody.

In 1948 you married again, this time thinking you were more circumspect in not allowing your heart to rule your head. When that marriage failed, were you beginning to think that perhaps you did not have, as it were, an aptitude for marriage?

No, I thought I was beginning to learn, I was gaining experience in it. And so, as I liked being married, I persevered with the institution. I knew that if it failed one could run a line over it, forget it. There are so many things to think about, there is no point in dwelling on things which are not particularly pleasant.

You claim to have followed Robert Kee's maxim: 'Any reasonably intelligent man not repellent to a woman can persuade almost any girl to go to bed with him if he is persistent.' Does that not imply a kind of contempt for women, the idea that women are invariably beddable no matter what?

No. I don't think it implies any contempt at all. I think it means that you can succeed if you are really interested in somebody – you can't do it if you're not seriously interested. As I'm sure you know very well, men fall in love through their eyes, and women through their ears, for obvious biological reasons.

What are the biological reasons?

At your age, you must surely know. First of all, it takes a man about ten seconds to impregnate a woman, not a very agreeable way of doing it, but that is the way it is. It takes the woman nine months to have the child, months in which she is somewhat incapacitated, and therefore over the ages she has evolved into someone who has certain ideas about the type of man she is going to allow to impregnate her. In the Stone Age no doubt the toughest guy around would just drag the woman off by the hair and batter everybody else with his club, but as time went on and we grew a little more civilized, ideas changed. Women may not always be conscious of this, but at the back of their minds they know that, despite all the contraception in the world, the sex act is designed to produce a child who has to have the protection of a father. That is fairly sensible. But a man does not have the same constraint: he can get an erection immediately he sees a pretty girl naked, even if he's hardly ever met her. It's not his biological job to rear children.

Did you always find it easy to seduce women?

Not at all. I'm not a great seducer, though I like women very much and I'd much rather be in women's company than men's.

Lord Wyatt

You also say that it would be biologically impossible for husbands and wives never to feel attracted outside their marriage after their mutual sexual excitement has calmed, and sometimes even before. Do you believe that marriages should rise above the odd infidelity?

Oh yes. The importance of the sexual act can be exaggerated, and it's not much good anyway if it isn't associated with love, but on the other hand people develop at different rates and it's obvious that the first fine careless rapture doesn't last indefinitely, and so people can be unfaithful without wanting to disturb their marriages.

Do you think the Establishment is very hypocritical about sex?

Of course, but then everybody is hypocritical about sex. The British are the greatest hypocrites in the world, but hypocrisy is necessary. If we went around telling the truth all the time, the place would be unbearable.

At the time of the Profumo scandal, you wrote an editorial in the Banbury Guardian *supporting him and dismissing the suggestion that 'one peccadillo' could make him a bad man. You were scathing about what you described as 'grave nonsense about morality'. Do you have that view generally about political scandals?*

Yes, absolutely. That's another part of the great British hypocrisy: you may tell a lie in the House of Commons about public matters – Eden and Selwyn Lloyd in attacking Egypt lied their heads off about collusion with Israel and the French – and that's all right, but poor old Profumo told a lie about a personal matter, mainly because he was terrified that if his wife found him carrying on with anybody else she would leave him. But the great British hypocrisy says that you must not tell lies about your personal life; you may only tell lies about things that really matter.

How do you react to the suggestion that those who cannot conduct their own private lives properly shouldn't be in charge of decisions which affect a great many other people's lives?

That would be ridiculous. We know very well that the people most prominent in leading nations have also had the greatest libido. That's been true throughout that ages. Lloyd George wasn't to be trusted in a room with any passable woman under 55; he couldn't help himself. Wellington and Napoleon were the same. What people do in their private lives has absolutely no relevance to what they do publicly. What to do about interest rates or how to deal with Yugoslavia are problems which you either have an aptitude for dealing with or you don't, but it's got nothing whatsoever to do with making love to the housemaid. The two are totally different activities.

You said of Harold Wilson: 'He should never have been Prime Minister, and I liked him better when he gave up and started to be a more wholesome man.' What did you mean by that remark?

Wilson carried hypocrisy too far. He was always pretending. He would say quite different things outside the Shadow Cabinet from what he said inside, and he was always sucking up to the lefties in his constituency, because these were the people he needed to get him elected one day as leader, although he never would have become leader if Hugh Gaitskell had not died so young. Like Macmillan, he didn't really care what happened, so long as he was Prime Minister; neither of them had any real feelings about what happened to the country, whereas somebody like Gaitskell or Mrs Thatcher cared very deeply, wrongheaded or not. Wilson let the extreme left into the Labour Party again; before Wilson came in you could not be a member of the Labour Party *and* a member of a Communist-front organization, but you could afterwards. He allowed the whole drift to go on with the trade unions which were being taken over by the Communists, and I thought he behaved terribly, very much against the interests of the country, and his whole government was a disaster. When he stepped down he became a much more wholesome person. His own personal morals were very good, but his morals when it came to politics were terrible.

You blame Wilson for the fact that – as you put it – 'the Labour Party turned rotten and the Marxist element became dominant'. Why did you later have such disdain for Neil Kinnock who stood up to the Marxist element and tried to tackle them?

Because he was also doing a Wilson in his own way. He got elected because he collected all the same people Wilson did, the extremists and the Communists and so on, and he attacked everything the Labour leaders were doing – they were all traitors to the working classes and God knows what else. When he became leader, he knew he would never get himself elected as Prime Minister carrying that baggage, so he then had to take a different tack. He was a similar character to Wilson. I don't think he really believed in anything very much.

The single reference in your book to Neil Kinnock describes him as 'a lightweight trendy – proof of the Labour Party's deterioration . . .'

That's exactly what he is. The Labour Party is never going to do any good until it's like the Democratic Party in America, where it's absolutely part and parcel of the Capitalist system, and not trying to turn everything upside down.

On the same page of your autobiography in which you say Wilson was totally cynical, you describe how you broke the rules of secrecy governing Party meetings by writing them up in the Daily Mirror. *Couldn't that also be interpreted as an act of cynicism?*

Of course it was. The leadership was leaking their version of events, so I though I would say what really did happen. It was a counter leak, if you like; all reasonable fun.

You also dismiss Callaghan as 'an inept Chancellor of the Exchequer, an indifferent Home Secretary, a poor Foreign Secretary and an unsuccessful Prime Minister.' What lies behind such a ferocious, and some would say unfair, assessment?

Observation. I'm quite fond of him in a curious way, and I don't want to upset him again, but I've got nothing whatsoever to add to what I said in my book.

By contrast, you obviously have considerable admiration for Ted Heath, of

Lord Wyatt

whom you say, 'I cannot blame him if he now seems ungracious – there is a noble soul there which has been grievously wounded.' Is this a sentiment which you would extend to others who have been similarly wounded... Mrs Thatcher, for example?

Certainly. She was abominably treated. That's one reason why – there are many others – I could never join the Conservative Party. They are a terrible lot of people, the MPs particularly. They treat their leaders appallingly. They're all cowards too; at the first sign of difficulties they all run for cover.

You were a great champion of Mrs Thatcher and her policies during the 1980s which went against the opinion of a great many objective commentators. What was the real basis of this admiration?

Because she reminded me very much of Hugh Gaitskell. I knew her on and off, and when she became leader of the Tory Party she asked me to go and see her. We talked for about two hours or so in her house and I told her how much her determination and honesty reminded me of Hugh Gaitskell. I said to her, 'If you're really going to stick to what you say, I'll back you'; which I did, always. I thought her party were total idiots to have got rid of her. I know she could be tiresome and difficult in some ways, but she would have won them the last election just the same, with a bigger majority than Major. She was the best peacetime Prime Minister since the 1832 Reform Bill. Winston was very good in many ways in a war, but not much good in peacetime. She really put Britain on the map again.

When you wrote about the Falklands War you said that she was in acute distress whenever anyone was killed, and that 'she was stricken far more than a man would have been'. Many people would consider that remark deeply insulting to men.

All these things about her not being compassionate are absolute balls. She felt it all very deeply, but you mustn't start breaking down and having tears about it. You have to be tough to win a war, and toughness is not necessarily a female attribute, and women are not usually placed in war situations. But that doesn't alter the fact that she always was a deeply compassionate and considerate person. The reason she didn't seem like that was that she had to grow a carapace in order to get things done; she couldn't show what might be called her feminine side. To control and master a cabinet of people, most of whom were at first hostile to her, was quite a difficult trick, and in order to do it she had to steel herself. But inside her nature wasn't like that at all.

Do you think that she has conducted herself well since her fall from power?

On the whole yes, but you have to remember that she's only in her sixties, still full of energy. She was a hands-on Prime Minister, and naturally she feels that things would be done better if she were there, and occasionally she can't resist saying so. I think that's extremely human and understandable. In fact in many ways she's been very supportive of Major and the government. After all, he was her anointed.

In your account of the proposed nationalization of steel under Wilson you paint a very convincing and disturbing picture of the pressure which chief whips can apply to MPs. Has that altered at all over the years, or would whips have resorted to similar tactics over the recent Maastricht vote for example?

All whips do that, and that is their reason for existing. It is their duty to make sure that the government wins a vote, and they must do it by every means available, and if people aren't tough enough to stand up to it, then they shouldn't be in politics. I've no sympathy whatsoever for people who say they were bullied, and their arms were twisted, and terrible threats were made. If you believe in something you must do what you think is right; by the same token the whips believe that the best thing for the country and their party is for the government to win. I don't know what they tell them in the Tory Party; perhaps they say you won't get a knighthood. In my case they were trying to get me out of my constituency.

Did you listen to them?

Of course not. I did exactly what I felt was right. This was at a time in the Labour Party when I was seeing more and more that the damned thing doesn't work. This kind of marvellous utopia where everybody would be working for everybody's good without any care of profit, and be motivated entirely like a lot of clergymen, was, I discovered, not going to happen. I should have realized it earlier, but I was very young. I told my constituency party in that election that I was going to oppose the nationalization of steel, that it would be a disaster, which it certainly was, and so it came as no surprise to Wilson when I refused to vote for the bill. Every kind of trick was used to get my vote, and harrowing stories were told; but that is the function of whips. The function of an MP is to be strong enough to take no notice.

In your book you describe politics as a sordid and often corrupt business. Were you ever dismayed by what Orwell called 'the ordinary dirtiness' of politics?

I didn't mean corrupt in the sense of money changing hands and that kind of business; only that people are a bit corrupted by wanting jobs, which is understandable. Part of the whole purpose of going into politics is to try and get somewhere and do something. A lot of intrigue goes on, as it does in everything, and perhaps I've been a bit too unkind to politicians; they're just human like everybody else, no worse than the rest.

As far back as 1947 you voted for a reduction in the proposed civil list allowance for Princess Elizabeth. Do you still take the same view now?

No, absolutely not. I really hadn't studied the problem enough. Now I take a totally different view. It's a great mistake for the Queen to pay income tax. Republicanism is being whipped up mainly by telling lies. You tell the lies first by saying, for example, that the Queen ought to pay for the restoration of Windsor Castle because she lives there, and you conveniently forget that the only parts that were burned down were state apartments which have been open to the public ever since George III. The country is in a discontented mood at the moment because after having had a very good ten years, people are now losing jobs and finding their houses are not going up in price, so they have to take it out on somebody, and why not on the Queen.

Lord Wyatt

Many people would think it demeaning to write for the News of the World. *Do you have no qualms about that at all?*

None whatever. Christ went among the publicans and sinners after all [laughs]. I like writing for the *News of the World*, because it has the largest circulation of any newspaper in the world. In a way I'm a kind of preacher who feels very strongly about many issues. I long for people to do what I think is right for them and for the country, and so I've got a marvellous pulpit from which to do it. When I write for *The Times*, which has a very small circulation, my article is lost in the mass of that paper, but in the *News of the World*, I have far more influence than ever I had in the House of Commons.

Your admiration for Rupert Murdoch borders on the reverential. You say: 'If I were not myself, I should most like to be Rupert...' You present him as an urbane, refined, educated man, knowledgeable of what you call 'the values of Western civilization'. Many people would regard him as a corrupter of these values.

Well, I don't. I think his activities have been beneficial in the main, although I haven't always agreed with the line the *Sun* and the *Sunday Times* have taken on the government or Norman Lamont or the Queen. Murdoch is a bit like Beaverbrook in some respects; they're both children of the manse with a puritan hellfire streak. I've always liked him, there's far more good in him than you think. He's not remotely like Robert Maxwell who was an obvious crook from start to finish. Rupert's not a crook.

Don't you think that as someone who writes for the News of the World *you are complicit in a general moral decline?*

They very often have archbishops writing for them, and when I'm away they go to John Smith or somebody like that. Any Labour leader who is asked to write for the *News of the World* is delighted, so why should it be so awful of me to write a weekly column?

Lord Wyatt

Are you at all uneasy about the relationship between the tabloids and the political parties; the knighting of tabloid editors, for example, in return for services rendered?

I don't think it's a very important subject; it doesn't matter one way or the other. It's been going on for a hundred years or so. And it doesn't seem to make editors particularly loyal – look at the way all the newspapers have been turning on Major and Lamont and the government.

But the principle is that if you support the government you're rewarded.

Is it so strange that governments show some gratitude to people who have helped them? It is normal, and it's been going on ever since human history began. On the whole you don't offer honours to your enemies.

The title of your column 'The Voice of Reason' is seen by many as adding insult to injury. Is it intended as a deliberate provocation to reasonable people?

Actually, I didn't invent it. The first time I saw it, I was quite amused, but on the whole what I write is logical and reasonable. Do you read my column?

Sometimes.

Well, you obviously don't read it enough, so you don't know what you're talking about. I think very much as ordinary people do.

While doing the research for this interview I borrowed your autobiography from the London Library. Near the end of the book you write, 'I shall be immodest . . .' and someone has written in the margin, 'You've never stopped.' Would you consider immodesty to be one of your failings?

No. I think what you tell me is very funny . . .

Lord Wyatt

You are a man who takes his horoscope seriously. Has astrology been a substitute for a more orthodox religion?

I don't think it's got much to do with religion. My opinion of religions is that none of them could possibly have got it all right. The Christian religion, for example, and the Muslim religion too, have this marvellous way of thinking that God has created man in his own image, and that isn't true at all. It was man who tried to create God in his own image, and all kinds of thoughts and feelings are attributed to this mysterious being which it couldn't possibly have. It all began with superstition and fear of the unknown. The idea of an afterlife seems to me inherently absurd; it's just sheer vanity on the part of man. And nobody today suggests that the sufferings of the wretched people in Yugoslavia, or the Kurds in Iraq, are because God is punishing them – it just has to be crazy. He is supposed to be omnipotent, but if so, he is really making a bad job of it. Astrology is also on the face of it fairly absurd, but there may just be something in it. 'There are more things in heaven and earth, Horatio, than are dreamt of in your philosophy'; and there *are*, but the idea that the imam of somewhere, or the archbishop of somewhere else, or the Pope, has any clue as to what they are, seems to me to be inherently ridiculous. I'm not in the least afraid of dying, though I'm annoyed that life is so damned short. I've wasted an awful lot of time by not working hard enough and now I feel 'Time's wingèd chariot hurrying near . . .'